Robert Brent Toplin is Assistant Professor of History at Denison University, Ohio. He has received fellowships from the Ford Foundation, the American Philosophical Society, the National Endowment for the Humanities, and Denison University, and has been a frequent visitor to Brazil.

THE ABOLITION OF SLAVERY IN BRAZIL

Robert Brent Toplin

THE ABOLITION OF SLAVERY IN BRAZIL

STUDIES IN AMERICAN NEGRO LIFE
August Meier, General Editor

New York ATHENEUM 1972

The author is grateful to the following publications for permission to reprint material which originally appeared, in part, in article form: Duke University Press, "Upheaval, Violence, and the Abolition of Slavery in Brazil: The Case of São Paulo," *Hispanic American Historical Review* (November 1969); and University of Wisconsin Press, "From Slavery to Fettered Freedom: Attitudes toward the Negro in Brazil," *Luso-Brazilian Review* (Summer 1970).

Library of Congress catalog card number 79–139329
Published simultaneously in Canada by McClelland and Stewart Ltd.
Manufactured in the United States of America by
Kingsport Press, Inc., Kingsport, Tennessee
Designed by Kathleen Carey
First Edition

To Aïda

Preface

COMPARING race relations in the United States and Brazil, always a favorite endeavor of travelers as well as historians, has become especially popular in recent years. No doubt the civil-rights movement and the "Black Revolution" in the United States provided a strong impetus for this interest. Growing recognition of the need to reverse the long history of injustice to the black man in America stirred interest in the story of blacks in Brazil. Suddenly the desire to know more about reports of racial tolerance in Brazil well surpassed American inquisitiveness concerning popular images of the land of coffee, beautiful cities, rhythmic music, and vivacious women. Was it true that Brazil lacked the virulent forms of racial hostility and strife that plagued the United States? Americans asked. Did the Afro-Brazilian find the doors of his society open to him, unobstructed by formal or covert discrimination? In the search for answers to these questions, many researchers have reexamined the history of slavery in Brazil, looking for the origins of the present-day racial situation in that country. Thus, studies of slavery became an important corollary of the general interest in comparing the black man's experience in the Americas.

I became a participant in this research "revolution" in the mid-1960s. Like many other students, I was greatly aroused by the implications of Frank Tannenbaum's ideas as developed in the provocative little book *Slave and Citizen: The Negro in the Americas*. Especially intriguing was Tannenbaum's observation that

> Wherever the law accepted the doctrine of the moral personality of the slave and made possible the gradual achievement of freedom implicit in such a doctrine, the

> slave system was abolished peacefully. Where the slave was denied recognition as a moral person and was therefore considered incapable of freedom, the abolition of slavery was accomplished by force—that is, by revolution.*

Tannenbaum's statement suggested that present-day concerns about the black man's experience in the Americas might be studied profitably not only in terms of the history of race relations, or of slavery, but also in view of the conditions under which societies abolished slavery and ushered the Negro into an era of freedom. Regarding the specific case of Brazil, it seemed that documents from the abolitionist era should be particularly rich. The prolonged abolitionist controversy in Brazil excited diverse groups into manifesting their views on slavery, emancipation, and race—views which, in more peaceful circumstances, they would have been less likely to express openly. Also, the abolitionist controversy pressed these groups into showing how far they would go toward turning their thoughts into action. In this context the Tannenbaum thesis raised a host of questions. For example, what was the status of slaves in late-nineteenth-century Brazil? How did various elements in the society view plans to change the Negro from slave to citizen? Were slaveholders amenable to the emancipation idea? Did changes in the economy and ideology influence the rise of abolitionism? Were abolitionists successful in finding moderate, gradual approaches to emancipation? Did abolition come about peacefully? How did abolition affect the lives of freedmen and their former masters?

If my own conclusions are at variance with those of Tannenbaum, as well as the conclusions reached by other scholars who have worked on the related topics of slavery and race relations, we still should acknowledge the late professor's important contribution. Though the answers Professor Tannenbaum suggested are not entirely satisfactory, he deserves credit for stimulating interest in comparative studies by asking the right questions.

* Frank Tannenbaum, *Slave and Citizen: The Negro in the Americas* (New York, 1946), Preface.

There is a more positive way of acknowledging Professor Tannenbaum's contribution. If we can excuse his failure to see that many of the problems of slavery and abolition existed, to a degree, in Brazil as well as in the United States, we can appreciate the value of his perception that "acceptance of the idea of the spiritual equality of all men [could make] for a friendly, an elastic milieu within which social change could occur in peace." Actually, both societies failed to meet Tannenbaum's terms. In both cases abolition did not really "occur in peace," and the change did not result fundamentally from widespread "acceptance of the idea of the spiritual equality of all men." If we argue, as I do in this study of abolition in Brazil, that moderate, gradualist approaches to emancipation failed and radical, often violent tactics proved to be necessary and effective abolitionist weapons, we should also remember that this approach did not lead to a lasting victory for the idea of equality. The political leaders who rushed to the abolitionist camp in 1888 acted out of an urgent need to placate agitators and check the danger of further disturbances. They were not especially concerned about the plight of the Negro. As liberated blacks soon discovered, emancipation from slavery marked the beginning of the struggle for freedom, not the end.

The interpretation which follows is in no sense a definitive study, but it is hoped that it will be a meaningful beginning toward a clearer understanding of the conditions that brought about the abolition of slavery in Brazil. Although Chapters I through VI deal, to some extent, with the pre-1879 period, the bulk of the material relates to developments in the nine years when the abolitionist campaign became a broad-based and well-organized movement.

A study of abolition should consider the diverse parties involved in the issue; it ought not to be limited only to an investigation of abolitionist activities. Slaveholders and slaves played important roles in the controversy as well as "middle-of-the-road" leaders who agonized, equivocated, and vacillated in efforts to find answers to the problem. The ideas and attitudes of all of these groups deserve serious attention in piecing together the puzzle of events and attempting to understand the motivation of the participants and the catalysts for change in the era of the antislavery campaign.

This monograph could not have been completed without the generous help of many people. Foremost among these are Professors Samuel L. Baily and Eugene D. Genovese. Professor Baily read the manuscript at several stages when it was in thesis form and improved the work at all points. He gave unsparingly of his time in advising, counseling, and guiding me through the labyrinths of research and writing. I am also appreciative of the assistance of Professor Genovese, with whom I began this investigation. His penetrating comments and questions served to highlight the broad implications as well as the limitations of my arguments. He also stimulated my interest in comparative study, an experience which has directed me toward a new project comparing the abolition of slavery in the United States and Brazil.

To the many other scholars who have passed numerous hours offering their impressions and suggestions, I am deeply indebted. As every student of Brazilian history quickly learns, the striking spirit of comradeship among Brazilians and "Brazilianists" is most genuine. With much gratitude I recall the assistance of Robert Conrad, Emília Viotti de Costa, Florestan Fernandes, Sérgio Buarque de Holanda, Octávio Ianni, and Stanley Stein. I also wish to acknowledge my indebtedness to those who made valuable suggestions during the early stages of the writing, particularly Robert J. Alexander, Lloyd Gardner, John Miller and David Ringrose. August Meier was especially helpful in suggesting improvements in the final drafts.

Financial assistance from the Ford Foundation, the American Philosophical Society, the National Endowment for the Humanities, and Denison University made possible three research trips to Brazil and the time necessary to complete the manuscript.

It is unfortunate that a word of thanks to my wife, Aïda, may seem anticlimatic after a long statement of sincere gratitude to many others. She well knows the depths of my appreciation. I dedicate this book to her.

ROBERT BRENT TOPLIN
Granville, Ohio

Introduction

HISTORIANS have often noted the contrast between Brazil's peaceful solution to the problem of slavery and its violent resolution in the United States. The Brazilians abolished human bondage through parliamentary legislation that was hailed with parades in the streets; in North America abolition came after a bloody civil war. Seen in this context, the Brazilian experience is a striking example of self-restraint, moderation, and political compromise.

Concentration upon the peaceful nature of the settlement of May 13, 1888, however, can be misleading, for it overlooks tensions prevailing in the epoch of the antislavery campaign in Brazil. As in the United States, the years of the antislavery movement in Brazil were years of crisis. A careful examination of Brazilian society in the 1880s reveals not only that abolition was a controversial issue but that violence and the threat of violence were important ingredients in the successful effort to end slavery. This turbulence, which undermined the law and threatened social order, forced the defenders of slavery to reconsider their positions. If they had to choose, these political leaders preferred abolition to social revolution. More than anything else, the environment of tension and upheaval explains the decision in favor of immediate abolition in May of 1888.

In the light of this thesis, the popular notion that the extinction of slavery in Brazil was a peaceful process needs reinterpretation. Certainly much of the misunderstanding can be traced to interpretations of slavery itself. For many years the myth that Brazilian slavery was far more humane than North American slavery passed as historical fact. Writers maintained that Brazilian slaveholders were very paternalistic toward their bondsmen and often emancipated them, that state laws and Church practices protected the slave and mitigated his condition, and that the absence of severe prejudice because of extensive miscegenation provided a kind of "racial democracy" for the Brazilian Negro. Such notions can be found in the diverse works of Gilberto Freyre, Oliveira Viana, Carolina Nabuco, Artur Ramos, Donald Pierson, Mary Wilhelmine Williams, Percy Alvin Martin, Frank Tannenbaum, and Stanley Elkins.[1]

Many historians moved from an interpretation of the mildness of Brazilian slavery to a view of the mildness of Brazilian abolition. The flexibility of the institution is the key to this kind of comparison. Writers argued that Brazilian slavery was not a severe and closed system. The legal and moral rights of the Brazilian slave were respected and manumission was common. Interpreting abolition along these lines, historians described Brazilian planters as amenable to emancipation, explained that opportunities existed for political compromise between abolitionists and slaveholders, and suggested that Brazilian society as a whole had fewer qualms about accepting the Negro freedman into civilian life than did American society. In a survey of Latin American society, historian William Lytle Schurz, drawing particularly on the work of Frank Tannenbaum, summarized these views:

> The emancipation of the slaves in Brazil was progressive. It was not cataclysmic and attended by civil war and its punitive aftermath, as it was in the United States. Manumis-

1. Gilberto Freyre, *The Masters and the Slaves* (New York, 1961); Oliveira Viana, *O império brasileiro, 1822–1889* (Rio de Janeiro, 1927), pp. 124–44; Carolina Nabuco, "*O elemento servil—a abolição,*" *Anais do Terceiro Congresso de História Nacional,* VI (1942), pp. 241–56; Artur Ramos, *The Negro in Brazil* (Washington, 1939), pp. 55–56; Donald Pierson, *Negroes in Brazil: A Study of Race Contact at Bahia* (Chicago, 1942), pp. 51–66; Percy Alvin Martin, "Slavery and Abolition in Brazil," *Hispanic American Historical Review,* XIII (May 1933), pp. 151–96; Frank Tannenbaum, *Slave and Citizen: The Negro in the Americas* (New York, 1946), pp. 39–66; Stanley Elkins, *Slavery: A Problem in American Institutional and Intellectual Life* (New York, 1963), pp. 63–80; Mary W. Williams, "The Treatment of Negro Slaves in the Brazilian Empire: A Comparison with the United States of America," *Journal of Negro History* (July 1930), pp. 315–36.

> sion was inherent in the very nature of Brazilian slavery, and the process of liberation was virtually contemporaneous with the history of the institution itself. For the slave, the door to freedom was always ajar and there were many occasions and pretexts, founded in humane custom and law, for opening it wide. . . . There were always slaveholders who questioned the justice of chattel slavery, and whom considerations of justice led to free their bondsmen.
>
> It was from this group that came part of the impulse for the abolitionist movement in the nineteenth century. . . .[2]

Arguing in similar fashion, historian Percy Alvin Martin concluded:

> The most difficult domestic problem which Brazil has ever been called upon to face was solved in a manner which reflects the highest credit on the good sense, self-restraint, and the humanity of the Brazilian people.[3]

Such interpretations lead us to believe that slaveholders in Brazil readily accepted the arguments of abolitionists and, with few reservations, prepared to divorce themselves from slavery. The flexibility of the servile institution in Brazil would provide room for an amicable settlement of the abolition issue.

We should not forget that the twentieth-century historians' favorable portrayal of Brazilian slavery and the high incidence of manumission derives much of its information from the words of nineteenth-century slaveholders. The far more critical literature

2. William Lytle Schurz, *This New World: The Civilization of Latin America* (New York, 1964), pp. 170–71.

3. Martin, "Slavery and Abolition," pp. 195–96. Also see Viana, *O império brasileiro,* pp. 125, 133, 143–44; Ramos, *The Negro in Brazil,* pp. 54–79; Pierson, *Negroes in Brazil,* pp. 51–66; Tannenbaum, *Slave and Citizen,* pp. viii, 93–107; João Pandiá Calogeras, *A History of Brazil* (Chapel Hill, 1939), pp. 253–56.

on slavery generated by Brazilian abolitionists as well as many travelers and foreigners residing in Brazil at the time offered a very different view of the subject. For example, abolitionist Joaquim Nabuco criticized the penchant for misleading comparisons, claiming that slavery in Brazil was "as severe, barbarous and cruel as it was in any other country of America." [4] An editor of an English-language newspaper published in the city of Rio de Janeiro stated the case more bluntly:

> Those who say that slavery is milder and more humane in this country than formerly in the United States are either grossly ignorant, or else they are guilty of deliberate falsehood—and the evidence is in favor of the latter supposition.[5]

In recent years such historical sources have been taken more seriously. The favorable picture of Brazilian slavery, which achieved great popularity in the decades after the *Lei Áurea* of 1888, has been effectively challenged by new scholarship, and this in turn suggests the need for a reinterpretation of some of the old views of Brazilian abolition. The studies of C. R. Boxer for the eighteenth century and Stanley Stein, Octávio Ianni, Fernando Henrique Cardoso, Florestan Fernandes, and Emília Viotti da Costa for the nineteenth century have put together a portrait of an institution much more coercive than the older historians would have us believe.[6] According to them, slaves ex-

4. Joaquim Nabuco, *O abolicionismo* (São Paulo, 1938), p. 130.

5. *Rio News,* December 15, 1882, p. 2. The editor was responding to an article in a Brussels newspaper claiming that slavery in Brazil could not possibly be as harsh as the institution described in *Uncle Tom's Cabin.*

6. C. R. Boxer, *The Golden Age of Brazil: 1695–1750* (Berkeley, 1962); Stanley Stein, *Vassouras: A Brazilian Coffee County, 1850–1900* (Cambridge, 1957); Octávio Ianni, *As metamorfoses do escravo* (São Paulo, 1962); Fernando Henrique Cardoso, *Capitalismo e escravidão: O negro na sociedade do Rio Grande do Sul* (São Paulo, 1962); Roger Bastide and Florestan Fernandes, *Relações sociais entre negros e brancos em São Paulo* (São Paulo, 1955); Emília Viotti da Costa, *Da senzala à colônia* (São Paulo, 1966). Also see David Brion Davis, *The Problem of Slavery in Western Culture* (Ithaca, 1966), and Robert Conrad's se-

perienced appallingly unpleasant conditions; often the treatment of bondsmen was downright brutal. While enslaving black people for 300 years, Brazilian proprietors showed little respect for Negro slaves as human beings; many, in fact, believed the black was innately inferior to the white. The principal interest of the masters was to exploit their servile workers and to reap profits from their labor. Indeed, some slaveholders were kinder than others, but little could be done against the severe master. The Church and the State interfered little, for despite some laws to the contrary, it was generally recognized that the *senhor* ruled supreme on his plantation. Slaveholders commanded great respect in the society and in the government. They were a powerful, jealous class, protective of their interests in slavery and resistant to any changes that might challenge their hegemony. Brazilian society was geared to the interests of the slave proprietors—to the barons of the land who acquired great economic wealth, social prestige, and political power through their possession of chattel labor.

As a result of the new works and new perspectives, we have a different and more accurate picture of the society engendered by the slave system, and consequently we can now develop a more accurate picture of abolition in Brazil. Recent studies of abolition by Octávio Ianni, Emília Viotti da Costa, and Richard Graham have focused on the broad social and economic transformations in the empire during the era of the antislavery movement.[7] New developments involving the commercialization of agriculture, industrialization, and urbanization provided dynamic forms of change that upset the old order. Advocates of

---

lection of readings as well as his own essay "The Brazilian Slave," in *History of Latin American Civilization: Sources and Interpretations,* ed. Lewis Hanke (1967), II, pp. 155–213. Also see Robert Conrad, "The Struggle for the Abolition of the Brazilian Slave Trade, 1808–1853" (unpublished Ph.D. dissertation, Columbia University, 1967).

7. Ianni, *As metamorfoses do escravo;* Octávio Ianni, *Raças e classes sociais no Brasil* (Rio de Janeiro, 1966); Costa, *Da senzala à colônia;* Richard Graham, "Causes of the Abolition of Negro Slavery in Brazil: An Interpretation," *Hispanic American Historical Review* (May 1966), pp. 123–37; Richard Graham, *Britain and the Onset of Modernization in Brazil, 1850–1914* (Cambridge, England, 1968).

the new arrangement viewed slavery as anachronistic, hence a hindrance to Brazil's modernization. Also, Brazil's increasing contact with the people and ideas of other Western nations provided an intellectual seedbed for a movement to challenge the slaveholders.

The new interpretations have the value of giving the student of abolition a broader perspective. Highlighting the general forces of change provides background for understanding abolition, but it does not fully explain how the slave regime crumbled so completely in a very short time. In the late 1870s hardly a word was heard in political circles about the early abolition of slavery. In May 1888, less than a decade later, Brazilians danced in the streets to celebrate the occasion of national liberation. It was the force of the abolitionist campaign, the turbulence that accompanied it, and the threat of further upheaval that brought the rapid demise of the pervasive institution. Authors of revisionist studies recognize the importance of upheaval in precipitating a settlement of the slavery question, but the details, the movement, and the significance of events which occurred during the crucial period of the 1880s need more elaborate treatment.[8] Moreover, despite the contributions of revisionist research, the view that Brazil found a "gradual" solution to abolition remains a popular interpretation. Even revisionists place heavy stress on the idea that slavery was already in a long-term state of decline by the early 1880s because of the termination of the Atlantic slave trade, the low reproduction rate of bondsmen, the common practice of manumission, broad-scale economic changes, the progressive position of some planters, and the effects of emancipation legislation. All of this evidence tends to support the conclusion that Brazilian slavery was severely weakened by the early 1880s and was declining significantly.[9]

8. Among the most important older studies that offer considerable information about individuals, clubs, and legislation are: Osório Duque-Estrada, *A abolição: 1831–1888* (Rio de Janeiro, 1918); and Evaristo de Moraes, *A campanha abolicionista: 1879–1888* (Rio de Janeiro, 1924).

9. See, for example, Viotti da Costa, *Da senzala à colônia*, pp. 154–220. Especially note the charts and commentary on pp. 203–208. This

It is clear that abolitionists viewed the situation differently in the 1880s. Statistics published during the decade exposed the fallacy of popular assumptions about the rapid disintegration of slavery. The institution was not dying except in the minds of the people. No viable solution seemed in the offing for those who planned to wait for liberation to come about "naturally." A policy of noninterference with slavery offered little hope to the generation of abolitionists. Hence, there is little reason to believe that slaveholders would have released their bondsmen in the forseeable future, whatever the general changes in the empire, were it not for the tremendous pressure placed upon them by the abolitionist campaign. In the end many slaveholders found resistance impossible as the antislavery movement closed in a wave of turmoil and violence that brought a surprisingly abrupt settlement of the problem.

Students of comparative slavery who seek to find in Brazilian history an example of a comfortable means of abolishing slavery are likely to be disappointed. Wherever the institution became deeply rooted, such as in Brazil and the United States, its eradication was an explosive issue. In Brazil the onset of the antislavery movement highlighted the salient contrasts in society: the city and the countryside; a capitalist economy and a precapitalist economy; free labor and slave labor; liberty and bondage. Contradictions developing out of these differences could not be resolved easily. A considerable amount of friction would be necessary before slavery could be eradicated.

---

interpretation clearly has influenced the views of many scholars outside of Brazil. For examples of similar assessments in some generally excellent studies of slavery, abolition, and race relations in English, see Graham, *Britain and the Onset of Modernization in Brazil,* pp. 160–61; Thomas E. Skidmore, "The Death of Brazilian Slavery, 1866–1888," in Frederick B. Pike (ed.), *Latin American History: Select Problems* (New York, Chicago, San Francisco, and Atlanta, 1969), pp. 169–70; Michael Banton, *Race Relations* (New York, 1967), p. 261.

Contents

I

The Rise of Abolitionism

1: The Masters and the Slaves

WRITING on the reciprocity of human relationships, Ralph Waldo Emerson observed that every situation had two sides, a good and a bad, and every advantage had its tax. "If you put a chain around the neck of a slave," he said, "the other end fastens itself around your own."[1] Emerson's proverb applies properly to the position of slaveholders in Brazil during the late nineteenth century. On the surface their status seemed secure; more than just masters over slaves, they appeared also to be masters over the economic, social, and political life of the empire. Below the surface, however, stood the shaky foundations of slaveholder power. If slave proprietors gave the appearance of wealth, in reality many of them were in financial difficulty; if they seemed to be politically unified, in reality their interests were diverse; if the free masses acted as though they were ever-ready to please them, in reality a significant number of non-slaveholders were unhappy about the existing order; and if the slaves seemed to be contented, in reality they harbored the seeds of rebellion. In time the abolitionist movement would destroy illusions about the blessings of slavery, exposing the liability side of the institution's ledger.

As late as the 1880s slavery remained well intact in Brazil. Until this time many people continued to be closely connected to the institution for a variety of economic, social, and political reasons. These individuals did not care to relinquish their interest in servile labor until they judged change convenient

1. Ralph Waldo Emerson, "Compensation," *Essays: First and Second Series—Emerson's Complete Works* (New York and Boston, 1929), pp. 109, 120.

and beneficial for them. If necessary, they would defend their multidimensional investment with all the forces they could muster. Commenting on this situation, the editor of an English-language newspaper in Rio de Janeiro reported in 1880, "There is fair indication that the old-fashioned slaveholding element will rule the country with but little opposition." Slave proprietors were so well entrenched, he thought, that abolition could not be achieved "except by revolution." Discounting that possibility, he concluded, "Businessmen may therefore count upon a continuation of the present state of affairs for a long time to come." Two years later the same editor offered a similar evaluation, suggesting that "were we to say that slavery would not continue 10 years, few if any Brazilians would believe the assertion."

To most observers at the time, the abolition of slavery seemed unlikely as an early prospect because the slave proprietors wielded tremendous influence and power. Brazilian society under Dom Pedro II was above all the dominion of slaveholders. Control over affairs of the nation rested indisputably in the hands of the people who possessed numerous slaves and vast areas of land.[2] Slaveholders watched over their local domains like feudal barons, and the *casa grande* (plantation mansion) became symbolic of their riches and importance. In the chambers of the provincial assemblies and the Imperial Parliament, the voices of slave proprietors commanded respect and deference. Not all of the ministers of government owned bondsmen, of course, but the slaveless political leaders usually had close family connections with slaveholders.[3] The great slave proprietors, then, were more than just masters over slaves; they were *senhores*—the lords, gentlemen, or aristocrats of the land—and their power rele-

2. This study will focus on the planters as the most important class of slaveholders. Urban citizens possessed slaves too, of course, but, on the average, they did not own as many slaves nor were they as politically powerful as the *fazendeiros*. The principal efforts in defense of slavery in the 1880s were made by the great rural slaveholders.

3. Evaristo de Moraes, *A campanha abolicionista, 1879–1888* (Rio de Janeiro, 1924), p. 104.

gated other social groups to dependent roles.[4] The poor rural proletariat struggled along feeding and servicing the plantations, often performing the dangerous tasks for which the planters did not want to risk employing their slaves. Clergymen sought to satisfy the planters' wishes in order to receive their social and financial support. Similarly, the slaveholding planters received good treatment from commercial agents who wished to export their crops, merchants who wanted to sell to the plantations, lawyers who sought the planters' patronage, and magistrates who wanted the planters' political support.[5]

Slave proprietorship appeared to offer extraordinary benefits of leisure and the freedom to participate in activities outside the plantation. Well-established *fazendeiros* frequently left the *fazendas* to visit friends in the cities or to gather together for social affairs and political meetings. They also indulged their sons, encouraging them to enjoy the comforts of the privileged class, often sending them to academies in the cities to acquire the culture, facility with language, and *savoir-faire* which their parents lacked. A degree in literature, law or medicine could enhance the status of the entire family. With economic security rooted in slavery and the plantation, a respectable family name, and some education, a young man could easily achieve social prominence.[6]

Slavery served as the foundation for this way of life. The system's attraction lay in its apparent offering of the most direct route to social prestige and political power.[7] Those who

4. Anyda Marchant, *Viscount Mauá and the Empire of Brazil* (Berkeley and Los Angeles, 1965), pp. 36–37, 209–210; *Annaes da Câmara* (1887), V, p. 379 (see the statement of Joaquim Nabuco); Francisco José de Oliveira Viana, *O ocaso do império* (São Paulo, 1925), pp. 73–75; Richard M. Morse, *From Community to Metropolis: A Biography of São Paulo, Brazil* (Gainesville, 1958), pp. 113–14.

5. *A Redempção,* March 3, 1887, p. 3; *Rio News,* May 24, 1882, pp. 4–5.

6. *Rio News,* November 5, 1882, p. 3; July 1, 1884, p. 2; *Congresso Agricola: Colleção de documentos* (Rio de Janeiro, 1878), pp. 249–51; Louis Couty, *L'esclavage au Brésil* (Paris, 1881), p. 80.

7. Celso Furtado, *The Economic Growth of Brazil* (Berkeley and Los Angeles, 1963), p. 133; Richard Graham, *Britain and the Onset of Modernization in Brazil, 1850–1914* (Cambridge, England, 1968), p. 9.

aspired to become members of the master class had few qualms about investing a large portion of their capital in servile labor, and once they made a sizable financial commitment, their allegiance to the institution hardened. Aristocrats and aspiring aristocrats viewed slavery as essential to establishing a comfortable and respectable life style.[8] The institution offered "a special pleasure of dominion to the master," explained a planter from Rio de Janeiro.[9] During hard times a slave proprietor might sell or free some of his bondsmen, but usually he would submit to great hardship before divorcing himself entirely from slaveholding.[10] As one writer from Minas Gerais observed in the 1860s, "A poor family will sell its house, its furniture—everything that is a vital necessity to it —before selling its slaves." [11]

The glitter of aristocratic status made possible through slaveholding masked slavery's hidden liabilities. Like moths drawn to light, proprietors plunged into attractive ventures without taking cognizance of the dangers of becoming prisoners of the system. As the son of one slaveholder described the deception of wealth:

> We senhores of slaves lived covered with the mantle of riches when in fact misery corrupts the core profoundly!
>
> No one takes profits from slavery in proportion to his capital! [12]

There was much truth in this description, for planters had tied up an inordinate amount of capital in slavery. Although the market prices of bondsmen rose significantly in the 1860s

8. Stanley J. Stein, *Vassouras: A Brazilian Coffee County* (Cambridge, 1957), p. 229.

9. Luiz Peixoto de Lacerda Werneck, *Idéias de colonização, precedidas de uma sucinta exposição dos princípios que regem a população* (Rio de Janeiro, 1855), p. 47.

10. Luiz Monteiro Caminhoá, *Canna de assucar e café: Relatório apresentado ao governo imperial pelo engenheiro Luiz Monteiro Caminhoá* (Rio de Janeiro, 1880), p. 105.

11. Joaquim Caetano da Silva Guimaraes, *A agricultura em Minas* (Rio de Janeiro, 1865), p. 15.

12. *Annaes da Câmara* (1879), March 5, p. 195.

and 1870s, they continued to invest heavily in slave labor. Bondsmen represented about one half of the capital of a typical slaveholding *fazendeiro,* while the value of the land made up a large percentage of the balance in assets.[13] Many found that slavery did not yield excellent returns in proportion to the size of their investment. The slave population of the estates included a large element that did not participate directly in agricultural production, often as much as 40 to 50 percent. *Fazendeiros* paid dearly for the numerous supplementary workers who rewarded them primarily in social rather than economic terms. Servants, cooks, blacksmiths, grounds keepers, the children, the old and the indigent all needed to be clothed, fed, and cared for by the proprietor. It is not surprising that *fazendeiros* frequently complained of a shortage of capital. They continued to concentrate their funds in land and slaves, sinking deeper and deeper into the economic quagmire.[14]

Excessive devotion to social and political affairs also affected the planters' economic position, leaving little time for plantation management. With large, servile labor forces at their service and a routinized work system based on cultivating and harvesting one principal crop, they often left their estates in the hands of overseers for long periods while they visited friends, attended political conferences, or served in the assemblies. Many expended large portions of their income in the cities by entertaining mistresses or gambling for high stakes.[15]

Finally, dependence on slavery often left planters lacking even the most rudimentary understanding of efficient and effective techniques for the cultivation of agricultural crops.

13. Stein, *Vassouras,* pp. 214–15, 225; Leôncio Basbaum, *História sincera da república, das origens até 1889* (Rio de Janeiro, 1957), pp. 156, 160.

14. Roberto C. Simonsen, *Aspectos da história econômica do café* (Rio de Janeiro, 1938), p. 50; *Congresso Agricola,* pp. 247–48; *Falla do presidente da província—October 4, 1887, João Capistrano Bandeira de Mello* (Bahia, 1888), p. 136; *Annaes da Câmara* (1879), March 5, p. 195.

15. *Rio News,* July 1, 1884, p. 2.

They did not devote much time to learning new methods of planting; in fact, some *fazendeiros* learned the basics of agriculture from their slaves.[16] The *fazendeiros'* educated sons could offer little help, for their training in literature, law and medicine hardly provided the practical knowledge necessary for plantation management. Relatively primitive farming techniques prevailed. Land was cleared by the traditional slash-and-burn methods, and *fazendeiros* exploited the soil without adequate rotation of crops. To a large extent the techniques of agriculture had not changed significantly from methods employed centuries before.[17]

Most planters chose to ignore these difficulties, or, if they recognized them, they argued that slavery was still worth the price. They could not imagine finding a post of wealth, comfort, prestige, and power without slaves. The servile institution had been a basic element in Brazilian society since the founding of the first important colonial settlements; how could the planters be expected to turn away from a class position that had come to be regarded as a way of life? By the nineteenth century, diverse groups had a stake in slaveholding. Planters, businessmen, friars, foreigners, the Emperor, his family and the Imperial Government all owned bondsmen. Even freedmen saved money to purchase a slave of their own.[18]

In the 1880s, however, slaveholding was, above all, the

16. Almelia de Rezende Martins, *Um idealista realizador: Barão Geraldo de Rezende* (Campinas, n.d.), p. 120.

17. Francisco Antônio Brandão Junior, *A escravatura no Brasil* (Brussels, 1865), pp. 124–26; Domingo Maria Gonçalves, *A instrucção agricola e trabalho livre* (Rio de Janeiro, 1880), pp. 61–62; Graham, *Britain and the Onset of Modernization in Brazil,* p. 12; Basbaum, *História sincera da república,* p. 129; *Congresso Agricola,* pp. 249–51; Couty, *L'esclavage au Brésil,* pp. 49–51. João Alfredo illustrated the backwardness of planters in a Senate speech by describing the case of a *fazendeiro* who fainted when first hearing the whistle of a locomotive in the countryside. See the *Rio News,* September 24, 1887, p. 4.

18. Basbaum, *História sincera da república,* p. 285; Guimaraes, *A agricultura em Minas,* p. 15; Robert Conrad, "The Struggle for the Abolition of the Brazilian Slave Trade, 1808–1853" (unpublished Ph. D. dissertation, Columbia University, 1967), pp. 20–21.

position of the rural landlords. For example, in 1887 the government's registration figures revealed that 90 percent of the bondsmen resided in Brazil's rural districts, and 85 percent of the total number of slaves were employed in agriculture.[19] The proprietors of *latifundio*—the owners of large plantation estates—ranked as the most prominent and politically powerful slaveholders in Brazilian society and assumed the major leadership positions in defending the servile institution when challenges to the system increased. Yet, because of economic, geographic, and historical distinctions, several different planter positions developed. While some slave proprietors viewed abolition as a serious threat to their interests, others became amenable to emancipation. As the reaction of the slaveholding planters to the rise of the antislavery campaign became significant in determining the nature of the final solution, these distinctions are relevant to an understanding of the politics of abolition.

Basically, three types of planters played the most significant roles in the crisis of abolition. These major groups can be identified as the "Traditional Planters," the "Hard-Core Slaveholders," and the "Progressive Planters." These categories represent a simplification of the situation, as the division is not all-inclusive, and in many cases the positions overlapped. Still, generally speaking, these categories are representative of the most salient differences among planter groups.

The first group, the Traditional Planters, were the representatives of many generations of slaveholding and plantation living. Most numerous in the sugar-cane regions of northeast Brazil, such as the provinces of Pernambuco and Bahia, these *senhores do engenho* (sugar planters) were the dominant classes in their communities. There the patriarchal, paternalistic plantation society developed which Gilberto Freyre so brilliantly describes in his classic study, *Casa Grande e Senzala* (*The Masters and the Slaves*). These Northeastern planters, who had become the richest and most

19. *Relatório* of the Minister of Agriculture, Commerce, and Public Works, Rodrigo Augusto da Silva, 1888.

powerful group in Brazil with the ascendancy of the sugar culture in the seventeenth century, were debilitated economically and declining politically by the 1880s. Sugar had experienced a temporary revival in the middle of the century from increased consumption in Europe and political upheaval in the United States and the Caribbean. But the development of beet sugar in Europe and the return of economic stability in North America and the islands threw the *senhores de engenho* back into serious difficulty. By the 1870s, the burgeoning coffee exports of the South well surpassed the value of exported sugar.[20]

Because of the long-term depression of the Northeastern sugar economy in the nineteenth century, traditional planters became increasingly interested in emancipation. Finding that they possessed more bondsmen than they could afford to maintain, they searched for ways to relieve themselves of their financial burden. They wanted to divorce themselves from the responsibility of feeding, clothing, and managing the superfluous Negro slaves who were not immediately needed for production purposes. Many of these planters sold their excess slaves to the South, where the *fazendeiros* of the rapidly expanding coffee regions were willing to pay high prices for them. Consequently, when the interprovincial slave trade drew to a close in the early 1880s, Northeastern planters had in their charge a disproportionately large number of very young, very old, or ill slaves who for various reasons were not attractive for sale in the interprovincial market of human property. As a result, the Northeastern planters increasingly freed their slaves during the 1880s.[21]

20. Graham, *Britain and the Onset of Modernization in Brazil,* pp. 13, 24; Basbaum, *História sincera da república,* pp. 135–37; Simonsen, *Aspectos da história do café,* p. 45.

21. Tobias do Rêgo Monteiro, *Pesquisas e depoimentos para a história* (Rio de Janeiro, 1913), p. 58; Jorge Freire, *Notas à margem da abolição* (n.p., n.d.), p. 6; *Rio News,* December 15, 1881, p. 3; P. Lopes de Leão, *Como pensa sôbre o elemento servil* (Rio de Janeiro, 1870), p. 9; *Importaçãó de Trabalhadores Chins: Memória apresentada ao Ministério da Agricultura, Commércio e Obras Públicas e impressa por sua ordem* (Rio de Janeiro, 1869), p. 6; *Brazil Agricola,* January 31, 1881,

With the long-term economic decline of the sugar economy and the close of the interprovincial slave traffic, the Negro freedmen came to represent a large segment of the total population of the Northeast. The increase in free labor and the decline of slavery did not, however, seriously alter the social and political position of the Northeastern planters. Freedmen did not frequently move away, because economic opportunities were limited in the depressed regions, and movement into the interior was restricted by the semi-arid *sertão* and *caatingas* backland conditions. Many freedmen remained connected to their old masters by both social and economic ties. By this arrangement, the planters of the Northeast discovered that they could work out a comfortable relationship with their free laborers. While the rural proletariat serviced the plantations or worked directly in the fields on a low-wage basis, the planters maintained their influence over the people of the region. Legal bondage gradually disappeared, but a quasi-slavery relationship took its place.[22]

A second group, the Hard-Core Slaveholders, were strongly committed to maintaining slavery and the slaveholders' regime for reasons of economic dependence, social prestige, and political power. Unlike the Traditional Planters, the Hard-Core Slaveholders did not feel that they could afford economically to move rapidly toward emancipation, nor did they have confidence that their other interests could be satisfied in a society without slavery. Hard-Core Slaveholders held prominent positions in all the areas where large-scale plantation

---

p. 74; Herbert H. Smith, *Brazil: The Amazons and the Coast* (New York, 1879), p. 470.

22. Furtado, *The Economic Growth of Brazil,* pp. 151–52; Charles Wagley, *An Introduction to Brazil* (New York and London, 1963), pp. 106–114. In an important article published after preparation of the above text, J. H. Galloway argues that by the late nineteenth century only a small portion of the population in the Northeast had a large financial stake in slavery. Essentially, Northeastern planters tried to hold on to their bondsmen for sociological rather than economic reasons. See J. H. Galloway, "The Last Years of Slavery on the Sugar Plantations of Northeastern Brazil," *Hispanic American Historical Review* (November 1971), pp. 586–605.

agriculture prevailed. For example, many *senhores* from the sugar and cotton-producing regions filled the ranks of this group as well as *fazendeiros* from the coffee-producing regions of central São Paulo, especially Campinas.[23] But the strongest base of Hard-Core Slaveholder power was concentrated in the region of the Paraíba River Valley, which runs through northeastern São Paulo, southern Minas Gerais, and a large part of Rio de Janeiro. It was the proprietors who lived near the "River of Slavery" who most vehemently expressed the political mentality of the intransigent slaveholders.[24] The province of Rio de Janeiro, particularly, contributed heavily to the leadership class of Hard-Core Slaveholders.

The coffee economy of the Paraíba Valley underwent tremendous development in the nineteenth century with labor obtained almost entirely from the Atlantic and interprovincial slave traffic. By mid-century the *fazendeiros* of Rio de Janeiro ranked among the richest planters in the empire, and the by-product of political power made the saying "Brazil is Rio de Janeiro" popular in parliamentary circles.[25] But economic decline set in and the coffee economy began to suffer severely from exhaustion of the soil and overdependence on inefficient slave labor and antiquated agricultural techniques. By the 1880s more than 50 percent of the *fazendeiros* in the valley were heavily in debt and without prospects of recuperation.[26] The sight of large mansions in glaring need of repair gave evidence of the rapid deterioration of their economic position. "Rich father, noble son, poor grandson," said the contemporaries in an oft-quoted statement which tersely described the rise and decline of many families of the Paraíba Valley.[27]

23. In the northern sections of Brazil, planters from Bahia and Maranhão, particularly, played important roles as Hard-Core Slaveholders.

24. Joaquim Nabuco, *Conferências e discursos abolicionistas* (São Paulo, n.d.), p. 311.

25. *O Paíz,* November 9, 1887, p. 1.

26. Emília Viotti da Costa, "A proclamação da república," *Anais do Museu Paulista,* 19, pp. 186–87.

27. Alcindro Sodré, *O elemento servil, a abolição* (Rio de Janeiro, 1942), p. 129.

The Rio planters depended almost exclusively on slave labor for work in the coffee fields. Despite severe financial difficulties in the 1880s, most refused to convert to a free labor system. They attached prestige to owning slaves, and neither the free Brazilian nor the European immigrant interested them much as laborers. Slavery represented a way of life to them—a leisurely and comfortable existence that gave the *senhor* of the plantation prestige and influence. The attitudes of the Hard-Core Slaveholders of Rio de Janeiro represented a classic example of the slavocrat mentality.

Hard-Core Slaveholders did not arrange a favorable accommodation with free labor as did the Traditional Planters because the economic difficulties of the planters in Rio de Janeiro were different from those of planters in the Northeast. While the demand for Brazilian sugar was declining in the world market, the demand for Brazilian coffee was rising. Despite their economic problems, the coffee *fazendeiros* of Rio de Janeiro did not desire to cut the size of their work force or risk disruption of production. They viewed abolition as a disastrous possibility, because they were not confident that the freedmen would remain on the *fazendas*. The Paraíba planters' social ties with the Negroes were not so secure as in the case of the Northeastern planters, and they feared that many freedmen would run off to seek new opportunities in the cities or in the richer, neighboring regions such as São Paulo. Moreover, the *fazendeiros* were not prepared to work with the freedmen that would remain. With indebtedness already increasing at an astounding rate, they did not wish to incur the new financial responsibility of wage payment.[28]

As long as slave labor remained prevalent in many parts of the empire, Rio de Janeiro planters could survive with some satisfaction. They could compete with other planters who operated within the slave system. But the trend toward employment of immigrants and other free workers seemed

28. Stein, *Vassouras,* pp. 214–15, 230, 237; Simonsen, *Aspectos da história do café,* pp. 17–31, 50; Sérgio Milliet, *Roteiro do café e outros ensaios* (São Paulo, 1941), pp. 19–20.

ominous for the Hard-Core Slaveholders, because they could not hope to produce the same products as cheaply or efficiently. And the most unpleasant prospect of all—total abolition of slavery—could prove a catastrophe from their standpoint, sweeping away the value of their heavy capital investment in bondsmen and the foundations of their work system. Finding themselves in a state of economic decline, they desperately needed new loans to remain solvent. Slaves were their primary source of collateral. Also, the antislavery movement represented a threat to their social aspirations. Financial difficulties notwithstanding, they expected to imitate the life style of older landed aristocrats, settling down in a system based on servile labor. Viewing slavery as essential to their well-being, the Hard-Core Slaveholders revealed a deeper commitment to the institution than any other planter group in Brazil. Politically, they stood out as the most inflexible opponents of the legislative proposals of the abolitionists.[29]

A third group, the Progressive Planters, resided in diverse regions such as the sugar plantation areas of Campos in Rio de Janeiro and Recife in Pernambuco and the central and western sections of São Paulo.[30] Since the importance of the Paulista *fazendeiros* well surpasses that of all other groups in this category, they deserve special attention. As the largest bloc of Progressive Planters, they played a crucial role in the crisis of the 1880s.

The powerful coffee barons of São Paulo found themselves trapped in a dilemma on the question of slavery. While they entertained thoughts adverse to slaveholding, in practice they

29. Eugene D. Genovese, *The World the Slaveholders Made: Two Essays in Interpretation* (New York, 1969), p. 84.

30. The *usinas* (centralized sugar factories) of Pernambuco represent an important example of new agricultural enterprises in the Northeast in the 1880s. Sponsored by foreign investments and employing improved methods of sugar production, these organizations aimed at cutting costs and strengthening the competitive position of Brazilian sugar in the world market. See Emília Viotti da Costa, *"O escravo no grande lavoura,"* in Sérgio Buarque de Holanda (ed.), *História geral da civilização brasileira* (São Paulo, 1966), V, pp. 172–74.

remained dependent on slave labor. Many Paulista *fazendeiros* did not have deep ties with the seignorial, slaveholding traditions. Drawn from the merchant trades and professions in the cities, they were essentially urban types in training and mentality. These individuals spent much of their time in the cities, and their ideas reflected a more modern outlook than those of other planter groups. On the other hand, a sizable number originated from rural backgrounds. Some had risen from positions as small farmers; others had migrated from older plantation regions where economic decline limited opportunities. Although they did carry notions about the slaveholding way of life in their intellectual and cultural baggage, they also demonstrated an ability to break from many of the traditional ties by moving to invest capital in developing areas where slave labor was not plentiful. By valuing land as capital and labor as a commodity they could begin to shake loose from the old system and adapt to a new economy. They came to view the plantation as a business enterprise rather than as a way of life.[31]

Historical circumstances also helped direct Paulista planters toward an interest in free labor. São Paulo expanded rapidly at a time when the province did not contain a slave population adequate to meet the *fazendeiros'* manpower needs. The end of the African slave trade in the early 1850s, rising slave prices, and the close of the interprovincial slave trade in the early 1880s forced the Paulista planters to invest their money in labor-saving machinery, banks, railroads, and other commercial and industrial enterprises instead of slaves. Technical advances made coffee production more efficient. *Fazendeiros* began replacing slow hand work with machinery to hull, blow,

31. Octávio Ianni, *Raças e classes sociais no Brasil* (Rio de Janeiro, 1966), pp. 79–80; Richard Graham, "Causes for the Abolition of Negro Slavery in Brazil: An Interpretive Essay," *Hispanic American Historical Review* (May 1966), pp. 123–37; Fernando Henrique Cardoso, "Condições sociais da industrialização em São Paulo," *Revista Brasiliense* (March–April 1960), pp. 31–46; Nícia Vilela Luz, *"A administração provincial de São Paulo em face do movimento abolicionista," Revista de administração* (December 1948), p. 97.

and classify the coffee. In relation to other planters, their economic expansion occurred late. In an earlier period they too could have lapsed into a deep commitment to a slaveholder's regime, but the shortage of slaves, the threat of abolitionism, and their experience with new forms of business enterprise convinced them that in their dynamic economy abundant investment opportunities existed that were more profitable than tying up capital in slaves.[32]

On the other hand, the serious labor shortage had a retarding effect on the Progressive Planters' attitude toward emancipation. Still dependent on slave labor for much of their production, these *fazendeiros* worried about the repercussions of widespread liberation. São Paulo attracted European immigrants, but not in sufficient numbers to satisfy the planters' demand for labor. The *fazendeiros* feared that abolition would deprive them of many workers and upset their economic prosperity. Consequently, many São Paulo politicians allied with the most adamant adversaries of abolitionism.

In spite of the Paulista planters' reluctance to proceed with rapid and extensive emancipation, they took pride in identifying themselves as "emancipators." Typical of the equivocation and inconsistency between thought and action is the position of Martinho Prado Junior, a prominent *fazendeiro* and political leader. In 1882 he labeled slavery "anachronistic" and a "horrible cancer," but not until 1887, when he saw abolition imminent, did he announce that he would liberate his fifty-two slaves within a year.[33] Like Prado, many Paulista *fazendeiros* described slavery as a dying institution in the long run and declared an interest in accelerating the provisions of the laws to bring about complete

32. Warren Dean, "The Planter as Entrepreneur: The Case of São Paulo," *Hispanic American Historical Review* (May 1966), pp. 142–44; Cardoso, "Condições sociais da industrialização em São Paulo," p. 35; Genovese, *The World the Slaveholders Made,* pp. 85–89; Emília Viotti da Costa, *Da senzala à colônia* (São Paulo, 1966), pp. 177–87; Anyda Marchant, *Viscount Mauá and the Empire of Brazil* (Berkeley and Los Angeles, 1965), pp. 220–21.

33. *In Memoriam: Martinho Prado Junior* (São Paulo, 1943), p. 184.

emancipation within suggested periods ranging from five to twenty-five years. The interim term, they said, would allow the planters to recruit workers and prepare for the transformation to free labor.

In short, the Progressive Planters approached the slavery question cautiously and defensively, but their interest in the system was primarily based on economic needs, not social and political considerations. The labor shortage influenced São Paulo *fazendeiros* in contrary ways. In the long run it forced them to familiarize themselves with capitalistic methods, and, consequently, they became less attached to slavery. But in the short run it increased their dependence on slave labor for the continuation of high production without disruption. Until 1887, just a year before abolition, the majority of the Paulista slaveowners were hostile to early emancipation, and statistics showed their province to have the slowest relative decline in the slave population in all the empire. It took a series of disruptive events in the 1887–1888 period to compel them to alter their position. Thus the epithet "progressive" was largely of the planters' own making. Preferring to view themselves in the vanguard of the fight for free labor, they tended to overlook their protective, temporizing attitude toward slavery. Terminology did not fool the abolitionists. They saw too many qualifications in the political rhetoric of the Paulista *fazendeiros* to describe their stance as "progressive."

Despite the reluctance of planters to liberate bondsmen, slaveholders, especially the Hard-Core and Progressive groups, frequently suggested that slavery was in a state of decline in Brazil, and, given the continued operation of a variety of depreciating factors, it would eventually disappear of a natural death. By trying to create an image of a strong trend toward diminution, slaveholders hoped to anticipate and undermine the arguments of antislavery groups. In particular, slave proprietors contended that manumission was common, that the close of the African slave trade cut off a major source of new bondsmen, and that the Rio Branco Law of 1871 further curtailed opportunities to replenish the declining slave population, thus dooming the institution to gradual extinction.

Cases of manumission could easily be advertised for partisan purposes. Slave proprietors enjoyed dramatizing events in which they liberated selected bondsmen with ceremony and color. Often they chose special occasions for their emancipatory acts, such as birthdays and religious and national holidays.[34] These celebrations obscured the real reasons for many of the manumissions: The slaves were old, sick, or no longer needed by their masters. Actually, these cases often represented abandonment, not liberation. The situation became so tragic in some areas that an important Bahian slaveholder introduced legislation in 1854 requiring masters to help sustain bondsmen they had freed.[35] In reality, manumissions did not effect significant diminution of the total slave population; they only gave the institution the *appearance* of decline because of the publicity that attended emancipations.

The termination of the African slave trade in 1850 also misled contemporaries about the status of the slave population. Planters believed it sounded the death knell for slavery. Before the 1850s, proprietors depended on the African trade as a primary source of workers. Male captives made up the majority of imported Africans. Planters worked them mercilessly, then replaced the effete laborers with new Africans purchased for low prices. Without a tradition of replenishing the labor force within the Brazilian slave system, masters believed the close of the Atlantic traffic would result in a fast decline of the slave population.[36] But they underestimated

34. Martins, *Um idealista realizador,* pp. 258–59.

35. Brandão, *A escravatura no Brasil,* pp. 57–58. The Bahian slaveholder, who later received the title of the Baron of Cotegipe, became noted for his virulent opposition to abolitionism in the 1880s. The motivation behind his action of 1854 deserves further study. For a different interpretation of the manumission issue, see Herbert S. Klein, "The Colored Freedmen in Brazilian Slave Society," *Journal of Social History* (Fall 1969), pp. 30–52.

36. Guimaraes, *A agricultura em Minas,* pp. 9–10; Agostinho Marques Perdigão Malheiro, *A escravidão no Brasil* (Rio de Janeiro, 1866–1867), Vol. II, pp. 157–58; Lacerda Werneck, *Idéias de colonização,* pp. 21–24.

their ability to adjust to the change. After 1850 planters gave more attention to the health needs of their bondsmen and encouraged breeding within the established slave community. To offer fewer than three meals a day or force slaves to work in the rain was to act against one's own interest, warned a Rio de Janeiro planter who stressed the need for more slave offspring shortly after the close of the African trade.[37] As slave prices doubled and tripled from the 1850s to the 1880s, proprietors increasingly spoke of providing better food, clothing, shelter, and medical care as well as a less exhausting work schedule. Improved treatment helped planters to cut down the slaves' high mortality rate while increasing the birth rate.[38] For example, between 1873 and 1885 the number of children born of slaves was more than adequate to replenish the slave population lost by death and emancipation during the period. Although these children of slaves were not categorized officially as bondsmen (a situation that will be explained shortly), inclusion of their numbers reveals a net increase of 6,643 slaves over the twelve-year period.[39] The slave population's fertility was clearly much greater than slave proprietors contended. Nevertheless, most slaveholders refused to acknowledge publicly that their efforts might have given renewed vitality to the institution of slavery. In the context of the emancipation question they continued to bemoan the difficulties supposedly imposed by the close of the African trade and predicted that these problems would eventually lead to the demise of slavery.

37. Barão do Paty do Alferes, *Memória sôbre a fundação e costeio de uma fazenda na província de Rio de Janeiro* (Rio de Janeiro, 1860), pp. 22–28.

38. Joaquim Nabuco, *Conferência do Sr. Joaquim Nabuco a 22 de junho de 1884 no Theatro Polytheama* (Rio de Janeiro, 1884), p. 28; *Rio News,* May 24, 1882, pp. 4–5; Couty, *L'esclavage au Brésil,* p. 51; W. D. Christie, *Notes on Brazilian Questions* (London and Cambridge, 1865), pp. 68–72; *Annaes do Senado* (1884), June 9, pp. 30–31.

39. The figure is obtained by adding the number of *ingenuos* ("free" children born of slave mothers after passage of the Rio Branco Law)—a total of 439,831 for 1885—to the slave population registered for that year (1,133,228). When this total is matched against the slave population registered for 1873 (1,566,416), it reveals a net increase of 6,643.

Finally, passage of the Rio Branco Law in 1871, which established an official emancipation fund and declared free all children of slave mothers born after the legislation went into effect, deceived many into believing that meaningful legislative action had been taken to doom slavery. The law appeared to be another strong blow at the source of slaves. Now even the propagation of slaves' offspring would not guarantee maintenance of the system. But the "free" children, or *ingenuos,* as they were called, continued to live under the care of their masters, to remain in a state of semibondage until the age of twenty-one. A few masters took the option of redeeming the children for money when they reached the age of eight; most chose to wait until the law would force them to release the *ingenuos.* Understandably, proprietors treated *ingenuos* much as they handled their regular slaves, and, in practical terms, the law could have little real significance until the children reached the age of twenty-one. This never happened, as the abolition law of 1888 preceded the first "maturity" date by four and one half years. Consequently, the population of *ingenuos* represented a hidden factor that did not appear in the official statistics on slavery. The Imperial Government reported a total of 439,831 *ingenuos* as of June 30, 1885, and the number probably climbed well above 500,000 before abolition brought complete freedom.[40] When these figures are added to the official slave statistics, they raise serious questions about the celebrated decline of the institution in the 1880s.

The data in Table I reveal no significant shift downward in the slave population until the mid-1880s. The figure then drops precipitously in 1887, just a year before abolition. These data require qualifications because of deficiencies in the recording of information. Government agents had great difficulty conducting a census of slaves in the empire because of the problems involved in obtaining accurate information concerning isolated plantations and the reluctance of some

40. *Relatório* of the Minister of Agriculture, Commerce, and Public Works, Antônio da Silva Prado, 1886, p. 35.

slaveholders to cooperate. In all the reports, ministers indicated that the returns did not include figures from certain communities, many situated in important slaveholding areas.[41] Because of these shortcomings in the recording system, the totals should be considered approximations of the real situation. Over-all, the information does not support the contention

TABLE I

Slave Population of Brazil *

1873	1,566,416
1875	1,419,966
1878	1,368,097
1883	1,346,648
1884	1,240,806
1885	1,133,228
1887	723,419

* Source: *Relatórios* of the Minister of Agriculture, Commerce, and Public Works.

Note: The totals do not include *ingenuos.*

that slavery diminished at a steady and meaningful pace from the time of the Rio Branco Law in 1871. In fact, by including the *ingenuos* in the slave totals of 1885, the sum shows, if anything, a slight increase in the slave population. These figures highlight the importance of the post-1885 events which abruptly brought the servile institution to a state of collapse. (See Figure I.)

A comparison of the decline in the number of slaves in sections of the empire between 1873 and 1887 reveals proportionately greater diminutions in major provinces of the Northeast compared with major provinces of the Central-

41. See the reports of the Minister of Agriculture, Commerce, and Public Works from 1882 to 1887. Also, see the *Rio News,* October 15, 1881, p. 1.

FIGURE I

Decline of the Brazilian Slave Population: 1873–1888 *

* Source: *Relatórios* of the Minister of Agriculture, Commerce, and Public Works. Note: These totals do not include *ingenuos.*

South. (See Table II.) The bulk of the slave population in Brazil was concentrated in Minas Gerais, Rio de Janeiro, and São Paulo; of the 743,419 slaves in Brazil in 1887, a total of 461,702, or 62 percent, were located in these three principal slaveholding provinces of the Central-South. São Paulo showed the most stable slave population totals of all the provinces. As indicated in Table III, its slave population actually increased in the 1870s and remained close to the peak until shortly before abolition.

Not only did the slaves' opportunities for liberation *from* the system remain limited until after the mid-1880s, but it

TABLE II

Decline of Slavery in the Five Largest Slaveholding Provinces in Brazil: 1873–1887 *

	1873	1887	Proportionate Decrease
Northeast			
Bahia	169,766	76,838	55%
Pernambuco	92,745	41,122	56%
Central-South			
Minas Gerais	356,254	191,952	46%
Rio de Janeiro	303,810	162,421	46%
São Paulo	168,002	107,329	36%

* Source: *Relatórios* of the Minister of Agriculture, Commerce, and Public Works.

is also true that bondsmen received little legal protection against abuses *within* the system of slavery until after the mid-1880s. On the question of treatment, just as on the issue of emancipation, slaveholders tried to create an image of the mildness and flexibility of Brazilian slavery.

Until antislavery pressure began to put teeth into Imperial, provincial, and local laws late in the abolitionist campaign, legislation designed to protect the slaves had very little meaning. In essence, the laws dealt with slaves as "things" rather than as "persons." Legislation which treated bondsmen as property carried much more weight than the isolated cases of laws which, indirectly, recognized their condition as human beings.[42] Legal guarantees for slaves appeared late, even though many believed that certain rights had long been commonly accepted. Despite much talk about respecting families in captivity, for example, the Imperial Government did not

42. Malheiro, *A escravidão no Brasil,* II, pp. 27, 163; Luiz Francisco da Camara Leal, *Considerações e projecto de lei para a emancipação dos escravos sem prejuizo de seus senhores, nem grave onus para o estado* (Rio de Janeiro, 1866), pp. 13–41.

prohibit the separation of slave families until 1869.[43] And not until the 1880s did legislation and judicial leadership provide semieffective means to guarantee the slave's right to save money toward his freedom, allow him to testify in court against his master, and protect him from brutal beatings. Many slaveholders evaded the laws. As late as one year before abolition, the president of the province of Minas

TABLE III

Slave Population of São Paulo Province *

1873	168,002
1875	154,861 **
1878	168,950
1883	174,622
1884	167,493
1885	153,270
1887	107,329

* Source: *Relatórios* of the Minister of Agriculture, Commerce and Public Works.

** The relatively low figure for 1875 is apparently due to incomplete registration.

Gerais renewed a warning against the separation of slave families, and a planter in Rio de Janeiro mortally flogged four bondsmen just a year after parliamentary legislation explicitly forbade whipping.[44] In most matters concerning the plantation the master ruled as the final arbiter; he was the legislature, the police, and the court all in one personage. Legislation framed outside his domain affected him little. Herbert H. Smith, a foreign traveler well acquainted with Brazil, offered poignant commentary on the ineffectual laws to protect slaves:

43. Costa, *Da senzala à colônia,* p. 271.

44. *Correio Paulistano,* October 25, 1887, p. 1; *O Paíz,* October 12, 1887, p. 1.

Practically they are almost useless, because they are not enforced. Everybody knows that there are cases of cruelty to slaves, maltreatment even to death, which are visited only by a light punishment, or with none. But no one knows, few even imagine, the vast number of *hidden* crimes which are yearly perpetrated under the slave system, and which never see the light of a court of justice. A slave may be maimed or killed on an island plantation, and no outsider will know of it; the master and the overseer, interested persons, will not proclaim their own crime, and the other slaves dare not give information, or have no one near to appeal to, or being brutalized by the hardships of their life, they do not care.[45]

Slaves suffered severe punishment for misbehavior. Masters and overseers sometimes employed crude devices resembling primitive torture instruments, but their favorite weapon, symbolic of authority and discipline, was the whip. Sometimes overseers flogged slaves simply for falling short of their daily quotas. Constant use of the whip was not necessary, however, for just the threat of its use was usually enough to cow the captives into obedience. On large plantations overseers typically assumed the responsibility of carrying out the punishments. Overseers were particularly harsh on the estates with more than one hundred slaves where problems of management and discipline could be especially acute. Some slaves achieved the status of overseers and became very severe taskmasters. Apparently they acted with a heavy hand in order to win the confidence of their masters.[46]

45. *Rio News, December* 15, 1881, pp. 1–2.

46. José Corrêa do Amaral to Joaquim Nabuco, September 3, 1881; José do Carmo Ferreira Chaves to Joaquim Nabuco, September 3, 1881, Instituto Joaquim Nabuco; C. B. Ottoni, *O advento da república no Brasil* (Rio de Janeiro, 1890), pp. 55–56. Notes of Joaquim Nabuco on *O eclypse do abolicionismo,* Instituto Joaquim Nabuco; Brandão, *A escravatura no Brasil,* pp. 34–37; Guimaraes, *A agricultura em Minas,* p. 41; Couty, *L'esclavage au Brésil,* p. 47; Joaquim Nabuco, *O aboli-*

It became common for slaves to work fifteen to eighteen hours a day on the huge coffee plantations where *fazendeiros* pushed production to the limits. After a long day of extensive labor, the men and women separated and returned to their respective *senzalas* (slave quarters) to be locked in for the night. These buildings served to incarcerate the bondsmen as well as to shelter them; to deter escape, *senzalas* usually did not have windows and contained only one door. The lack of adequate ventilation produced extreme discomfort in hot and humid weather.[47]

Even when the planter permitted slaves to leave the estate, authorities and citizens carefully watched and circumscribed their activities. Provincial and municipal regulations prescribed curfews, required bondsmen to carry passes signed by their masters, and prohibited them from carrying weapons, participating in carnival festivities, and selling goods without a license.[48]

Only a small minority of slaves were married. The 1872 census listed 8.8 percent in this category compared to 26.5 percent of the free population. By 1887 the figure increased slightly to 10.8 percent.[49] Many masters discouraged marriage among their captives because formal recognition of the relationship could preclude the possibility of selling the man and woman to separate buyers.[50] To avoid this restriction while

---

cionismo (São Paulo, 1938), pp. 125–31. Slaves frequently died from whippings. For example, see the *Rio News,* June 24, 1880, p. 3; June 24, 1881, p. 3; March 15, 1882, p. 4; June 15, 1882, p. 4; December 15, 1882, p. 2.

47. Martins, *Um idealista realizador,* pp. 245–57; Costa, *Da senzala à colônia,* pp. 243–44; Smith, *Brazil, The Amazons and the Coast,* p. 526.

48. Milliet, *Roteiro do café e outros ensaios,* pp. 161–63; Costa, *Da senzala à colônia,* p. 232; Smith, *Brazil,* p. 526; Gilberto Freyre, *The Mansions and the Shanties: The Making of Modern Brazil* (New York, 1963), pp. 260–66.

49. These figures are based on the 1872 census returns and the report of the Minister of Agriculture, Commerce, and Public Works, Rodrigo Augusto da Silva, in 1888.

50. Malvino da Silva Reis, *Situação econômica do Brasil: Exposição apresentada a commissão especial nomeada pela assembléa geral da Associação Commercial em 2 de maio de 1884* (Rio de Janeiro, 1884),

also insuring against the dangers of the slaves' pent-up frustrations, proprietors often allowed sexual promiscuity as an alternative to wedlock. This social order probably affected the psychological development of slave children. Many knew only a single parent: the mother.[51]

Distinctions within the system of Brazilian slavery should not be overlooked. The condition of the captives was not uniformly bad; indeed, some slaves enjoyed privileges which gave them considerably more freedom and comfort than other bondsmen experienced. The contrast between the status of field hands and that of slaves in the "Big House" is a significant example. Field hands worked long hours tending the crops, performing simple, boring, and exhausting tasks. They received little or no formal education or vocational training. Visitors often had difficulty understanding the field hand's crude language, a bastardized form of Portuguese that could be described as plantation vernacular. Servants and domestics who worked in the master's home condescended toward the field hands, believing they had achieved a status of some distinction within the limits of the system. House slaves usually received better food, clothing, and shelter and were more articulate and better acquainted with the social graces than their brothers who worked in the fields.[52]

Urban slaves also enjoyed opportunities beyond the reach of most plantation slaves. They experienced more freedom of movement than their rural counterparts and frequently found time to take on additional jobs for their own economic benefit. Employment as newspaper salesmen, janitors, and part-time workers at other odd jobs afforded them opportunities to

---

p. 25; Costa, *Da senzala à colônia,* p. 268. Of 2,535 slaves listed in the southern city of Florianópolis in the year 1841, for example, only ten were married. See Fernando Henrique Cardoso and Octávio Ianni, *Côr e mobilidade social em Florianópolis: Aspectos da relações entre negros e brancos numa comunidade do Brasil meridional* (São Paulo, 1960), pp. 128–29.

51. Couty, *L'esclavage au Brésil,* p. 75.

52. Martins, *Um idealista realizador,* p. 261; Couty, *L'esclavage au Brésil,* pp. 82–83, 86; Costa, *Da senzala à colônia,* pp. 276–77.

increase their *pecúlio* (savings), income which enabled many urban slaves to purchase their freedom. Slaves in the cities also mastered complicated trades and dominated some important artisan occupations. The development of vocational talent, contact with urban culture, and the opportunity to accumulate savings gave city slaves a sense of dignity and self-confidence that few of their brothers in the rural areas could share. They enjoyed superior physical comforts too in terms of food, clothing, and living conditions. Also, urban bondsmen were less likely to suffer from extreme physical punishment. In the countryside plantation authorities could beat a slave severely and escape public attention. But the proximity of the courts gave the urban slave some hope of redressing grievances if he could obtain legal assistance. It is significant that masters found the threat of returning recalcitrant Negroes to the plantations one of the most effective means of disciplining urban slaves.[53]

It is also generally true that by the time of the abolition campaign, slaves in northeastern Brazil received better treatment than slaves in the coffee regions of the Central-South. Where the institutions of the plantation society had developed patriarchal traditions over several centuries and the depressed sugar economy allowed proprietors to work at a moderate pace, the demands of labor did not tax slaves as greatly as in the regions of the expanding coffee frontier. The *senhor de engenho* was often a resident planter who developed fairly close relationships with the workers on his estate. More than a businessman, he became a *patrão*—the leader of a community or small society in itself. On the other hand, the exploitation of bondsmen became severest in the areas of high capitalization and rapid development where social rela-

53. Nabuco, *O abolicionismo,* pp. 39–40; Freyre, *The Mansions and the Shanties,* pp. 46, 130; Costa, *Da senzala à colônia,* pp. 276, 284; Couty, *L'esclavage au Brésil,* pp. 45, 82; Fernando Henrique Cardoso, *Capitalismo e Escravidão: O Negro na sociedade do Rio Grande do Sul* (São Paulo, 1962), pp. 269–70; *Rio News,* December 15, 1881, pp. 1–2; Malheiro, *A escravidão no Brasil,* II, p. 115.

tionships between master and slave were less intimate and coffee *fazendeiros* "on the make" pushed their laborers hard for quick and sizable profits.[54]

The manifold personalities and attitudes of *senhores* also distinguished the treatment of bondsmen. Some slaveholders showed little concern for the fate of their workers, exploited them terribly, and addressed them with contempt. Others developed a genuine sense of interest and attachment toward their human property. Some *fazendeiros* and their families considered favorite slaves "friends," gave them favored treatment, and grieved by their side in times of illness. Religiously devout masters did not work their bondsmen on Sundays or on numerous Catholic holidays. Ironically, some of the most vehement opponents of abolitionism had established reputations as very kind masters. Within the confines of a system which they could control, these slavocrats were willing to display generosity.[55]

The condition of slaves who worked in the Big House, lived in the cities, resided in the older plantation regions or labored under benevolent masters represent experiences which mitigated life in bondage, providing some relief from the harshest aspects of servility in contrast to the plight of the masses of slaves. Yet the lives of those who enjoyed certain privileges and immunities could hardly be described as attractive. Regardless of the opportunities available *vis-à-vis* other bondsmen, almost all slaves would opt for freedom if they had a choice. In fact, some observers believed the "privileged" groups felt a more intense desire for freedom than most because their chances of obtaining liberty, however

54. Luiz Luna, *O negro na luta contra a escravidão* (Rio de Janeiro, 1968), pp. 121–25; Smith, *Brasil,* pp. 444, 468; Magnus Mörner, *Race Mixture in the History of Latin America* (Boston, 1967), pp. 119–20. Genovese, *The World the Slaveholders Made,* pp. 75–80.

55. Smith, *Brazil,* pp. 82, 468, 526; Christie, *Notes on Brazilian Questions,* p. 101; Costa, *Da senzala à colônia,* pp. 245, 280; Brandão, *A escravatura no Brasil,* pp. 42–44; Couty, *L'esclavage au Brésil,* p. 47; Malheiro, *A escravidão no Brasil,* II, p. 123; Dr. Orlando de Almeida Prado, *Em defeza da raça negra: O preconceito de raça não existe no Brasil* (São Paulo, n.d.), p. 10.

remote, were greater than in the cases of most bondsmen. The glimmer of hope only aggravated the frustration.[56]

Slaveholders demanded obedience and allegiance from their workers as imperative for maintaining effective master-slave relationships. Slaves well understood these expectations and the power and force behind them. By obsequious and deferential behavior they tried to satisfy the desires of the master and win his affection. Many slaveholders so thoroughly enjoyed the manners of respect engendered by the system that they forgot the stimulus-response basis of the relationship. They reached the point of believing that bondsmen were content with their status, unaware of the depths of the slaves' longing for freedom. But in the moments of great pain and anguish slaves broke their silence and revealed their true feelings. The drama of this situation is revealed in the reminiscences of a *senhora* who recalled the experiences on her family's plantation in São Paulo. In spite of her father's general record of good treatment of workers, she could not forget painful scenes when, after a severe lashing, slaves raised their hands to the sky and exclaimed, "God free me!"[57]

Many slaves refused to submit passively to servility. The provinces of Bahia, Minas Gerais, Espirito Santo, Rio de Janeiro, and São Paulo, to name outstanding examples, witnessed serious slave uprisings in the nineteenth century. Sporadic clashes in Bahia involving recent arrivals from Africa and led by urban slaves imbued with Islamic religious ideas marked the most notable insurrections of the first half of the century. In the last decades of slavery the incidence of servile rebellion shifted to the southern coffee regions, particularly affecting São Paulo and Rio de Janeiro during the period of the abolitionist movement. The most widespread disruptions occurred in 1887–1888, a subject for later consideration. But it is significant that the tremors which shook

56. *Annaes do Senado* (1888), June 9, pp. 30–31; Brandão, *A escravatura no Brasil,* pp. 42–44.

57. Adir Gigliotti, "*Libertação dos escravos foi a festa mais bonita a que alguem ja assistiu!,*" *Ultima Hora,* June 23, 1960.

these same provinces in 1882 foreshadowed the larger-scale insurrections which followed, showing the dangers of revolt and the contagious nature of its appeal to the captives.

The first signs of turbulence in 1882 appeared in the area of Rezende, Rio de Janeiro. These slave uprisings quickly spilled over into the plantation communities of the northeastern lip of São Paulo, forcing apprehensive *fazendeiros* to gather their families and flee from their homes. The revolts finally subsided after provincial police forces arrived to restore order.[58] Slave insurrections near the city of Campinas proved more dangerous. When a *fazendeiro* learned of his slaves' insurrection plot, he assembled a party of thirty friends to invade the slave quarters during the night and secure the ringleaders. But the slaves learned of the plan, armed themselves and established an effective communications network between the *senzalas*. They succeeded in driving off the attackers, killing one and wounding several. Then the slave group set out for the city of Campinas shouting *vivas* to emancipation and republicanism. Some from the group engaged in violent acts along the road to Campinas, mortally shooting four free citizens, including a woman and two children. Shortly after, another uprising occurred in the neighboring area of Caldas when 100 slaves killed their overseer and abandoned the plantation. Police from the larger municipality of Campinas were unable to answer the distress call of the Caldas citizens because of difficulty suppressing the revolt in their own area. "The whole countryside is in a state of terror," cried one panicked resident. Eventually a combined force of provincial troops and policemen from the capital city of São Paulo succeeded in quelling the revolts and containing the fugitives.[59]

Slaves also participated in numerous individual acts of violence during the period of abolitionism. From towns such as Barra Mansa and Carangola in Rio de Janeiro, Ponba

58. *Relatório* presented by the vice-president of São Paulo, Conde de Tres-Rios (Santos, 1882), p. 10.

59. *Rio News,* November 15, 1882, pp. 2, 4–5.

in Minas Gerais and Itabapana in Espirito Santo came reports of horrible assassinations by angry slaves. In one case a captive slipped into his master's bedroom during the night to commit the act. In another, a fifteen-year-old boy secured the proprietor's own gun, then shot him. Some slaves resorted to poison. Wives and children of *fazendeiros* also fell victim to slave assassins. Overseers faced the greatest dangers, especially becoming targets after administering punishment or trying to impede escapes.[60]

Slaves frequently fled from the plantations to join fugitive communities in the hinterland or to try to conceal themselves in the urban centers. Many escaped with little preparation or idea of where they could go to seek safety. Within a short time they were usually captured by the *capitaes do mato,* the rough-hewn men who earned handsome rewards for returning runaways to their masters.

When the most desperate slaves saw all avenues of escape closed, some chose suicide. Several reports of such extreme action appeared in the newspapers during the era. A fugitive in Pernambuco tore open his bowels when captured. A slave in Campos cut his throat with a piece of iron and ripped it open after his master placed him in jail; another threw himself under a railroad car rather than return to his mistress.[61]

These shocking examples of hatred, violence and self-destruction led contemporaries to offer grave warnings of future danger. Francisco Antônio Brandão, who wrote one of the first books on slavery in Brazil, worried that without strong preventive measures "the slave will sign his letter of liberty with the blood of his oppressor and, to the disbelief of all, the decayed edifice of our society will fall." Brandão viewed

60. *Rio News,* February 15, 1881, p. 3; February 24, 1881, p. 3; April 15, 1881, p. 3; June 15, 1881, p. 3; August 24, 1881, p. 3; September 15, 1881, p. 3; September 24, 1881, p. 3; December 24, 1881, p. 3; October 15, 1882, p. 4; December 15, 1882, p. 4; *Gazeta de Campinas,* January 21, 1881, p. 2; January 22, 1881, p. 2; *Revista Illustrada,* 1884, *Ano* 9–382, p. 2; *Brazil,* June 3, 1884, p. 1; Luna, *O negro na luta contra a escravidão,* p. 79.

61. *Rio News,* November 15, 1881, p. 3; December 15, 1882, p. 4; October 24, 1887, p. 3.

the cataclysmic events of Haiti and the United States as examples of the kind of horrors that could occur in Brazil.[62] Another foreboder of trouble, Senator Christiano Ottoni, considered violence on the plantations not only frightening as an institutional crisis for slavery but because "these horrors are aggravated and exacerbated by race hatred!" Ottoni feared that confrontations could lead to an ugly blood bath, a "civil war" or "race war." [63] Brandão, Ottoni, and other Cassandras of Brazilian society well understood the perils of slaveholding, for in reality the regime of the master class was much less secure than it appeared to be on the surface. The greatest danger lay in the possibility of new antislavery movements appearing to shake the structure and stir the slaves to manifest their discontent.[64] As long as *fazendeiros* could keep the captives isolated from contact with numerous other slave communities or abolitionist agitators, they could expect to maintain relative tranquility. Should slave hostilities ignite into massive action, the planters' tenuous control would be exposed. In many rural areas black bondsmen greatly outnumbered the *fazendeiros,* and law-enforcement officials were ill prepared to counteract servile revolts.[65] A planter from Rio Preto in Rio de Janeiro noted that his community depended on only twenty policemen to watch over the activities of 28,000 slaves. In the event of trouble, even overseers and other agents of the *senhores* could offer little help, he said, because many *fazendas* relied on as few as two to five managers to guard and discipline from 100 to 1,000 slaves.[66] A. Scott-Blacklaw, a British businessman, gave a detailed and frightening description of the planters' situation:

62. Brandão, *A escravatura no Brasil,* pp. 44, 53, 95–96.

63. *Annaes do Senado,* June 9, pp. 30–31; C. B. Ottoni, *Autobiographia de C. B. Ottoni,* p. 270.

64. *Annaes da Câmara* (1880), November 11, p. 258; *Brazil,* May 20, 1884, p. 2; *Congresso Agricola,* pp. 47, 248–49; Reis, *Situação econômica do Brasil,* p. 21; *Rio News,* August 24, 1882, p. 2; November 5, 1882, p. 2.

65. *Annaes da Câmara* (1879), March 5, pp. 194–95.

66. *Congresso Agricola,* pp. 204–205.

> A few laborers by entering the lock-fast slaves' quarters, on a few estates, and telling the slaves how easily they could get freedom, if they could revolt, could put the whole country in a blaze. There is no police force that could quell a slave disturbance. Around the town near where I lived, there were only some twelve policemen that could be taken to help the authorities. These policemen were used for nothing but to keep watch over the jail. It would take two days to get some two hundred soldiers from the capital. The slave does not know how easily the thing could be done, else he would free himself. Slaves are locked up at night, and the overseer is over them all day: so they have no way of knowing anything. The Brazilian government do not calculate on such an event as a negro insurrection and are not prepared for it. The slaves would succeed with no other weapon than their own hands. There is a very small organized army to bring against them. The police force is so small and inefficient that the beginning of a disturbance, however small, could not be stopped.[67]

Scott-Blacklaw concluded with the suggestion that "a slave rebellion will not happen, unless influences from outside the plantations were brought to bear on the minds of the slaves. This is not a likely event for some time." [68] Like many other observers who wrote in the early 1880s, he did not foresee an early termination of slavery. The hesitancy of diverse groups to manifest strong opposition to the institution led him to believe that slaveholders might maintain their regime, albeit shaky, for a considerable length of time. As mentioned before, many clergymen, lawyers, magistrates, business and commercial leaders who could have offered important voices to the abolitionist cause remained apathetic or silent on the slavery question. They were dependent on the planter's eco-

67. This excellent article entitled "Slavery in Brazil" was first published in the *Ceylon Observer* and later reprinted in the *Rio News,* May 24, 1882, pp. 4–5.

68. *Ibid.*

nomic, social, and political support and found opposition costly. Although some began to see attractive new possibilities as they contemplated a society based entirely on free labor in the latter part of the nineteenth century, they were not ready to break from the prevailing order, for independent action would leave them at the mercy of planters who could cut the relationships, favor more amenable clients, and drive the dissidents into social and economic bankruptcy. Without dramatic political changes and new mass support for their position, many individuals would not risk antagonizing the lords of the land.

The situation of small merchants in the interior cities well illustrates the dilemma of those who found their interests on both sides of the slavery issue. Shopkeepers complained that wealthy planters spent much of their money in the large coastal or capital cities, bypassing small enterprises in their own area. Moreover, the presence of abundant slaves performing the major work prevented development of a large rural population of wage-earners. If the land could be cultivated by free laborers, a much more dynamic market economy would open up for the merchants of the interior. As long as the system continued unchallenged, however, they would not chance a cut-off of the *fazendeiros'* purchases. It would take a "revolution," thought Scott-Blacklaw, to break them from their cautious posture and provide the confidence necessary to side with the Negro.[69]

The poorest classes of free Negroes and mulattoes were also dependent on the support of *fazendeiros* and victimized by the system of slavery. Their position was particularly precarious in the regions of the large plantations where slavery excluded free workers from most of the main productive activities.[70] In the 1875–1880 period, for example, slaves represented about five-sixths of the workers in the coffee fields and two-thirds of the hands in the sugar fields—a situation which left free coloreds in fierce competition for the

69. *Ibid;* Basbaum, *História sincera da república,* pp. 142–56, 170.
70. Malheiro, *A escravidão no Brasil,* II, p. 134; Guimaraes, *A agricultura em Minas,* p. 11.

occasional employment proprietors would give them as day laborers or supplementary workers at harvest time.[71] This situation was especially evident in some sections of important slaveholding provinces such as Rio de Janeiro and Minas Gerais, where slaves greatly outnumbered the free population.[72] The close of the African slave trade and subsequent elevation of slave prices stimulated demographic changes which precluded significant improvement in the status of free blacks and mulattoes.[73] The planters' desire to satisfy rural manpower needs resulted in the purchase of urban bondsmen for transference to plantation districts.[74] In turn, some freedmen migrated from the countryside to the cities, often filling artisan and service positions previously held by slaves. These changes kept the doors shut on major employment opportunities for the rural freemen who continued to live on the fringes of the plantations, eking out a living. *Fazendeiros* permitted some to reside and work on sections of their property in return for the food they produced to supply the slave population. The rural poor could also be valuable to the *fazendeiro* at election time, delivering their part of the bargain by casting votes according to instruction. Other freemen did not work with the land or reside in one particular place. Instead, they passed away idle hours until *fazendeiros* called upon them to undertake temporary, dangerous jobs. In this group were slave-catchers, thugs, and, particularly, hired laborers who handled tasks the planters judged too hazardous for the engagement of their high-priced slaves.[75]

The weakness and dependence of the free rural poor left

71. Roberto Simonsen, *Aspectos da história econômica do café* (Rio de Janeiro, 1938), p. 51; Reis, *Situação econômica do Brasil,* p. 4.

72. See the ratios of slaves to free citizens in provinces of the empire reported in *Annaes da Assembléa Legislativa Provincial de São Paulo* (1878), March 27, 1878, p. 470.

73. Paula Beiguelman, *Formação política do Brasil,* Vol. I: *Teoria e ação no pensamento abolicionista* (São Paulo, 1967), p. 24.

74. Costa, *Da senzala à colônia,* p. 231.

75. Caminhoá, *Canna de assucar e café,* pp. 106–107; *Rio News,* January 15, 1881, p. 2; Costa, *Da senzala à colônia,* p. 29; Beiguelman, *Formação política do Brasil,* I, p. 24; Werneck, *Idéias de colonização,* pp. 35–39; Couty, *L'esclavage au Brésil,* p. 57; *Brazil Agricola,* October 15, 1882.

them reluctant to join the ranks of the abolitionists. They relied on the ruling classes for their livelihood, as meager as it was, and they would not dump the existing system without clearly seeing what they could understand to be a viable alternative. Sharecroppers feared expulsion from the plantations; indeed angry *fazendeiros* were known to evict uncooperative residents summarily and burn their cabins. Part-time workers worried about the prospect of liberating the large slave population, looking at the immediate threat of further weakening their competitive position and lowering wages rather than the larger problem of the predominance of slaves in the pool of regular rural laborers. And, understandably, slave-catchers and other hirelings who supported themselves by serving as auxiliary policemen for the planters were hardly inclined to challenge the order. In the broadest sense the system victimized all of these groups, leaving them politically weak and limiting them to marginal occupations. But their vision was narrow. They lived from day to day, preoccupied with the profound importance of the power *fazendeiros* held over their lives. Tampering with slavery seemed to be a highly dangerous business. It could lead to severance of a precious economic relationship or the more serious consequence of death at the hands of a hired killer.[76]

Until the 1880s, slaveholders succeeded in holding the allegiance of diverse free classes, and, despite some economic difficulties and rumblings from the servile population, it appeared that they could maintain control over slavery for a considerable length of time. Beneath the surface, however, existed the realities which posed threats to their hegemony: divaricating interests among planter groups, the growing disillusionment of some non-slaveholders with the system of slavery, and the pent-up frustrations of restive, potentially rebellious bondsmen. The appearance of a well-organized antislavery movement would bring these conditions out into the open, splitting traditional loyalties and, eventually, triggering the breakdown of the slaveholders' regime.

76. *Rio News,* May 24, 1882, pp. 4–5; André Rebouças, *Abolição immediata e sem indemnisação* (Rio de Janeiro, 1883), pp. 18–19.

2: The Search for a Gradual Solution

IN SEPTEMBER 1871 the United States minister to Brazil witnessed a scene of celebration that left a deep and lasting impression. The Imperial Parliament had just passed legislation for gradual emancipation of the slaves, inviting a roar of approbation from a huge crowd of citizens situated in the galleries of the assembly hall and outside in the streets. As the jubilant, cheering citizens rained flowers down on members of Parliament, the American minister knelt down, picked up some of the articles of celebration, and said to a friend, "I am going to send these flowers to my country in order to show how a law was made here, in this manner, which cost so much blood there." Implicit in the minister's statement was the view that Brazil had found a political solution to the nagging and volatile problem of slavery. With time, patience and adherence to the legislation's progressive principles, it seemed that slavery could be extinguished without the dangerous forms of confrontation and strife which troubled society in the United States.[1]

Time would reveal that the parliamentary act of September 28, 1871, which became known as the Rio Branco Law, offered much less promise for abolition than the American minister and the Brazilian citizens saw in it on the day of festivities. At the time of its passage, the celebrants did not recognize the conservative nature of the law's provisions or the potential loopholes it offered slave proprietors. They did not understand that it could quickly be turned into an obstacle to emancipation rather than a stimulus to abolition.

1. Tobias do Rêgo Monteiro, *Pesquisas e depoimentos para a história* (Rio de Janeiro, 1913), p. 34.

Within a decade, antislavery leaders would denounce the Rio Branco Law as "the apple of the eye of the slavocracy."[2]

Why did the gradualist approach to abolition fail? To search for the answer to this question, it is helpful first to view the Rio Branco Law against the background of developments in Brazil during the decades preceding the parliamentary decision. The stimuli which produced criticisms of slavery in the earlier years and the outcome of related political disputes influenced the form of settlement attempted in 1871. Ideas about emancipation used during the pre-1871 period were frequently expressed in the gradualist frame of mind, and the realities of political power in Brazilian society tended to reinforce this tone of analysis. Both aspects helped to condition expectations that fell short of a radical approach to abolition. Second, it is important to examine the process of political compromise which brought a settlement in 1871, producing a law replete with provisions that could be weakened or evaded. The frustrations that resulted from these shortcomings gave rise to a new turn in the Brazilian antislavery movement, a change in strategy that led to a more forceful approach to abolition in the 1880s.

As in the British West Indies and the United States, most of the early attacks on slavery in Brazil focused on the slave trade rather than slavery itself. In the first half of the nineteenth century important political leaders such as José Bonifácio de Andrada e Silva and Padre Diogo Antônio Feijó spoke out against the human traffic from Africa. Brazil signed a treaty with Great Britain on November 7, 1831, banning the African slave trade, declaring free all persons henceforth illegally imported, and establishing heavy penalties for those convicted of importation. Despite the treaty, African slaves continued to pour into Brazil in numbers greater than ever before. Probably more than half a million slaves entered the country illegally between 1831 and 1850, when, after

2. Nicolão Joaquim Moreira made this comment in a speech delivered to the *Associação Central Emancipadora* on September 19, 1880. *Rio News*, October 15, 1880, p. 4.

immense British pressure, the Brazilians passed a law to make the prohibition effective.[3] A few traditional planters from the Northeast who already had sufficient slaves to satisfy their needs welcomed the change, but most Brazilians believed the act would trigger economic depression. They viewed the decision as an unfortunate necessity, a capitulation forced upon them by the threat of British naval power. But no great economic problems materialized from the end of the traffic, and, after a few years, Brazilians began celebrating their role in a decision they described as humanitarian and sensible. Eusébio de Queiroz, who had steered the legislation through Parliament, even pointed out that passage of the law exempted planters from tremendous debts they had accrued with foreign slave traders, thus freeing large sums of capital for other forms of investment.[4]

In the heat of discussion over the slave trade, some critics began to talk also about a frontal attack on domestic slavery, but manifestations of this kind of approach occurred infrequently once Parliament took a decisive step against the African traffic.[5] The prohibition against the African trade

3. Evaristo de Moraes, *A escravidão africana no Brasil: Das origens à extinção* (São Paulo, 1933), pp. 47–99; Jane Elizabeth Adams, "The Abolition of the Brazilian Slave Trade," *Journal of Negro History*, X (October 1925), pp. 607–37; Lawrence F. Hill, "The Abolition of the African Slave Trade to Brazil," *Hispanic American Historical Review*, XI (May 1931), pp. 169–97; Caio Prado Junior, *História econômica do Brasil* (São Paulo, 1949), p. 155; Leslie Bethell, *The Abolition of the Brazilian Slave Trade* (Cambridge, England, 1970), pp. 327–95; Philip D. Curtin, *The Atlantic Slave Trade* (Madison, Milwaukee, and London, 1969), pp. 47–49, 269; *Homagem da Sociedade Emancipadora Academica* (São Paulo, 1883), p. 4; Robert Conrad, "The Contraband Slave Trade to Brazil, 1831–1845," *Hispanic American Historical Review* (November 1969); Robert Conrad, "The Struggle for the Abolition of the Brazilian Slave Trade, 1808–1853" (unpublished Ph.D. dissertation, Columbia University, 1967).

4. Edison Carneiro, *Ladinos e crioulos: Estudos sôbre o negro no Brasil* (Rio de Janeiro, 1964), pp. 91–96; Edison Carneiro, *Antologia do negro brasileiro* (Rio de Janeiro, n.d.), p. 39; *Annaes da Câmara* (1879), March 5, p. 195.

5. For some early examples of efforts to challenge both the slave trade and domestic slavery, see João Severino Maciel da Costa, *Memória sôbre a necessidade de abolir a introducção dos escravos afri-*

appeared to be of monumental importance for the future of Brazil. So prevalent was the belief that the slave population could not replenish itself or expand without constant imports from Africa that many believed slavery had been put irreversibly on the road to extinction. In the aftermath of the 1850 legislation, slavery lost its place in the political limelight. During the 1850s and into the early 1860s Brazilian politics stayed relatively stable and peaceful, and government leaders gave little attention to the slavery issue.

New developments in the 1860s broke quickly, however, throwing the emancipation question before the Brazilian public with great force, pressuring politicians to recognize that maintenance of the *status quo* was no longer a tenable policy. One of the first shock waves resulted from the outcome of the American Civil War. News of the sudden demise of the Western Hemisphere's largest slave society frightened Brazilian leaders. Abolition in the United States, a settlement which required much bloodshed, was "a fact deserving meditation," said one political leader in an obvious understatement.[6] Brazilians interpreted the American experience as an example of the foolishness of adamantly resisting reform. By taking the hard line and allowing no avenue for change, the American South cornered itself into a position which left abolitionists with no alternative but to resort to violent language and behavior. The outcome was ruinous to the planters and brought blood and tears to the whole society. It was terribly disconcerting, then, for Brazilians to recognize that, in many ways, their own slave society resembled that of the

---

canos no Brasil (Coimbra, 1821), pp. 39, 50, 71–76; J. E. P. da Sa, *Memória sôbre a escravatura e projecto de colonisação dos europeos e prêtos da Africa no Império do Brasil* (Rio de Janeiro, 1826), pp. 7, 14–19; José Bonifácio de Andrada e Silva, *Representação a Assembléa Geral Constituinte e Legislativa do Império do Brasil a escravatura* (reprint by the Faculdade de Filosofia, Ciências e Letras de Santos, Santos, 1965), pp. 26–29; Caetano Alberto Soares, *Memória para melhorar a sorte dos nossos escravos—lido na sessão geral do Instituto dos Advogados Brasileiros* (Rio de Janeiro, 1847), pp. 9–22.

6. José Antônio Pimento Bueno (Marquis de São Vicente), *Trabalho sôbre a extincção da escravatura no Brasil* (Rio de Janeiro, 1868), p. 4.

United States more than any other slave society in the Americas. Reflecting on the great civil catastrophe that divided North Americans, Silva Netto pondered Brazil's situation nervously: "The life we have passed was without great worry; the present is easy; the future I do not know!"[7]

Abolition in the United States also left Brazilian slaveholders feeling much more isolated as a social type, and news of progress toward abolition in Spanish-held Cuba only added to their sense of discomfort.[8] Brazil's anomalous position as the last great slaveholding country was becoming increasingly conspicuous. "How can Brazil, isolated and only of its kind on the globe, resist the pressure of the entire world?" asked José Tomaz Nabuco.[9] Others, too, spoke vaguely of "European pressure" working to force Brazil into taking action against domestic slavery, and it appears that Brazilian diplomats and businessmen did experience some nudging on the matter, particularly from Britain and France.[10] But Europe's more important contribution was also more subtle; it came from the impact of ideas rather than direct political interference. "The eyes of the world are upon us, judging us barbarians, savages . . ." exclaimed a senator.[11]

7. Silva Netto, *Estudos sôbre a emancipação dos escravos no Brasil* (Rio de Janeiro, 1868), pp. 31–32; *Elemento Servil: Parecer e projecto de lei apresentados à Câmara dos Senhores Deputados na sessão de 16 de Agôsto de 1870 pela Commissão Especial nomeada pela mesma Câmara em 24 de Maio de 1870* (Rio de Janeiro, 1870), pp. 7, 74; Taveres Bastos, *A Província: Estudo sôbre a decentralisação no Brasil* (Rio de Janeiro, 1870), pp. 278–79; *Annaes do Senado* (1871), September 5, pp. 61–62; *Annaes da Câmara* (1871), May 29, p. 108; May 30, p. 148; August 2, p. 32.

8. Ypiranga, *Breves considerações histórico-políticas sôbre a discussão do elemento servil na Câmara dos Deputados* (Rio de Janeiro, 1871), p. 17; Augusto de Carvalho, O *Brasil: Colonisação e emigração* (Pôrto, 1876), p. 94.

9. Pimento Bueno, *Trabalho sôbre a extincção da escravatura no Brasil,* p. 62.

10. T. Alencar Araripe, *O elemento servil: Artigos sôbre a emancipação* (Paraíba do Sul, 1871), p. 9; *Pareceres do Conselho de Estado no anno 1868 relativos ao elemento servil* (Rio de Janeiro, 1871), p. 16; A. F. de Mello Moraes, *O Brasil, social e político: O que fomos e o que somos* (Rio de Janeiro, 1872), pp. 64–66.

11. *Annaes do Senado* (1871), September 26, p. 251.

The "world" opinion which particularly concerned Brazilians was the view of people in the "civilized" world, especially the French and British. In Europe the new spirit of intellect and science had reached its highest form, said the Brazilians, and in the advanced countries the word *slavery* carried ignominious connotations. The best minds in Europe condemned slavery unflinchingly, describing it as an immoral institution which made one man the property of another. Whether judged against the principles of modern philosophy or the ideals of Christianity, slavery now appeared to run clearly against the current of opinion in the "civilized" nations.[12] "Slavery has been the black mark on our civilization," said one writer.[13] If Brazilians were to steer their society into the mainstream of what they saw as modern, nineteenth-century culture, something would have to be done about slavery. "The age!" exclaimed Silva Netto; "it is now more than 1,867 years since the era of Christ and slavery still exists. The age!" [14] From a worldwide perspective, the hour for slavery was turning late.

While these self-doubts began to make many Brazilian leaders more flexible toward a policy change, it took pressure from the French Emancipation Committee to prompt the government into making a formal statement on the issue. In response to a highly publicized letter from the committee, which appealed to the Emperor to use his powers of intervention to help the cause of emancipation, the Brazilian government explained that a decision on the problem was simply "a question of form and opportunity" and indicated that appropriate steps would be taken to accomplish emanci-

12. Araripe, *O Elemento Servil,* pp. 5–7; José Antônio Pimento Bueno, "Escravidão no Brasil" (1867?), Instituto Histórico e Geográfico Brasileiro, Lata 436, Doc. 16; Pimento Bueno, *Trabalho sôbre a extincção da escravatura no Brasil,* pp. 35, 69–70.

13. Um Conservador, *Cartas aos fazendeiros e commerciantes fluminenses sôbre o elemento servil, ou refutação do parecer do Sr. Conselheiro Christiano Benedicto Ottoni acerca do mesmo assumpto* (Rio de Janeiro, 1871), p. 3.

14. Silva Netto, *Segundo estudos sôbre a emancipação dos escravos no Brasil* (Rio de Janeiro, 1868), p. 9.

pation upon conclusion of the Paraguayan war.[15] Some conservative figures criticized this attempt to answer the French inquiry as a precipitous act which could be interpreted as a distinct commitment. But the leader of the Brazilian cabinet, Zacharias de Góes Vasconcellos, was already sympathetic to the emancipation idea, and, besides, it was imperative to make some kind of formal reply. Paraguay's agents were busy in Europe trying to convince the powers that the war then raging in South America was a battle between freedom and slavery.[16]

The disputes emanating from the Paraguayan war helped to bring the slavery question out into the open. It was a long, costly, and frustrating contest in which Brazilian forces worked with the armies of Argentina and Uruguay to battle Paraguay's frenzied dictator, Francisco Solano Lopez. The Brazilian military was poorly prepared for a large-scale, protracted conflict and suffered some humiliating losses. The countries of the Triple Alliance finally overwhelmed Paraguay and brought the war to a close in 1870, but embarrassments and squabbles over Brazil's war efforts produced new political cleavages and raised questions about the empire's resiliency in responding to critical problems of war mobilization. In the process, leaders began to focus new attention on slavery. First, the war exposed slavery as a potential Achilles' heel. During the hostilities, numerous rumors circulated suggesting that Lopez might try to move into Brazil's southernmost province of Rio Grande do Sul and incite slave rebel-

15. Monteiro, *Pesquisas e depoimentos para a história,* pp. 11–18; Osório Duque-Estrada, *A abolição: 1831–1888* (Rio de Janeiro, 1918), pp. 41–48; Moraes, *A escravidão africana no Brasil,* pp. 103–24; *Rio News,* August 15, 1880, p. 1; Agostinho Marques Perdigão Malheiro, *A escravidão no Brasil* (Rio de Janeiro, 1866, 1867), II, pp. 207, 223–27; Luiz Francisco da Camara Leal, *Considerações e projecto de lei para a emancipação dos escravos sem prejuizo de seus senhores, nem grave onus para o estado* (Rio de Janeiro, 1866), pp. 16–17.

16. *Pareceres do Conselho de Estado no anno 1868 relativos ao elemento servil,* pp. 18–19; *Annaes da Câmara* (1871), July 10, p. 88; Pimento Bueno, *Trabalho sôbre a extincção da escravatura no Brasil,* p. 33; Joaquim Nabuco, *Uma estadista do Império: Nabuco de Araujo* (São Paulo, n.d.), III, p. 219.

lions. Second, as parties, interest groups, and personalities clashed over the government's conduct of the war, positions on other issues, including the emancipation question, became part of the disputes. Finally, the work of war mobilization directed attention to the Negroes in bondage. The army had to resort to thousands of slaves to fill the soldiers' ranks, and many bondsmen received promises of liberty in return for their enrollment in defense of the empire. The blacks' contribution to the war effort raised new issues regarding the justice of slavery.[17]

The combination of progress toward emancipation in other countries and tensions created within Brazil by the Paraguayan war catapulted the slavery issue onto the political arena. For the first time it became a major preoccupation of both the Conservative and Liberal parties. One influential statesman, Pimento Bueno (later named the Viscount of São Vicente), presented no less than five major emancipation projects for the government's consideration. In 1868 the Prime Minister, Zacharias de Góes, recommended study of Pimento Bueno's proposals and preparation of a report suggesting a constructive course of action. In this manner he became the first head of state to take a sympathetic and forceful stand on emancipation.[18]

Senator José Tomaz Nabuco, a distinguished Liberal party leader, prepared the report, and, after some minor changes, the Zacharias ministry adopted it as its program. But Zacharias quickly fell under fire, first for embroiling himself in a personal clash with the popular Duke of Caxias over

17. Richard Graham, *Britain and the Onset of Modernization in Brazil, 1850–1914* (Cambridge, England, 1968), p. 23; Carneiro, *Antologia do negro brasileiro,* pp. 46–48; Malheiro, *A escravidão no Brasil,* II, p. 118; Orlando de Almeida Prado, *Em defenza da raça negra: O preconceito de raça não existe no Brasil* (São Paulo, n.d.), pp. 3–4.

18. Evaristo de Moraes, *A lei do ventre livre* (Rio de Janeiro, 1917), pp. 9–15; Pimento Bueno, *"Escravidão no Brasil"; "Cartas do Marques de São Vicente (1870–1871) a Ourem,"* Lata 157, Doc. 11; *"Carta do Visconde do Rio Branco ao Conde d'Eu sôbre o projecto de Visconde de São Vicente* (Rio de Janeiro, June 21, 1867), Lata 276, Doc. 16, Instituto Histórico e Geográfico Brasileiro.

conduct of the Paraguayan war, then for an argument about constitutional procedures in filling a vacant Senate seat. The second controversy, which was related to the slavery question, brought his downfall. Although a Liberal supported by the Zacharias cabinet had received the largest number of electoral votes, a group of elderly, antireform members of the Council of State who were apprehensive about the growing slavery issue urged Dom Pedro to select a Conservative to fill the seat. The Emperor succumbed to the pressures of his advisers. Zacharias protested angrily, viewing the decision as a capitulation to the reactionary groups that would undermine his efforts to pass emancipation legislation. When the Emperor refused to reverse his decision, Zacharias and his ministry resigned. Dom Pedro then appointed a Conservative, pro-slaveholder politician to head the new government. As a final defiant gesture, the pro-Zacharias Chamber of Deputies passed a stinging resolution expressing "no confidence" in the government. Dom Pedro had little choice but to dissolve the Chamber and call for new elections. Since Zacharias' successor now controlled the political machinery, the elections delivered the expected Conservative majority.[19]

The crisis of the Zacharias cabinet became a *cause célèbre* among reformist groups which described the incident as a *coup d'état* and used the issue to criticize the traditional political system and influence of the "oligarchy." Dissident Liberals organized a Reform Club in 1868. Their newspaper, *A Reforma,* featured virulent indictments of the government, including articles written by Zacharias. This movement generated the Liberal Manifesto of 1869 which hammered at the institutions that kept political power in the hands of an oligarchy and called for more individual liberty and electoral reform. The writers of the document also proclaimed support for gradual emancipation of the slaves. A splinter group, the Radical Club, elevated the slavery question to a higher posi-

19. José Maria dos Santos, *Política geral do Brasil* (São Paulo, 1930), pp. 92–128; Francisco José de Oliveira Viana, *O ocaso do império* (São Paulo, 1925), pp. 13–17; *Breves considerações histórico,* pp. 12–14.

tion in the list of priorities. Another offspring of the organizational activity appeared in 1870 in the form of a Republican Club. This organization, made up primarily of professional people from the Imperial capital of Rio de Janiero, composed a Republican Manifesto which subscribed to many of the currently popular reform ideas, including interest in accelerating emancipation. But the sister republican organization formed shortly after in the province of São Paulo spoke more directly to the interests of the *fazendeiros* and hedged on the slavery issue.[20]

The Zacharias Affair opened a Pandora's box of troubles for the Emperor. Dom Pedro became caught in the crossfire of political volleys between parties and factions. By personal sentiment, the Emperor inclined toward emancipation reform, but he could not disregard the vehement outcries of powerful pro-slaveholder advisers and political leaders. The pressure of antislavery groups continued to rise. Within Parliament, some reform-minded Liberals persisted in chastising the government for lack of action, while outside, students, professors, and interested citizens gathered together at public meetings to debate the issues. Among the participants was a brilliant young Negro, Castro Alves, who roused the audiences by reading his emotional antislavery poetry.[21]

With the slavery question now in the open for public debate, government leaders and other influential figures began to disseminate pamphlets and reports announcing their own suggestions for emancipation reform. With few exceptions, these plans were cautiously worded and represented moderate, gradualist approaches to the emancipation problem. For example, Pimento Bueno's ideas, which had attracted the interest of Zacharias, asked that all future children of slave mothers be declared free and, after operating a gradual pro-

20. Leôncio Basbaum, *História sincera da república, das origens até 1889* (Rio de Janeiro, 1957), pp. 187–88; Santos, *Política geral do Brasil,* pp. 120–28.

21. Richard Morse, *From Community to Metropolis: A Biography of São Paulo, Brazil* (Gainesville, 1958), pp. 146–48.

gram for liberating adults over many years, slavery should be declared extinct on December 1, 1899. He also expressed concern that complementary measures be included to insure that the liberated would not quickly become vagabonds.[22] Another reformer, José Tomaz Nabuco, endorsed Bueno's ideas concerning free births and gradual emancipation and warned that any plans for immediate abolition would have tragic consequences. The freedmen would work lethargically or refuse to labor at all to the disgust of the planters, and the resulting animosities could lead to grave confrontations, Nabuco explained. "Simultaneous and immediate abolition is an abysm," he warned, "because of the brusk transition of two million men from the state of slavery to that of liberty! A fatal transition, in relation to the dangers to public order, fatal, in relation to the disorganization and anarchization of labor." To avoid disaster, Nabuco supported a gradual emancipation program with indemnification to the slaveholders, a process which, he admitted, might take fifty or sixty years to complete.[23] Another prominent Brazilian widely considered a proponent of emancipation, Taveres Bastos, expressed similar hopes and reservations. He particularly criticized the idea discussed by some advocates of emancipation which involved setting a fixed termination date for slavery in twenty or thirty years. Bastos warned that such a plan would be imprudent, dangerous, and unnecessary because better results could be achieved by leaving the decline of slavery to the work of deaths, voluntary manumission, and the plan to free future children of slave mothers.[24]

Conditions were now propitious for a new departure in slavery legislation. Individual efforts quickly merged into political programs. In 1869 Parliament passed a law prohibiting the sale of slaves in public and the separation of husbands and wives and children under the age of fifteen. More important, other major goals emerged from the heated political

22. Pimento Bueno, *"Escravidão no Brasil."*

23. Pimento Bueno, *Trabalho sôbre a extincção da escravatura no Brasil,* p. 64–67; *Annaes do Senado* (1871), September 26, pp. 250–52.

24. Bastos, *A Província,* pp. 256–57.

exchanges of the 1860s which demanded attention: freedom for slaves belonging to the Imperial Government; protection of the slave's right to maintain private savings (the *pecúlio*) in order that he might eventually purchase his freedom; establishment of an emancipation fund from the proceeds of taxes and government lotteries; registration of all the slaves in the empire; and, finally, freedom for all children henceforth born of slave mothers (such children would be called *ingenuos*). These proposals represented the most salient demands of the growing political tempest. In 1871 Emperor Dom Pedro cautiously acquiesced to the call for a change in the government's policy toward slavery. Since he realized it would be extremely difficult to convince a Parliament made up of many slaveholders to give the proposals a favorable hearing, he had to use his best political acumen in selecting the minister who would lead the effort. He finally decided to appoint the Viscount of Rio Branco as head of the new ministry. Rio Branco, a Conservative, was known to be more flexible on the slavery question than many other members of his party. With the difficult decision made, the Emperor conveniently slipped out of the picture by traveling to Europe before the great debates. This would help relieve him of association with the decision, whatever the outcome of the discussions.[25]

Intense forensic battles ensued in Parliament as spokesmen for the slaveholders began attacking the Rio Branco proposals. To observers it seemed that no government recommendation had ever suffered from such prolonged and bitter debate. The exchanges were particularly fierce in the Chamber of Deputies, where politicians hurled biting insults at one another and sometimes seemed on the verge of rushing into a physical encounter. The noisy people in the galleries, some of whom came armed with pistols, only augmented the tensions. On several occasions their shouting interrupted the sessions and resulted in tumultuous incidents.[26]

While attacking the Rio Branco program, many of the

25. Moraes, *A lei do ventre livre,* pp. 16–40.

26. *Annaes da Câmara* (1871), May 31, p. 142; June 7, p. 33; J. M. Pereira da Silva, *Memórias do meu tempo* (Paris, n.d.), II, p. 140.

pro-slaveholder politicians expressed ideas that would form important elements in the defense of slavery in the 1880s. In the most general terms, they charged that government interference in matters of slavery was unnecessary, unconstitutional, and dangerous. It was unnecessary, they said, because the slaveholders were already convinced of the rightness of the emancipation idea and frequently liberated their own slaves without any government prodding. They were not intransigent slavocrats, nor racists like the slaveholders in the United States. Slavery in Brazil was defended largely on the basis of economic necessity, they explained, and, therefore, was flexible enough to change when the economic circumstances permitted. The issue was not a question of whether slavery should be perpetual; rather, it was a question of the method by which it could be abolished.[27] The government's approach to this problem represented unconstitutional means toward a desirable end because it would rob the slaveholders of their legal property. Slavery had been a legally recognized institution for over 300 years, and this condition, which the present-day proprietors found when they sunk their capital into slave property, could not now be swept away by government decree.[28] Moreover, even moderate programs designed by the government to encourage gradual emancipation were fraught with danger because, once a third party was introduced into master-slave relationship, the delicate system of authority and discipline could be fatally weakened. As deputy Almeida Pereira explained the problem:

> Slavery cannot depend on half-measures, because, when one gives rights to the slaves, one imposes duties on the masters. Discipline, the only moral tie that binds the slave to his master, and the respect which determines

27. *Annaes do Senado* (1871), September 5, p. 62; September 14, p. 130; September 27, pp. 276–77; *Elemento Servil: Parecer,* pp. 76, 92.

28. *Annaes da Câmara* (1871), May 29, p. 116; August 2, p. 27; Pimento Bueno, *Trabalho sôbre a extincção da escravatura no Brasil,* p. 39; *Pareceres do Conselho de Estado relativos ao elemento servil,* pp. 18–19.

> the master's superiority, naturally slacken. With such half-measures obedience and subordination will disappear completely on the rural establishments. I will ask your honor, Mr. President of the Council: What farmer of our country will be able to maintain his establishment, once these ties of subordination loosen and break? [29]

Defenders of slavery gave specific reference to recent examples of servile insurrection and warned that government interference could stir the bondsmen with unrealistic hopes about freedom, producing anxieties, frustration, and rebellion.[30]

Applying these ideas to the specific points in the Rio Branco program, the critics charged that government laws "forcing" the master to honor the *pecúlio,* register his slaves, and accept the consequences of an emancipation fund would, in the eyes of the bondsman, undermine his image of absolute authority.[31] But it was over the implications of freeing all future children of slave mothers that the conservative interests reacted most angrily. The reform touched directly on the issue of the sanctity of slave property. Slaveholders emphasized the same complaints about this proposal that they had registered repeatedly when special government commissions discussed slavery reform in 1868 and 1870—namely, that freedom by birth would set a precedent for liberation without compensation to the proprietors. If such legislation could now be passed regarding the newborn, who could guarantee in the future that amendments would not be added extending freedom without indemnification to other groups such as the old? Was this not the beginning of a new policy, signaling

29. *Annaes da Câmara* (1871), August 2, pp. 31–32.

30. Araripe, *O elemento servil,* p. 33; *Annaes da Câmara* (1871), June 10, pp. 62–65; June 28, p. 206; July 11, p. 97; *Annaes do Senado* (1871), September 4, p. 26; *Elemento Servil: Parecer,* pp. 98–99; Um Magistrado, *Analyse e commentario critico da proposta do governo imperial às camaras legislativas sôbre o elemento servil* (Rio de Janeiro, 1871), p. 16.

31. *Annaes da Câmara* (1871), July 10, p. 90; August 1, pp. 9–10; *Pareceres do Conselho de Estado relativos ao elemento servil,* p. 33.

the end of legal support for slavery?[32] Slaveholders thought they saw this suggestion in one of the government commission's statements which used the words "present servile property." Just how long would the "present" last?[33] Consequently, they described the idea of emancipation by birth as "immoral," "criminal," and tantamount to "decreeing robbery."[34]

To placate these critics and, indeed, to express their own reservations about reform measures, supporters of the Rio Branco plan emphasized that they had no intention of removing the legal sanction for slave property. True, the new legislation implied that a distinction could be drawn between property in man and property in "things." Property in man was "exceptional property." It was not absolute, but subject to restrictions, particularly restrictions that required the owners to conform to the needs of the public good. But slave property would remain legal as indicated by the provisions for an emancipation fund and the option to be given to the owners of slave women who gave birth to free children: Masters would have the right of retaining the children for services until the age of twenty-one or turning them over to the state at the age of eight, receiving 600 milreis (about $300) in exchange. The state's explicit guarantee of 600 milreis gave evidence that the government would continue to endorse the principle of indemnification, said Rio Branco's supporters.[35]

The importance of these issues, with all the innuendos or interpretation that could be drawn from them, influenced two prominent Brazilian figures, Augustinho Marques Perdigão Malheiro and Zacharias de Góes Vasconcellos, to take surprising stands in the debates. Perdigão Malheiro, eminent lawyer and interpreter of constitutional law, had written a

32. Araripe, *O elemento servil,* p. 17; *Annaes da Câmara* (1871), May 29, p. 119; *Pareceres do Conselho de Estado relativos ao elemento servil,* pp. 20–21; *Elemento Servil: Parecer,* pp. 97–99.

33. *Annaes da Câmara* (1871), May 29, p. 110.

34. Araripe, *O elemento servil,* p. 17.

35. *Annaes do Senado* (1871), September 26, p. 252; Nabuco, *Uma estadista do Império,* III, pp. 202–203.

monumental study of Brazilian slavery in the 1860s. In his book as well as in important speeches delivered while he was president of the Lawyers' Institute, Malheiro had condemned slavery as immoral and illegitimate and urged the government to establish new machinery to emancipate the slaves. As deputy in Parliament in 1871 representing a constituency of powerful slaveholders from Minas Gerais, however, Malheiro had to reverse his position considerably. He opposed the Rio Branco plan, worrying that governmental action could lead to complete anarchy in the labor system and economic disaster for the country. The planters feared not only for their prosperity but also for their security, he said, rehashing the oft-stated apprehensions about maintaining the "moral" force behind slavery. On the issue of property, he tried to draw a distinction between the ideas he had expressed in earlier years and his new interpretation. Malheiro insisted that there was a difference between studying a problem and legislating on it, between desiring a certain end and working out the means to accomplish it. Although he had condemned slavery as "illegitimate," he still maintained that it was legal in view of the nation's laws. Therefore, it would be more appropriate not to tinker with the institution's legal foundations. The "emancipation idea," which was moral and Christian, could be better realized by leaving the matter to manumission and deaths—the processes of "natural extinction." Understandably, Malheiro received several tongue-lashings in Parliament for his intellectual inconsistency.[36]

From a very different perspective, the pressures of politics and the pattern of parliamentary debate drove another well-known spokesman for slavery reform, Zacharias de Góes Vasconcellos, into opposition against the Rio Branco plan.

36. *Annaes da Câmara* (1871), May 30, p. 148; June 10, pp. 51–54; July 12, p. 118; August 9, pp. 94–103; *"Papeis do Dr. Agostinho Marques Perdigão Malheiro,"* Instituto Histórico e Geográfico Brasileiro, Lata 436, Doc. 16; A. M. Perdigão Malheiro, *Illegitimade da propriedade constuida sôbre o escravo—Natureza de tal propriedade—Justica e conveniência da abolição da escravidão—Em que termos* (n.p., 1863), pp. 5–11.

During the time of his controversial tenure as chief minister, Zacharias had thrown his support behind many of the moderate proposals that came to form the core of the Rio Branco program. But during the 1871 debates Zacharias took a much more radical stand on the need for change and lambasted the government's plan as far too "imperfect" to win his acceptance. His trenchant criticisms cut right to the heart of the reform's weaknesses. Slavery in its most naked form was the condition of man holding property in man, said Zacharias. All the constitutional mumbo-jumbo that characterized the debates was an effort to evade facing the uncomfortable realities. Slavery was not created by law as much as it was created by the force, ignorance, and prejudice of men. Besides, if political leaders insisted on arguing that slavery had been instituted by law, then it might also be argued that slavery could be abolished by law—and without indemnification. Zacharias believed the legislation being proposed was much too conservative in form. The government was using the wrong political approach by suggesting reforms be made only in very cautious ways and leaving more progressive changes to developments in later years. It would be far better to write a definitive solution into the present legislation, he thought. Finally, Zacharias asked whether the Rio Branco plan's principal reform contribution—the free-birth idea—represented reform at all. Zacharias charged that the *ingenuos* (the supposedly "free" children) would, in effect, be slaves until age twenty-one since they would not be paid for their labor and would have little protection from the government against cruel treatment. Moreover, he judged "immoral" the provision for turning eight-year-old *ingenuos* over to the government because it could tear children away from their families.[37]

37. *Annaes do Senado* (1871), September 4, pp. 29–36; September 12, pp. 1–11. For other radical criticisms of moderate reform proposals, see Elzeario Pinto, *Emancipação dos escravos: O.C.D. As sociedades maçonicos e abolicionistas do Império* (Bahia, 1870); Carlos Benjamin da Silva Araujo, *A escravidão: Questão da actualidade* (Rio de Janeiro, 1871); Netto, *Segundo estudos sôbre a emancipação dos escravos no Brasil,* pp. 56–60, 70–81, 104.

Many colleagues tried to dismiss the strident tone of Zacharias' criticisms as due to an effort to embarrass the government and avenge the political defeats he had suffered earlier as chief minister. Others thought he was simply acting as a fierce party partisan who was angry that the Liberal party had not been given an opportunity to design the reforms. Undoubtedly both of these factors influenced Zacharias' sense of alienation, but they could hardly give full explanation to his motivation. The Zacharias attack contained too many elements of truth to be written off lightly, for the emotional reformer had pinpointed the shortcomings of compromise.

In the midst of these significant expressions of criticism and reservation, it remained for the chief minister himself to make the most impressive effort to push the reform through Parliament. The Viscount of Rio Branco countered powerful resistance with twenty-one discourses in a Herculean effort to win acceptance of his program. To the conservative critics, Rio Branco reaffirmed his view that the legislation respected the interests of property and suggested that his right-wing opponents were sounding paranoid by grossly exaggerating its potential effect. The chief minister also turned upon his critics on the left, preaching the need for calm and prudence and cautioning them against using the political tactics of the emotional agitator.[38]

The long and excited debates finally came to a close in late September. Rio Branco's proposals passed in the Chamber of Deputies by 65–45 and by a more impressive score in the Senate, 33–7. On September 28, 1871, the Princess Regent made the Rio Branco Law (or Law of Free Womb, as it was sometimes called) official. Rio Branco had succeeded not only because members of Parliament responded to the pressures of changing public opinion but also because, essentially, his plan represented a moderate compromise. Many Conservatives realized that defeat of the program could pave the way for a more radical solution under the auspices of a Liberal minis-

38. *Annaes da Câmara* (1871), May 9, pp. 31–34; May 29, pp. 107–108; July 10, pp. 84–85.

try. Even beyond the issue of party politics and programs, slaveholders feared that prolongation of the debates and agitation might stir the free masses and slaves into disruptive and dangerous activities.[39]

Against the background of tremendous slaveholder opposition, passage of the Rio Branco Law appeared to be more of a reform than it really was. In the mood of enthusiastic celebration, many reformers gave a sigh of relief, believing that the greatest source of tension had been removed, and slavery was now on the way toward gradual extinction. One of these figures, Senator Nabuco, praised the legislation as a successful outcome of conciliation between the country's economic interests and the pressing humane considerations of the century. To be sure, Nabuco saw certain inconsistencies and undesirable sections in the program, but these were minor difficulties compared to the law's over-all value. A means had been found, he thought, to turn the country from slave to free labor without running the danger of making a brusque, uncontrolled transition.[40] Much less convinced of this was Charles Sumner, the prominent American abolitionist and politician, to whom Nabuco had written explaining the aims of Brazil's antislavery reformers. Sumner replied through a note to one of Nabuco's friends, expressing his criticism of projects which postponed emancipation for a long time. Sumner finished by saying, "I hope Senator Nabuco will forgive me, if I express the opinion, that he too is wrong in not requiring it [abolition] *at once*. . . . The *will* only is needed."[41] Although Sumner's advice was overly simplistic because it did not take into account the complexities of Brazilian politics, there was still an important element of

39. Moraes, *A lei do ventre livre,* pp. 40–74; Duque-Estrada, *A abolição,* pp. 65–75; Monteiro, *Pesquisas e depoimentos para a história,* pp. 21–34; *Breves considerações histórico,* p. 106; *Annaes do Senado* (1871), August 18, p. 183.

40. *Annaes do Senado* (1871), September 26, pp. 250–52; Nabuco, *Uma Estadista do Império,* III, pp. 201–212.

41. Undated manuscript written by Charles Sumner, Instituto Joaquim Nabuco.

truth in his recommendation. If "will" represented the immediatist frame of mind, it was clearly missing in the thinking of most of the 1871 reformers. Evidence of the failure of the gradualist approach would have to accrue and a new generation of more impatient reformers would need to appear before the call for change could move into a truly abolitionist position.

3: The Rise of Moderate Abolitionism

UNLIKE THE SITUATION in years past, when the term "antislavery" was commonly used to describe leading critics of slavery, the new, outspoken critics in the 1880s became more typically identified as "abolitionists." Moreover, these new leaders accepted the label with pride. The unifying goal which bound them together as abolitionists was a search for an early, definitive solution to the abolition question. The reform philosophy of 1871 no longer would suffice. Abolitionists were too impatient to allow slavery to die the slow death envisaged by framers of the Rio Branco Law. Exactly when the mortality of the existing slave population and the very gradual accumulation of results from the emancipation fund and self-purchase would bring complete abolition was not at all clear. Many predicted that slavery would last well into the twentieth century, even if all the Rio Branco Law's provisions worked reasonably well. If the demand for early emancipation marked the unifying characteristic of abolitionists, these individuals differed in defining the specific means to achieve abolition. Appreciating the economic, social, and political realities, they remained cautious and, sometimes, indecisive in determining strategies for the new campaign. Cognizant of the slaveholders' weighty power and the difficulty of arousing support from apathetic or hostile non-slaveholders, abolitionists usually adhered to moderate tactics in the early 1880s. They wished to achieve change within the political system and indicated a willingness to compromise in order to achieve their goals. It was only after 1885 that the combination of abolitionism's increasing popularity and its leaders' frustrations brought an abrupt shift in the character of both abolitionist demands and action.

The political environment immediately following passage of the Rio Branco Law appeared relatively relaxed compared to the tension and clashes that marked the period from 1866 to 1871. Although some squabbles interrupted the post-1871 calm, such as a heated controversy between the Imperial Government and the Church, an aura of placidity prevailed on the slavery question. Slaveholders became satisfied that they could continue exploiting servile labor without difficulty, especially as they learned that the Rio Branco Law was weak and there were abundant opportunities to evade it. Also, many antislavery leaders were deluded into thinking that they had established an effective instrument for emancipation that could expand according to the needs of the situation. For eight years after Rio Branco's success, political leaders maintained general silence on the slave question, while the public expressed little concern for the cause of the captives.[1]

In the late 1870s, however, rising discontent became evident. The slave proprietors themselves were partially to blame for the new developments. They became apprehensive about signs of unrest on the plantations, particularly cases of assassinations committed by slaves and servile insurrections in the province of Rio de Janeiro, and demanded that the government strengthen the repressive powers of the laws. In 1878 planters convoked an Agricultural Congress of the South to discuss their problems under the auspices of the new Liberal ministry of the Viscount of Sinimbú. They suggested diverse means of increasing the production of their labor forces and complained that a "manpower shortage" made rapid emancipation impossible under existing conditions. Repeating the antireform arguments of the 1871 debates, some described the Rio Branco Law as dangerous because it inspired the slaves with a flicker

1. José Maria dos Santos, *Política geral do Brasil* (São Paulo, 1930), p. 138; Augusto de Carvalho, *O Brasil, colonização e emigração* (Porto, 1876), pp. 259–60; notes of Joaquim Nabuco, *"Livro: Livro I"* in the Instituto Joaquim Nabuco.

of hope for freedom, a frustrated desire which could undermine the regime of the plantations. Then, in 1879, *fazendeiros* called for new legislation to increase the severity of punitive measures against slaves who committed crimes. On the day this proposal was submitted to the Chamber of Deputies, São Paulo slaveholder Moreira de Barros angrily declared that slavery was a legal institution and that slave proprietors were in no way obligated to deal with it according to philanthropic principles. Barros also demanded that the newspapers refrain from discussing the sensitive issue of slavery.[2]

The audacious efforts of reactionary *fazendeiros* prompted a swift response from a small group of bright, young, idealistic new representatives in the Chamber of Deputies who had been elected as Liberals to work with the Sinimbú ministry. Figures such as Jeronymo Sodré, Joaquim Nabuco, and Rui Barbosa would play key roles in the abolitionist movement in the next decade.

The Chamber opened in 1879 with an exchange of ideas about the means of actuating an old Liberal party promise: electoral reform. After a fast and impressive start, the meetings bogged down in a debate over the problem of maintaining order on the plantations, an issue of greater immediate interest to the *fazendeiros*. Slaveholders wanted to revise the criminal laws to make punishment for offenses more severe. They argued that capital punishment was no longer practiced in Brazil and, therefore, did not serve as an effective deterrent to violent crimes committed by slaves against their masters and overseers. Support began to coalesce around a new proposal suggested by Lafayette Rodrigues Pereira, asking for fifteen years' imprisonment in the most serious cases, including solitary confinement during the first five years.[3]

2. *Congresso Agricola: Colleção de documentos* (Rio de Janeiro, 1878), pp. 54, 140, 204; Evaristo de Moraes, *A escravidão africana no Brasil: Das origens à extincção* (São Paulo, 1933), pp. 150–52.

3. *Annaes da Câmara* (1879), March 3 and March 5; Joaquim Nabuco, *Discursos parlamentares: 1879–1889* (São Paulo, 1949), pp. 6, 10–11.

On March 5, 1879, Jeronymo Sodré, a young professor of medicine from Bahia, touched off a political explosion. Disgusted by the clamor for repressive measures and the plan to subject slaves to the most horrible conditions of incarceration, Sodré protested that prisons were not the answer to the problem. He acknowledged the danger of violence, saying, "Everyone knows it, Brazilian society is sitting on a volcano. Let us not delude ourselves." [4] But emancipation was the proper solution, he insisted, not repression and extreme penalties. He predicted that the rural provocations would stop on the day of abolition, bringing tranquility and prosperity to the country. Sodré then spoke to the other proposals under consideration. With emotion and eloquence, he claimed that the plans to reform and modernize the country would prove fruitless unless Parliament tackled the central issue of slavery:

> You are asking for educational reform? You are asking the government to guarantee the rights of non-Catholics? You are asking for liberation of the citizen through direct elections? You want all these things while conserving the cancer which deteriorates all, and corrupts all! [5]

Sodré's bold challenge broke the silence of antislavery groups and brought latent emancipation sentiment into the open. In the following years political leaders would find it difficult to discuss electoral reform, monetary reform, recruitment of immigrants, and other changes without taking the risk of prompting comment from abolitionists who sought to relate the issues to the fundamental problem of slavery. Furthermore, Sodré's speech attracted widespread attention outside the halls of government, triggering discussions among many people who previously had not given voice to their inclinations. Through 1879, most of the activity remained in Parliament, with deputy Joaquim Nabuco delivering important orations for the emancipation cause. Outside of the Chamber,

4. *Annaes da Câmara* (1879), March 5, pp. 194–96.
5. *Ibid.*

a few journalists made significant contributions.[6]

In the next year, 1880, a new awakening of pro-emancipation opinion took place in the major cities in Brazil. Anti-slavery leaders appeared to form societies, hold meetings and prepare newspapers to drum out the propaganda of a new attack. Although they were only a small minority, they succeeded in laying the foundations for a dynamic, viable movement. For the first time in Brazilian history, large groups of people worked together to mount a broad-based, organized, and popular campaign to attack slavery in the most fundamental way—that is, to challenge its right to exist. These agitators would not be satisfied simply with making arrangements to accelerate emancipation. They wanted to set a date to extinguish slavery in Brazil completely. It was a campaign for *abolition.*[7]

The abolitionist campaign was primarily an urban movement. It was in the cities that the idea of modernization excited numerous Brazilians whose changing views increasingly set them apart from the rural proprietors. The leaders in the cities, who looked outward, wishing to emulate the ways of the modernizing nations, believed the vision of the *senhores* was aimed inward and toward the past. In the eyes of the new urban elites, slavery was a vestige of the old Brazil. Though urban groups differed on the question of *how* slavery should be eradicated, many of them frankly stated their disapproval of the traditional order of masters and slaves and criticized it as an obstacle to Brazil's transformation into a modern country. Here was the nucleus for a growing and serious threat to the slaveholders: a geographically concentrated element representing diverse occupational positions which saw its interests lying outside the sphere of the slaveholders' society.

6. *"A abolição,"* notes of Joaquim Nabuco, Instituto Joaquim Nabuco.

7. *Perseverança e Porvir* (Fortaleza, May 24, 1883), in the Instituto Joaquim Nabuco; Nabuco, *O abolicionismo,* pp. 5–6; Evaristo de Moraes, *A campanha abolicionista, 1879–1888* (Rio de Janeiro, 1924), pp. 11–13.

The extraordinary economic developments of the 1870s and 1880s prepared the way for changes in attitudes. Especially in the decade of the Eighties, Brazil was swept into the current of worldwide capitalistic expansion with force far surpassing earlier developments. In the capital city of Rio de Janeiro, the largest metropolitan center in the empire and the country's principal gateway to the outside world, business moved at a feverish pace. Coffee sacks from neighboring provinces filled the city's docks. Through the streets of the capital signs and advertisements offered abundant evidence of the new enterprises designed to feed, supply, and service the expanding urban population. To the south the rapid spread of coffee cultivation across São Paulo's rich central and western sections spurred tremendous increases in exportation and the growth of cities such as São Paulo, Campinas, and Santos. Because of the slow and costly transportation of the product to the port city of Santos, British and Brazilian investors built railroads which lowered the shipping costs and also facilitated the transportation of foreign-made commodities into the interior. Moreover, railroad building opened new possibilities for internal development, making coffee planting in the backlands possible and stimulating the growth of interior cities.[8]

New organizations appeared to service the expanding businesses. Banks, insurance companies, and transportation companies were established not only through capital from foreign investors but also from the surplus profits of the Brazilian coffee planters. Rural entrepreneurs and town merchants began directing new capital into small-scale manufacturing enterprises such as hat-making, textile production, and food processing in order to sell to the growing urban market. These developments—the rise of new businesses and industries and the growth of port and interior cities—

8. Emília Viotti da Costa, *Da senzala à colônia* (São Paulo, 1966), pp. 184–87; Anyda Marchant, *Viscount Mauá and the Empire of Brazil* (Berkeley and Los Angeles, 1965), pp. 220–21; Morse, *From Community to Metropolis*, pp. 115–16.

produced an enlarged group of managers and small proprietors who associated themselves with popular nineteenth-century concepts of "liberal" economics. Translated into views on slavery which evaluated the economic rather than the moral aspects of the institution, this meant emphasis on the importance of free-market labor relationships and the superior value of free labor over slave labor. The idea that free labor was more productive and profitable than slave labor became axiomatic in the thinking of Brazil's new business elites. Slavery seemed glaringly incompatible with the goal of expanding modern capitalistic enterprise.[9]

Increasing ties with Europe and the United States contributed significantly to making the cities into centers not only for the exchange of goods but also for the exchange of ideas. In the 1880s publications multiplied, the expansion of steamship lines made travel abroad easier, railroads opened connections between the cities, and the telegraph speeded the communication of news events. All of these developments closed the gaps of intellectual isolation. Current trends in European thought received increasing attention as diverse groups in the urban environment embraced new views on economics and philosophy. When the participants in this cultural awakening employed the popular concepts to examine their native institutions, slavery appeared as an embarrassing anachronism. An antislavery stance became a necessary part of their call for modernization. In this condition of intellectual ferment, the cities became pockets of abolitionist agitation.[10]

The individuals who led, staffed, and supported the

9. Richard Graham, "Causes for the Abolition of Negro Slavery in Brazil: An Interpretive Essay," *Hispanic American Historical Review* (May 1966), pp. 123–37; Roberto C. Simonsen, *A evolução industrial no Brasil* (São Paulo, 1939), pp. 24–25; Stanley J. Stein, *The Brazilian Cotton Manufacture: Textile Enterprise in an Underdeveloped Area, 1850–1950* (Cambridge, 1957), pp. 7–8, 18.

10. José Maria dos Santos, *Os republicanos paulistas e a abolição* (São Paulo, 1942), p. 170; Graham, *Britain and the Onset of Modernization in Brazil,* pp. 31–32; Octávio Ianni, *Raças e classes sociais no Brasil* (Rio de Janeiro, 1966), pp. 78–93.

abolitionist campaign were largely from the urban areas and had no personal stake in slave property.[11] Diverse groups found places in the movement which appealed to a great variety of people of high, middle, and low social and economic status. Some of the most respectable citizens of urban society led the campaign. News reports of abolitionist meetings were filled with comments about the attendance and participation of members of "high society," "distinct gentlemen," and individuals identified with the deferential title of "Doctor."[12] Important abolitionist leadership also came from the professional schools. For example, in Ouro Preto (Minas Gerais) students in the School of Mines and the School of Pharmacy organized antislavery clubs, while in the cities of Rio de Janeiro and São Paulo, law students and engineering students became active abolitionists. In many cases these youths were sons or nephews of slave masters, and their expressed attitudes represented blatant rejection of traditional family interests. Throughout the campaign, the educated youth of the cities joined their professors as vigorous activists. Writers also played important roles in the movement. Journalists, novelists, and poets penned books, tracts, articles, and broadsides and participated in the organizational activity.[13] Representatives from business and professional classes filled the leadership ranks of abolitionist organizations too. Lawyers, doctors, merchants, manufacturers, engineers, commercial exporters and importers, printers, and notaries held promi-

11. João Dornas Filho, *A escravidão no Brasil* (Rio de Janeiro, 1939), p. 136; Almelia de Rezende Martins, *Um idealista realizador; Barão Geraldo de Rezende* (Campinas, n.d.), p. 358; Graham, *Britain and the Onset of Modernization in Brazil,* pp. 31–34.

12. See, for example, *O Paíz,* November 24, 1887, p. 1; Benedicto Pires de Almeida, *"Tiete, os escravos e a abolição," Revista do Arquivo Municipal de São Paulo,* XCV, No. 9 (1944), pp. 54–55.

13. Santos, *Os republicanos paulistas e a abolição,* pp. 181–82; Oliam José, *Abolição em Minas* (Belo Horizonte, 1962), pp. 93–94; Ciro Viera da Cunha, *No tempo de Patrocínio* (São Paulo, 1960), p. 73; Edmar Morel, *A dragão do mar: O jangadeiro da abolição* (Rio de Janeiro, 1949), p. 57; Luiz Luna, *O negro na luta contra a escravidão* (Rio de Janeiro, 1968), p. 74; Raimundo Girão, *A abolição no Ceará* (Fortaleza, 1956), pp. 233–50.

nent positions. The high status of these people in their communities gave respectability to the abolitionist campaign and significantly strengthened its political potency.[14]

Individuals from the lower social and economic strata did not usually find places in the organizational hierarchy of the movement, but they made significant contributions by attending meetings, supporting abolitionist candidates in political campaigns, and, especially, taking direct action against slavery. Through protest meetings in the streets and public squares and venturing out into the countryside to encourage slaves to escape, they effectively threatened and undermined the servile institution. In this group, for example, were coachmen, railroad conductors, fishermen, painters, harbor workers, artisans, and common laborers.[15]

From 1880 on, many abolitionist clubs appeared in the cities to stimulate public interest in emancipation and advance the cause in legislative bodies. Modeled on forms of association which had worked effectively in England and the United States, these clubs gave abolitionists a sense of camaraderie in the face of stiff opposition and helped keep the momentum of their campaign going. One of the first important clubs to develop out of the new wave of antislavery activity formed on November 7, 1880. Abolitionists in the city of Rio de Janeiro organized the Sociedade Brasileira Contra a Escravidão (Brazilian Anti-Slavery Society), electing Joaquim Nabuco president and André Rebouças treasurer. The effectiveness of the organization and its official organ *O Abolicionista* was short-lived, especially after Nabuco

14. Antônio Manuel Bueno de Andrada, *"Depoimento de uma testamunha," Revista do Instituto Histórico e Geográfico de São Paulo,* XXXVI (1939), pp. 210–13; Fernando Henrique Cardoso, *Capitalismo e escravidão* (São Paulo, 1962), p. 257; Costa, *Da senzala à colônia,* pp. 429–34; Roger Bastide and Florestan Fernandes, *Relações sociais entre negros e brancos em São Paulo* (São Paulo, 1955), pp. 102–103; Alaor Malta Guimaraes, *Campinas: Dados históricos e estatisticos* (Campinas, 1953), pp. 33, 59; Girão, *A abolição no Ceará,* pp. 233–50.

15. Andrada, *"Depoimento de uma Testamunha,"* pp. 210–13; Costa, *Da senzala à colônia,* pp. 429–34; *A Redempção,* May 13, 1889, pp. 3–4.

stepped down from the presidency in 1881, but other clubs quickly superseded it.[16] New organizations sprang up throughout the country such as the Sociedade Cearense Libertadora (Cearense Liberator Society) in 1880, the Sociedade Abolicionista Ouropretana (Abolitionist Society of Ouro Prêto) in 1882, and the Sociedade Libertadora Bahiana (Bahian Liberator Society) in 1883. In May 1883 João Clapp assumed the presidency of an important new organization, the Confederação Abolicionista (Abolitionist Confederation), which coordinated the work of several antislavery societies. The titles of the various clubs reflected the diversity of their personnel, such as the Club Abolicionista dos Empregados no Commércio (Abolitionist Club of Employees in Commerce), the Club dos Libertos de Niteroy (Freedmen's Club of Niterói), the Libertadora da Escola de Medicina (Liberator of the Medical School), and the Libertadora da Escola Militar (Liberator of the Military School). The manifesto of the Confederação Abolicionista, written by Patrocínio, Rebouças, and Aristides Lobo, was read to a cheering crowd of 2,000 people in the Dom Pedro II Theater. Capitalizing on the political leverage gained by this impressive gathering, abolitionists succeeded in presenting the document in Parliament and publishing it in the *Diário Oficial* (Official Record).[17]

The opportunities provided by the extraordinary expansion of the newspaper industry turned into a windfall for the abolitionists' propaganda campaign. As a consequence of the introduction of new inexpensive presses and technologically more sophisticated printing methods, newspapers could be sold to the public at less cost and in greater quantity than

16. *O Abolicionista,* November 1, 1880, p. 1; Carolina Nabuco, *The Life of Joaquim Nabuco* (Stanford, 1950), p. 75. Also important in Rio de Janeiro in the early 1880s was the Associação Central Emancipadora (Central Emancipation Association) under the leadership of Nicolão Moreira. It stressed "emancipation" rather than outright "abolition." Several public liberation ceremonies were held under the aegis of the association.

17. Duque-Estrada, *A abolição,* pp. 19–97, 104; *O Propulsor,* April 9, 1883, p. 1.

ever before. During the 1880s, numerous abolitionist groups started their own press in cities and towns across the empire. Among the most significant abolitionist periodicals were: *O Libertador* of Fortaleza, established in 1881 and published by the Liberator Society of Ceará; the *Vinte e Cinco de Março* of Campos, established in 1884 and edited by Carlos de Lacerda; and *A Redempção* of São Paulo, established in 1887 and edited by Antônio Bento. Newspapers in the city of Rio de Janeiro were particularly important because of the city's position as hub of political operations in the empire. Several abolitionist organs appeared there. *O Paíz,* established in 1884, was vehemently abolitionist; it contracted Joaquim Nabuco as a regular columnist and featured many important antislavery tracts. Some of the older periodicals of the capital city which had been established before the advent of the abolitionist movement also made significant contributions to the campaign. The *Gazeta de Notícias,* for example, was not radically abolitionist, but its editor, Ferreira de Araujo, did frequently feature important antislavery articles. Also, the English-language newspaper *Rio News* was boldly opposed to slavery from the first years of the movement. Abolitionists frequently quoted its reports and acclaimed the work of its editor, A. J. Lamoureux.

Most influential of all the abolitionist newspapers was the *Gazeta da Tarde* of Rio de Janeiro, established in 1880. Under the editorship of the mulatto Ferreira de Menezes, it openly criticized slavery, but the tone of its attack became noticeably harsher when Menezes died and the darker complexioned abolitionist José do Patrocínio assumed control. Patrocínio's dramatic rise to fame as Brazil's most influential black journalist and abolitionist deserves special attention. He was the illegitimate son of a popular *fazendeiro,* clergyman, and politician from Campos and a free Negro grocery huckster. Although the father did not legally recognize his son, he gave the youngster favored treatment and partially subsidized his education in pharmacy school. Patrocínio's financial situation remained precarious through the school years, necessitating considerable assistance from friends and a charitable organization. Even the degree in pharmacy did not provide a ticket to success, as he dipped into his last savings after graduation while trying to find employment. Then, suddenly, his career took a more favorable turn. A sympathetic friend from pharmacy school invited Patrocínio to his home for a night. The next day the family offered him a position as tutor of the children in the household. He remained in the home, eventually married his friend's sister, and found a job as political journalist for the influential Rio newspaper *Gazeta de Notícias.* When the editor of the newspaper *Gazeta da Tarde* died, Patrocínio quickly bought the enterprise with the help of his father-in-law. The editorship gave him an instrument to release the anger he had built up against slavery since the days when he witnessed brutal lashings on his father's own *fazenda.* Within a short time, Patrocínio increased the newspaper's daily circulation from 2,000 to 12,000 and established it as the major antislavery organ in the country. With twelve antislavery societies contributing information from various parts of the empire, the newspaper's staff was able to present a comprehensive coverage of the development of the campaign. Along with news reports and articles representing diverse approaches to abolitionism, it featured excerpts from other newspapers, including the editorials of slavocrat gazettes. The principal editorials of the *Gazeta da Tarde,* titled *Semana Política* (Politics of the Week), were written by Patrocínio under the pseudonym "Proudhomme." After quarrels with a co-editor of the newspaper in 1887, Patrocínio left the *Gazeta da Tarde* to begin publication of a new newspaper, *Cidade do Rio,* through which he carried on his fervent style of journalism. Following Patrocínio's resignation, the *Gazeta da Tarde* published very little information on the antislavery movement, while *Cidade do Rio* became an important new organ of abolitionist invective. Throughout this period of journalistic activities, Patrocínio also served as an active leader in the antislavery movement. His fiery style spilled over into other activities, and he acquired fame as a powerful, charismatic orator in the streets and squares of the capital city, particularly for his provocative diatribes before large audiences of Negroes and mulattoes.[18]

André Rebouças, a mulatto and close friend of José do Patrocínio, was also active in penning articles for the anti-slavery cause. Taciturn by nature, Rebouças did not attract great public attention as a forensic duelist as did Patrocínio. Instead, he made his greatest contributions to the movement by preparing manifestoes and radical antislavery literature and working "behind the scenes" to organize meetings in Rio de Janeiro. Rebouças was the son of a mulatto politician who had achieved considerable distinction as a lawyer, jurist, and member of Parliament, although he lacked a formal, professional degree. The younger Rebouças became an engineer, winning a degree in Physical Science and Mathematics from the Military School. He served the empire commendably, planning construction projects during the Paraguayan war and helping to build some of Brazil's first railroads. Rebouças achieved recognition for his technical ability and intellectual endowments and won the friendship and respect of the Imperial family. With the appearance of a new abolitionist movement in Rio in 1880, Rebouças entered the thick of battle as an intense partisan, identifying with the cause of his black "brothers." [19]

Another important mulatto, Luiz Gama, achieved con-

18. Moraes, *A campanha abolicionista,* pp. 355–76; Osvaldo Orico, *Patrocínio* (Rio de Janeiro, 1935); João Guimaraes, *Patrocínio: O abolicionista* (São Paulo, 1956); Ciro Viera da Cunha, *No tempo de Patrocínio* (São Paulo, 1960); Dorothy B. Porter, "The Negro in the Brazilian Abolition Movement," *Journal of Negro History,* 1952, pp. 61–62; *Gazeta da Tarde,* May 29, 1884, p. 1; Edison Carneiro (ed.), *Antologia do negro brasileiro* (Rio de Janeiro, n.d.), pp. 398–404. Because of the newspaper's comprehensive coverage of slavery, it serves as an excellent source for historians interested in the Brazilian antislavery movement.

19. André Rebouças, *Diário e notas autobiográficas,* ed. Ana Flora and Inácio José Veríssimo (Rio de Janeiro, 1938); Inácio José Veríssimo, *André Rebouças através de sua autobiografia* (Rio de Janeiro, 1939); Porter, "The Negro in the Brazilian Abolition Movement," pp. 66–70; Moraes, *A campanha abolicionista,* pp. 34–37.

siderable fame as an outspoken abolitionist before his untimely death in 1882. Gama was the illegitimate son of an aristocratic Bahian planter and a free Negro street vendor. His mother, the famous Luiza Mahin, had been a princess in Africa. While in Bahia, she was implicated in several planned slave insurrections. When Gama's father fell into debt, he sold his ten-year-old son into slavery. The traders shipped Gama to the expanding slave markets in São Paulo. Fortunately, he was purchased by a friendly family which treated him well. At the age of seventeen, Gama befriended a boarder at his master's home. The visitor, a law student, taught Gama the skills of reading and writing. Eventually, Gama fled from his master and obtained proof of his free birth. In the following years Gama served in the militia, then worked arduously in São Paulo establishing a career as a writer and lawyer. By the 1870s he became well known as a tough abolitionist and republican. He successfully argued several legal cases in behalf of slaves and became a dynamic leader of antislavery organizations before death interrupted his work.[20]

Many other Negroes and mulattoes played important roles in the abolitionist campaign, but aside from Patrocínio, Rebouças, and Gama, few achieved major leadership positions. The disparity troubled Rebouças, who in 1882 lamented the presence of only three mulattoes in the "Abolitionist Party" operating in Rio de Janeiro.[21] Even in the northern provinces, where the proportion of Negroes and mulattoes to the total population was very high, few people of color appeared in the top echelons of the organizations. For example, a catalogue of biographies concerning eleven prominent figures in an abolitionist club in Pernambuco lists only one individual as a

20. Sud Mennucci, *O precursor do abolicionismo no Brasil: Luiz Gama* (Rio de Janeiro, 1938); Moraes, *A campanha abolicionista,* pp. 250–58; Morse, *From Community to Metropolis,* p. 146; Porter, "The Negro in the Brazilian Abolition Movement," pp. 61–62.

21. Rebouças, *Diário e notas autobiográficas,* p. 295; Fernando Henrique Cardoso and Octávio Ianni, *Côr e mobiliadade em Florianópolis: Aspectos das relações entre negros e brancos numa comunidade do Brasil meridional* (São Paulo, 1960), p. 275.

"descendent of Africans," and he is identified only as an "auxiliary" member.[22] Similarly, in a study of twenty-seven abolitionist leaders in Ceará, historian Raimundo Girão describes only one person specifically as a "mestizo." [23] White elites directed many of the antislavery organizations, and free blacks could not usually meet the common prerequisites for high office: prestigious family background, formal education, and independent wealth. Moreover, blacks were usually excluded from important positions in political parties and the Imperial and provincial governments. In the face of obstacles to major participation in the political system, outspoken black opponents of slavery had to direct their energies largely to pressure-group activities. The situation directed them into the role of agitators, and, generally speaking, black abolitionists revealed more radical postures on the slavery issue than white abolitionists.

Many leading white abolitionists of distinguished family background who presided over antislavery organizations and held seats in Parliament exhibited a more cautious attitude when broaching the subject of slavery. Joaquim Nabuco is an outstanding example of the type of abolitionist who, especially in the early years of the campaign, agonized greatly over questions of strategy. For a while he showed strong reservations about adopting radical positions on issues such as indemnification for the slaveholders, demanding immediate rather than gradual abolition, and the tactic of employing extralegal measures to lure slaves away from their masters.

The scion of an important Brazilian family of Portuguese descent, Nabuco received a good education at exclusive schools and had opportunities to travel to the United States and Europe. Like many other prominent abolitionists, Nabuco was fascinated by European culture. He greatly admired the British, espousing the ideas of Walter Bagehot, imitating the political

22. *Cincocentenário da abolicão em Pernambuco. Catologo da exposição realizada no Teatro Santa Isabel de 13 a 31 de Maio de 1938* (Pernambuco, 1938), pp. 7–19.

23. Girão, *A abolição no Ceará,* pp. 233–250.

manner of William Gladstone, and dressing in the "British cut." He graduated with a law degree but was unable to establish a clear idea of his career goals while he worked in the shadow of his famous father, Senator José Tomaz Nabuco, a leader of the Liberal party. Through the 1870s Nabuco practiced law with his father in Rio de Janeiro, dabbled in journalism, and served with the Brazilian legations to the United States and Great Britain. After the death of his father and his own election to Parliament as deputy, Nabuco suddenly emerged as a public figure in his own right. In 1879 at the age of thirty, he fanned the flames of debate first lighted by Jeronymo Sodré, making slavery an issue for national consideration. Bright, handsome, and gifted in the forensic arts, the talented young man of distinguished heritage seemed to possess the major prerequisites for a fruitful career in Brazilian politics. He quickly became leader of the abolitionist group in Parliament, distinguishing himself as the most outstanding proponent of a political solution to abolition. Through eloquent speeches, prolific writing, and diligent work in the Chamber of Deputies, he left his mark as a principal contributor to the abolitionist victory.[24]

Nabuco's abolitionist activities were the manifestation of sentiments nurtured over a long period. He spent much of his youth on his family's sugar plantation in the northeastern province of Pernambuco, and the scenes he witnessed there left a deep impression. Nabuco was particularly moved by the experience of facing an anxious young slave who had fled from

24. The literature on Nabuco is voluminous. See, for example, Carolina Nabuco, *The Life of Joaquim Nabuco;* Alceu Marinho Rego, *Nabuco* (Rio de Janeiro and São Paulo, 1951); Celso Viera, *Joaquim Nabuco, libertador da raça negra* (São Paulo, n.d.). The *Revista do Instituto Histórico e Geográfico Brasileiro* published a special issue on Nabuco (V [July–September 1949], p. 204). Also see *O direito e a moral: Conferência realizada na sessão exotérica de 21 de março de 1932, na sede do "Circulo Esotérico" em S. Paulo, na Praça Almeida Junior n. 20* (São Paulo, 1932), pp. 4–18; *Cincocentenário da abolição em Pernambuco,* p. 9; Joaquim Nabuco, *A escravidão* (n.p., 1870), original manuscript in the Arquivo do Instituto Histórico e Geográfico Brasileiro.

a neighboring plantation after receiving severe castigation. The trembling bondsman knelt down, embraced Nabuco by the legs and pleaded that the young aristocrat purchase him from his harsh master. A reading of *Uncle Tom's Cabin* intensified Nabuco's concern. As a student he began to put his sentiments into writing, and in 1870, during the time of discussions that led to the Rio Branco Law, Nabuco prepared an unpublished manuscript, describing slavery as a criminal institution that corrupted and degraded society.

Through most of the campaign Nabuco stressed the importance of directing abolitionist activities through legal channels. He warned against making bitter denunciations of masters, politicians, or the Emperor. Nabuco wanted the debate to be kept on a high level, with the ultimate goal a victory in Parliament. He also wished to keep propaganda channeled toward the free masses, not the slaves. The contrary, said Nabuco, "would be the end of the abolition of Wilberforce, Lamartine, and Garrison and the beginning of the abolition of Spartacus or John Brown." [25]

Another rising young intellect of the period, Rui Barbosa, also stressed the importance of directing protests through the political machinery. A brilliant lawyer, intellectual and political figure from Bahia, Barbosa made his principal contributions to the antislavery cause through speechmaking and writing. In 1884, when he was a member of the Chamber of Deputies, he penned an important report on the emancipation problem that was presented to Parliament during the debates of the Dantas administration. Although hastily written, it offered a cogent, well-documented summary of legal precedents that supported the case for emancipation.[26] Barbosa was a magnificent public speaker. He enjoyed the intellectual challenge of humoring and awing his abolitionist audiences through

25. Carolina Nabuco, *The Life of Joaquim Nabuco,* p. 105; Joaquim Nabuco, *O abolicionismo* (São Paulo, 1938), p. 25; *Gazeta da Tarde,* October 4, 1882, p. 1.

26. Ruy Barbosa, *Emancipação dos escravos: Parecer formulado pelo deputado Ruy Barbosa (projecto N. 48)* (Rio de Janeiro, 1884).

speeches replete with witticisms, *double-entendres,* and quotations from the classics. Aristocratic and somewhat haughty, Barbosa preferred the company of law-abiding abolitionists.

At the other extreme were the radical abolitionists who advocated extralegal tactics to undermine slavery. Most outstanding was Antônio Bento, a pharmacist and public prosecutor who centered his activities in the city of São Paulo. He succeeded in bringing both white citizens and black freedmen together to create a radical movement. Bento's nocturnal agents went directly to the plantations to counsel slaves to flee, and he established an extensive network of "underground railroad" stations to guide fugitives to safety.

Bento was born in the city of São Paulo in 1843, the son of a pharmacist. He remained close to the Church during his school years, serving as choir boy and later as Chaplain of the Holy See after being nominated for the post by the bishop of the diocese. As Bento prepared for his graduation from an academy at the age of twenty-one, he seemed highly touted for an impressive professional career. During his last year in school, the Baron of Itauna nominated him to the position of public prosecutor. On graduation day, however, the young Bento shocked officials of the academy by refusing to offer the traditional expression of gratitude to the faculty. In response to this rebellious gesture, the school suspended him, and a councilman canceled the Baron's nomination. Thereafter, Bento followed a checkered career, serving in small cities outside the capital as lawyer, police delegate, public prosecutor, and municipal judge. He returned to São Paulo in 1877, continuing his ties with the legal profession but devoting an increasing amount of time to Church-related work. In the early 1880s the new currents of abolitionism captured his interest. Bento particularly admired the popular mulatto abolitionist Luiz Gama, and when Gama died in 1882, Bento pledged himself to leadership in the antislavery cause. His unorthodox style and attitude soon drew the attention of other Paulista antislavery figures. They found him an exciting, inspiring leader but, at the same time, a severe, cold, distant, and somewhat mysterious man. Bento's apparel of a long black cape and a tall black hat reflected a bizarre personality—religious, intense, and given to expressions of extreme indignation. As the abolitionist mood changed to interest in extralegal tactics, Bento's extreme approach gained increasing appeal.[27]

The Church served as Bento's base of operations. Working through the Church of Nossa Senhora dos Remédios, he developed a powerful *irmandade* (lay brotherhood) composed primarily of blacks, both slave and free. He established excellent rapport with the Negroes, calling in *padres* to hear their confessions, creating a special fund to help the poor, and organizing the brotherhood to stage large processions through the streets to demonstrate against slavery. Through careful planning, Bento expanded his efforts, developed a multipronged attack, and climbed to the chief position in the abolitionist movement in São Paulo. He became president of the local Abolitionist Association and edited his own newspaper, *A Redempção.* Most important, Bento directed the secret operations to help slaves escape from the plantations, a program which soon developed into the best organized underground movement in Brazil.[28]

Carlos de Lacerda served as Bento's counterpart in the province of Rio de Janeiro. A journalist and son of a medical doctor in the city of Campos, Lacerda concealed fugitives in his home with great risk to his life. He also directed the strategy of agitation in the area of Campos and encouraged slaves to burn the sugar-cane fields.

Many abolitionists bridged the gap between the leaders who advocated political efforts and those who demanded direct

27. *Revista do Instituto Histórico e Geográfico de São Paulo* (1914), XIX, pp. 635–36; *São Paulo e a sua evolução: Conferências realisadas no Centro Paulista em 1926* (Rio de Janeiro, 1927), pp. 33–35; *A Redempção,* May 13, 1899, pp. 3–4.

28. Antônio Manuel Bueno de Andrada, *"Depoimento de uma testemunha," Revista do Instituto Histórico e Geográfico de São Paulo,* XXXVI (1939), p. 221; José Maria dos Santos, *Os republicanos paulistas e a abolição* (São Paulo, 1942), pp. 179, 310–15; *A Redempção,* January 27, 1887, pp. 1–2, May 13, 1899, pp. 3–4; *Cidade do Rio,* April 30, 1888, p. 1.

action. Such was João Clapp, who served as president of the Confederação Abolicionista (Abolitionist Confederation). The owner of a china shop and other merchant enterprises, Clapp centered his antislavery operations in the cities of Rio de Janeiro and Niterói. While working to impress the political leaders through organizational work and the dissemination of propaganda, he also secretly arranged to have fugitive slaves spirited out of Rio de Janeiro. José Mariano of Pernambuco also sanctioned both approaches. An outspoken abolitionist in the Chamber of Deputies, Mariano was very popular with the masses in the city of Recife. With great personal magnetism, he harangued large crowds on the streets, pleading in favor of the abolitionist cause. Mariano championed a parliamentary solution to abolition, but he also spoke bravely in defense of those who were engaged in illegal operations with fugitive slaves. In fact he participated directly in clandestine activities through membership in a secret abolitionist society in Pernambuco.

Thus, abolitionists differed in their campaign tactics. Some advocated moderate, political approaches; some stressed radical, extralegal methods; and others sanctioned various combinations of the two. For example, though Nabuco and Patrocínio were compatriots in the antislavery movement, Nabuco sometimes looked askance at Patrocínio's appeals to the large urban element of Negro freedmen, because he feared that these masses might resort to violence. Yet even Patrocínio did not counsel a brazen extralegal approach to abolitionist agitation in the early 1880s. Both of these leaders as well as most other abolitionists evolved into less compromising positions during the decade. Abolitionists debated strategy among themselves, but, despite individual differences, there was a general tendency for all to become increasingly radical during the 1880s. By 1887 even the "moderate" abolitionists such as Nabuco and Barbosa would endorse the efforts to encourage slaves to run away or protest their status. These changes in attitudes point up the complexity involved in defining and identifying political positions in the antislavery controversy. Dates are important factors in such a discussion, for not only did significant changes develop within the abolitionist camp during the 1880–1888 period but also among other groups in the population. Therefore, it is necessary to consider a flexible taxonomy in identifying major groups in the struggle—one which accounts for the position of individuals on major issues *relative* to the stance of others during the same time period.

The title of "abolitionist" was used frequently in the 1880s. At any given time it was generally recognized who among the political leaders was an abolitionist and who was not. Abolitionists were the prime movers of the assault on slavery. These individuals were not satisfied with the existing legal apparatus for emancipation of the slaves; they wanted to expedite the emancipation process and make it a definitive solution. Throughout the 1880s the abolitionists took the most advanced positions on the slavery question. Abolitionism was, then, not one specific program but rather a *movement* that actively challenged slavery throughout the 1880s in a manner more radical than was acceptable to other parties in the controversy. The strategy of the abolitionist movement evolved to the point where, finally, almost all of them demanded the immediate end of slavery without any compromises.

Standing at the extreme of reaction in the face of the abolitionist challenge were the "slavocrats." As possessors of many slaves or as political spokesmen for slaveholders, these individuals adamantly defended slavery with all the forces they could muster. In principle, the slavocrats of the 1880s did not defend slavery as an everlasting institution, because the Rio Branco Law of 1871 had provided for its eventual extinction. But slavocrats latched onto that legislation as the final answer to the question. Similarly, when other emancipation legislation passed against their wishes, slavocrats insisted that it too would be the last word on the matter. In short, slavocrats denied the need for further compromise; they were the vehement defenders of the *status quo*.

Many individuals involved in the slavery question stood in a flexible position between the extremes of the abolitionists and the slavocrats. They were frequently identified as "emancipationists." Basically, the emancipationists believed that the existing legislation for liberating the slaves was inadequate. They were willing to pass new reforms to facilitate and speed the process of emancipation, but they were concerned that the arrangement still be gradual and respect property. Emancipationists cautioned Parliament to "go slow" on the sensitive issue and to resolve it in a way that would be at least partially satisfactory to the slaveholders. Unlike the "abolitionists" who were initiating the attack against slavery, the emancipationists were responding to the controversy by attempting to find a compromise solution.

With the rapid progress of the antislavery movement in the 1880s, many individuals changed their positions. Slavocrats became emancipationists and emancipationists became abolitionists. By May 1888 the ranks of the abolitionists swelled with recent converts. Consequently, the original group of out-and-out, hard-line abolitionists was dwarfed in a large movement that included many of the most powerful planters in the country.

In examining the stance of the active, organized group of "abolitionists" in the early 1880s, however, it is important to keep in mind that they were a small minority at the time. The position of the majority of the politically active figures in the empire ranged between the stances of the emancipationists and the slavocrats. In Parliament, especially, formidable obstacles existed which abolitionists would have to overcome before carrying their cause to victory in the Imperial Government. Many abolitionists believed this situation left them little choice but to direct policies along moderate channels.

Effective political power in the period usually rested in the hands of the party that controlled the ministry. Parliament passed a reform bill in 1881 to provide direct elections, but the law only strengthened the influence of the party in power because it could still control the election machinery. It gave suffrage to 145,000 out of a population of about nine million.[29]

29. C. B. Ottoni, *Autobiographia de C. B. Ottoni* (Rio de Janeiro, 1908), p. 260. Ottoni underestimated the population of the empire at the time of the electoral reform law by basing his figure on the 1872 census.

One superficially attractive feature of the law made freedmen eligible to vote, but an income stipulation made the clause almost insignificant.[30] In reality the electoral reform bill did not attack the interests of the landed oligarchy; in fact, it received support from many powerful slaveholders. Joaquim Nabuco suggested that the law turned Parliament into a bona fide Agricultural Congress (alluding to the controversial 1878 meeting).[31] Nabuco had reason to be sarcastic; in the first elections after the new "reform" law, he and many of his abolitionist friends lost their seats in the Chamber.[32] In the hands of the Baron of Cotegipe's Conservative ministry (1885–1888), which was sympathetic to the slaveholders, the law permitted almost complete exclusion of the Liberal party from power, placing 103 Conservative deputies in the Chamber, compared to only twenty-two from the opposing party.[33]

At the onset of the abolitionist movement there had been no clear-cut differences between the two parties on the issue of slavery. Some traditional antislavery sentiment was concentrated in the Liberal party, but this represented a minority position. The alignment, such as it was, could be traced back to the debates during the Paraguayan war and the political battles which led to the Rio Branco Law. Nevertheless, in 1880, outspoken, abolitionist Liberal leaders were few in number. Basically, the parties of the empire divided over the quests for power and the spoils of victory but rarely over ideological issues. This situation led some to question whether the Liberals and Conservatives represented real parties at all. As the *Gazeta de Noticias* noted:

> In Brazil there are *really* no parties. The two constitutional parties, the liberal and the conservative, are simply ag-

30. Basbaum, *História sincera da república*, p. 192.
31. Joaquim Nabuco, *Conferências e discursos abolicionistas* (São Paulo, n.d.), p. 272.
32. *Rio News*, May 24, 1882, pp. 4–5.
33. Luis Anselmo Fonseca, *A escravidão, o clero e o abolicionismo* (Bahia, 1887), pp. 616, 620; João Pandiá Calogeras, *A History of Brazil* (Chapel Hill, 1939), pp. 239–41, 249–51; Clarence Haring, *Empire in Brazil* (Cambridge, 1958), pp. 111–12.

gregations of men, and they are the outcome of convenience, circumstances, or opportunities, but they have no leading ideas.[34]

The absence of sweeping differences between the parties on the slavery question in the early years of the abolitionist campaign is also demonstrated by the fact that Liberals occupied the post of chief minister exclusively from 1878 to 1885 yet, with the exception of the Dantas ministry (1884–1885), they did little or nothing to help the antislavery cause. Dom Pedro's choices for the important post reflected his desire to placate the sensitive slaveholders. Shortly after the onset of the abolitionist movement, the government leader José Antônio Saraiva stepped down from his post, and on January 21, 1881, the Emperor named Martinho Campos of Minas Gerais to replace him. Martinho Campos had achieved notoriety as the empire's most frankly slavocrat politician. Both friends and foes understood the new leader's goals. He would try to hold the line on the emancipation issue and, if possible, exert great pressure to silence the abolitionists in Parliament. He succeeded in weakening antislavery activity within the government, but outside the Chamber, abolitionist sentiment continued to grow. Ironically, the presence of Martinho Campos in the position of Prime Minister served as a boon to the antislavery movement, since his undisguised attitudes made him an easy target of criticism.[35] After a brief and undistinguished term, Campos resigned, to be replaced by another Liberal known to be slightly more flexible on the emancipation issue, the Viscount of Paranaguá. The new minister threw sops to the antislavery forces by sponsoring piecemeal reforms to increase the emancipation fund, tax the sale of slaves, and prohibit the interprovincial slave traffic. Most abolitionists judged these programs inadequate, viewing them as insignificant changes designed to give some semblance of action.[36]

34. *Gazeta de Notícias,* April 30, 1883.
35. *Rio News,* July 5, 1882, p. 2.
36. *Ibid; Rio News,* August 24, 1882, p. 2; C. B. Ottoni, *Autobiographia de C. B. Ottoni* (Rio de Janeiro, 1908), p. 263.

Paranaguá's successor, Lafayette Pereira Rodrigues, tried a different policy. He sidestepped the emancipation issue, giving the appearance that it did not exist. During his tenure from May 24, 1883, to June 4, 1884, the government said and did little about slavery.[37]

If the strength of opposition in Parliament during the early 1880s made abolitionists hesitant about adopting proposals for immediate and unqualified emancipation, the lack of abolitionist enthusiasm among some important members of the intellectual community only added to their difficulties. When the antislavery movement suddenly burst forth with new popular support in the 1880s, some prominent teachers and writers were not prepared to embrace abolitionist philosophy. They could commend the humane sentiments which motivated abolitionists but worried about the constitutional and social implications of their programs. For example, some intellectuals opposed government action in the emancipation process through rigid adherence to "principle." Dr. José Maria Corrêa de Sâ, a professor, viewed manumission a necessity but called the emancipation fund created by the Rio Branco Law illegal and socialistic because the state had no business assuming a "moral" commitment to indemnify slave proprietors. He also asked for resistance to the abolitionists, claiming their impetuous, revolutionary approaches would bring more harm than good.[38] Another intellectual, the famous literary critic Sílvio Romero, stressed the idea of "autonomous emancipation," arguing that liberation should be encouraged but left to the slaveholder's initiative. Romero could not condone the government's "meddling" in the affairs of slavery.[39]

The Positivists particularly annoyed abolitionists, because their ambivalence on the slavery issue precluded full-fledged support from a small but influential school of philosophy.

37. Ottoni, *Autobiographia de C. B. Ottoni,* p. 263; *Brazil,* May 15, 1884, p. 1.

38. *Homagem da Sociedade Emancipadora Academica* (São Paulo, 1883), p. 3.

39. Luna, *O negro na luta contra a escravidão,* pp. 180–83; Moraes, *A campanha abolicionista,* p. 32.

Several Brazilian intellectual leaders had become disciples of the French writer August Comte, and by the 1880s Positivism came into vogue in the empire. "Order and Progress" were the precepts of the Positivists, but on the abolition issue many of them put greater stress on the first principle. Only a few Positivists acted as outright abolitionists during the early 1880s, while most of them displayed varying degrees of readiness to temporize on the question.

Luís Pereira Barreto, one of the leaders of the Brazilian Positivist school and author of the important book *As Três Filosofias* (*The Three Philosophies*), was a slaveowner. He opposed abolitionism and argued that neither the planters nor the Negro slaves were prepared for an abrupt change in the system.[40] Another important Positivist, Raimundo Teixeira Mendes, was considerably more progressive on the question than Pereira Barreto, but, in the early years of the controversy, he too warned that the foundations of the national economy were too solidly based on slavery to survive a sudden transition to free labor and that the slave, by his "mental and moral state," was not yet ready for successful assimilation into Brazilian society. Yet Teixeira Mendes converted quickly once abolitionism became a full-fledged movement, and this response disturbed his colleague, Miguel Lemos, the most prominent leader of the Positivist Church in Brazil. Lemos cautioned his friend not to embrace the idea of immediatism without serious consideration of the problems of the master class. The whole country was to blame for the institution, he said, not just one group. And the entire nation would suffer should a rash program be adopted. "In an essentially agricultural country such as ours," explained Lemos, "the ruin of the rural proprietors would be nothing less than the ruin of our country." He urged that the solution take all points of view into account: the "scientific," the "social," and the "moral." Lemos suggested working within the framework of the Rio Branco Law, empha-

40. Ivan Lins, *História do Positivismo no Brasil* (São Paulo, 1964), pp. 45–94; *Província de São Paulo,* November 20 to November 30, 1880.

sizing the importance of improving the education and work habits of the *ingenuos* who would become free at the age of twenty-one. It was the duty of the Positivist, he said, to impress *fazendeiros* with the need to improve the plantation milieu.[41] In the years to follow, however, Lemos, too, succumbed to the new intellectual ferment and became an abolitionist partisan. He penned a poignant indictment of the "monstrous crime" of slavery in his introduction to *O positivismo e a escravidão moderna* (*Positivism and Modern Slavery*) and joined his friend Teixeira Mendes in appealing for immediate abolition.

Over-all, the Positivists' contribution to the abolitionist movement was not great. They were too cautiously concerned about making emancipation an orderly process and too absorbed in internal disputes over leadership and religion to take an aggressively abolitionist stand.[42] For the most part, Positivists changed their attitudes in response to changes in public opinion —the more progressive ideas stirred up by leaders in the vanguard of the antislavery movement. This tendency of Positivists and other groups to react rather than to act on the slavery question proved to be a handicap to abolitionists during the early years of their campaign. While division and indecision persisted among important members of the intellectual community, the antislavery movement lacked the kind of philosophical endorsement it needed to isolate slavocrat ideology. Abolitionists wanted to expose the slaveholders' reservations about emancipation as invalid and untenable in the context of current thought, but they could not muster a solid front on this issue from the intellectual camp in the early 1880s. The equivocation of influential teachers and writers tended to bolster the position of pro-slaveholder leaders in government who challenged the purportedly "radical" programs

41. João Cruz Costa, *A History of Ideas in Brazil* (Berkeley and Los Angeles, 1964), pp. 105–106, 140; *Cartas de Miguel Lernos a R. Teixeira Mendes* (Rio de Janeiro, 1965), pp. 177–78, 185–86; Ivan Monteiro de Barros Lins, *Três abolicionistas esquesidos* (Rio de Janeiro, 1938), pp. 24–35; Miguel Lemos, *O positivismo e a escravidão moderna* (Rio de Janeiro, 1934).

42. Costa, *A History of Ideas in Brazil,* p. 138.

of abolitionists as unconstitutional and unworkable.

While confronting the formal and informal problems of indifference or opposition to their movement in the early years, abolitionists remained cautious and moderate in their approach. They recognized their position as a small but vocal minority. Acquiring greater mass support was imperative, but this required discretion. They would have to answer to the fears, common at the time, that a radical termination of slavery would prove dangerous. Abolitionists spoke of "immediatism," but almost all of them indicated willingness to compromise on this matter. They thought in terms of delayed emancipation, believing that most people were not prepared to accept immediate abolition. Consequently, many leaders who declared themselves "abolitionists" in the early 1880s were quick to add that they were not intransigent abolitionists. As the editors of the *Gazeta da Tarde* explained their position, "Intransigent in principles, we are, however, transigent in facts." [43] Acknowledging that slavery was a deep-rooted problem, abolitionists were willing to wait awhile for the complete realization of their hopes. For example, the Carlos de Lacerda Abolitionist Club of Campos announced in 1884 that its goal was immediate abolition but stated paradoxically that until that could be achieved, it would work to promote liberty and to better the slaves' living conditions.[44]

Emancipation plans suggested by antislavery leaders reflected this interest in compromise. A proposal by J. I. Arnizaut Furtado in 1883 called for immediate liberation of slaves over age fifty and four- to eight-year terms for the rest.[45] A plan submitted in the Chamber of Deputies in 1883 by Leopoldo de Bulhoes of Goiás suggested immediate liberty for slaves over age fifty and six-year terms of service for the rest.[46] Similarly, a petition circulated by José da Costa Azevedo and Joaquim

43. *Gazeta da Tarde,* July 6, 1882, p. 1.

44. *Vinte e Cinco de Março,* July 17, 1884, p. 1.

45. J. I. Arnizaut Furtado, *Estudos sôbre a libertação dos escravos no Brasil* (Pelotas, 1883), pp. 84–85.

46. *Camara dos Srs. Deputados—discurso proferido na sessão de 5 de Setembro de 1883—Leopoldo de Bulhões,* pp. 5–7.

Nabuco in 1882 recommended immediate emancipation "or a short term." [47]

The moderate approaches of abolitionists in the early years is also reflected in the activities of abolitionist organizations. Abolitionist clubs held many large public conferences to stimulate interest in the campaign and collect contributions for the emancipation of particular slaves.[48] Most of the oratory at these conferences remained respectful to the slaveholders, stressing the need to convince planters that slavery was morally wrong and economically disadvantageous to them. The first major emancipation conference in Rio de Janeiro, held at the São Luiz Theater on July 25, 1880, set the style for other meetings. Conspicuous in the box seats of the theater were elegantly dressed ladies, while many prestigious members of the urban society sat in the capacity crowd on the main floor. After honoring the presence of Carlos Gomes, the highly regarded composer of the Brazilian opera *Guaraní,* and hearing an eloquent antislavery speech by the noted orator Dr. Vicente de Souza, the assemblage contributed to a liberation collection for some selected slaves. The conference idea quickly spread to other cities, where the programs similary included musical and dramatic performances by professional and amateur artists, speeches by important personalities, and emancipation ceremonies.[49] These conferences proved so successful in stimulating interest in emancipation and generating antislavery attitudes in the cities that soon the abolitionists turned their sights outside the meeting halls to mount a broad-based propaganda campaign involving the distribution and sale of broadsides, pamphlets, and newspapers. They disseminated materials in the streets, cafés, theaters, and other gathering places. André Rebouças even passed out abolitionist literature at a cemetery

47. Furtado, *Estudos sôbre a libertação,* pp. 77–82.

48. *Rio News,* October 24, 1882, p. 4; *Gazeta do Porto Alegre,* April 26, 1884, p. 1.

49. Duque-Estrada, *A abolição,* pp. 89–90. For information on other meetings, see *Gazeta da Tarde,* January 8, 1881, p. 2; January 15, 1881, pp. 2–3; January 23, 1881, p. 1; February 7, 1881, p. 1; October 3, 1883, p. 2; Rebouças, *Diário e notas autobiográficas,* p. 290.

during interment ceremonies for the Viscount of Rio Branco.[50] Most of this abolitionist literature contained polemical arguments on the "wrongs" of slavery. The information was intended both to establish a dialogue with slave proprietors and to stir up antislavery enthusiasm among the free urban population. Authors of the materials usually shied away from making direct appeals to the bondsmen.

The difficulty of confronting Parliament with a precise political program for abolition in the early years of the campaign can be seen in the reaction prompted by a modest proposal Joaquim Nabuco submitted to the Chamber of Deputies in 1880. In one of the first legislative projects of the abolitionists, Nabuco asked for complete liberation of the slaves by January 1, 1890. He reasoned that the plan was a good compromise because

> an unchangeable term, such as the 1st of January, 1890, would leave time for the planters to prepare for a great revolution, while it would give rise directly in the hearts of the slaves to an invaluable hope, which would render life less and less hard for them at every step and bring them nearer to freedom.[51]

It was exactly that "hope" of freedom that the slaveholders feared. They believed that the establishment of an official date of liberation would stir the slave population to impatience and bring dangerous disturbances to the plantations. Also, in 1880 the slave proprietors considered ten more years of slavery far too short a term. When *fazendeiros* from the provinces of Rio de Janeiro and São Paulo heard of Nabuco's proposal, they marched on the capital to lobby against it. Parliamentary leaders attempted to make all discussion of the measure secret to preclude press coverage, and on the day scheduled for its consideration many deputies boycotted the Chamber, forcing cancellation of the meeting for lack of a quorum. After these

50. Veríssimo, *André Rebouças através a sua autobiografia,* pp. 202–203.

51. Carolina Nabuco, *The Life of Joaquim Nabuco,* p. 58; *O Abolicionista,* January 1, 1881, p. 6.

political antics, the deputies soundly defeated Nabuco's plan by a vote of 77–16. Significantly, twelve of the sixteen proponents represented the northern provinces.[52]

After the abortive effort to pass a comprehensive abolition law in Parliament, antislavery leaders turned much of their attention to piecemeal changes. In the 1880–1884 period abolitionists suggested a variety of reforms designed to eliminate some of the worst abuses of slavery and to expand the opportunities for liberation. They proposed prohibition of the interprovincial slave trade throughout the empire, increases in the emancipation funds through lotteries and new taxes, an end to the employment of slaves in public-works projects, and prohibition of slave-trade businesses. Many of these proposals began on the local level through attempts to pass laws in the municipal and provincial legislatures.[53]

Bringing the interprovincial slave traffic to a halt was one of the major interests of abolitionists in the 1880s and also the first of their moderate reform proposals to achieve some legislative success. The challenge to Brazil's domestic slave traffic developed as a response to tremendous demographic changes in the servile population which had occurred during the 1860s and 1870s. After the close of the African slave trade, *fazendeiros* in the expanding coffee regions of the Central-South found new sources of slave labor through purchasing bondsmen from proprietors in the Deep South and, especially, from planters in the economically depressed regions of the Northeast.[54] Abolitionists viewed this commerce as appallingly reminiscent of the African traffic. Almost all of the bondsmen

52. Campos Salles in *"A propaganda abolicionista e a lavoura," Província de São Paulo,* December 4, 1880, p. 1; Nabuco, *Conferências e discursos abolicionistas,* pp. 293, 310–11; Moraes, *A escravidão africana no Brasil,* p. 156.

53. *Gazeta da Tarde,* April 9, 10, 11, and 12, 1883.

54. The significance of the slave traffic from the Northeast is well known, but the importance of the emigration of slaves from the Deep South to the Central-South provinces has not been adequately explored. The diminution in the slave population in Rio Grande do Sul, for example, did provide a favorable environment for abolitionism. See Fernando Henrique Cardoso, *Capitalismo e escravidão* (São Paulo, 1962), pp. 80–81. Also, many slaves were transferred from the cities to the rural districts during the 1870s and 1880s.

from the distant coastal provinces were transported to the coffee lands by ship, and the stories of crowded vessels with human cargoes shackled to chains and balls sounded similar to the tales of the notorious Atlantic passage.[55] Abolitionists believed that prohibition of the interprovincial traffic would check this disgusting business and also give the *fazendeiros* of the Central-South an opportunity to concentrate on manumission rather than augmenting their slave forces. In late 1880 and early 1881 most of the interprovincial traffic was closed, as the provincial legislatures of São Paulo, Rio de Janeiro, and Minas Gerais all passed laws establishing heavy taxes on slaves brought in from outside the provinces.

The success of this reform, however, was due less to the support of abolitionists than to other groups. Most important, the slaveholders themselves became seriously interested in the prohibition. They realized that as northern planters and other slaveowners sold many bondsmen, they became less attached to the servile institution and more inclined to support emancipation projects. If the trend toward concentration of slaves in a few major provinces of the Central-South continued, the political "equilibrium" might be broken.[56] One spokesman for the coffee *fazendeiros* manifested his fears in the Chamber of Deputies of the Imperial Government by shouting to a representative from a northern province, "You want to sell your slaves, then to ask us to liberate ours." [57] Legislators in the provincial assembly of São Paulo frankly admitted their purposes in framing the law shortly after its passage. In an open discussion, representative R. Lobato recalled, "What we wanted to evade [by passing the prohibition law] was that the provinces of the North, after throwing all of their slaves in São Paulo, would be the first to give the shout of emancipation!" [58]

55. W. D. Christie, *Notes on Brazilian Questions* (London and Cambridge, 1865), pp. 76, 93; Nabuco, *Discursos Parlamentares,* pp. 11–13; Carneiro, *Antologia do negro brasileiro,* p. 43.

56. *Rio News,* May 24, 1882, pp. 4–5; *Annaes da Assembléa Legislativa Provincial de São Paulo* (1881), June 18, pp. 469–70.

57. *Rio News,* October 15, 1880, p. 4.

58. *Annaes da Assembléa Legislativa Provincial de São Paulo* (1881), June 18, pp. 315–17; *In Memoriam: Martinho Prado Junior* (São Paulo, 1943), pp. 190–94.

Fazendeiros of the Central-South also worried about the danger of bringing great numbers of uprooted slaves into their communities. In the 1870s these recent arrivals were responsible for frightening acts of violence on the plantations, and many *fazendeiros* believed that Northerners had purposefully sold them the most insubordinate and incorrigible slaves. As one representative to the São Paulo provincial assembly warned, "You *fazendeiros* who buy slaves from outside are placing assassins in your homes, not laborers."[59] The editors of the *Província de São Paulo* saw legislation against the traffic as necessary to ensure that the "black wave" from the north would not put the province in serious jeopardy.[60]

Many of the most vehement supporters of legislation against the interprovincial traffic were *fazendeiros* who already had a slave labor force adequate to satisfy their needs. They felt that the prohibitive taxes would make slaves scarce in their provinces, and should the government some day pass abolition with indemnification, they would be paid for liberations on the basis of a high market value.[61]

Consequently, the established slavocrats found a variety of reasons to reverse their position on the issue from intransigent opposition to acceptance of reform. The posture of the planters of Campinas reflected this attitude. Situated in the "central" coffee zone of São Paulo, they had long fought as leaders in the battle against prohibition through the powerful Planters' Club of Campinas. But the club changed its position in 1881 and helped to pass the new law. From the standpoint of the Campinas *fazendeiros,* the labor problem no longer seemed as important as the danger of northern abolitionism, slave insurrections, and the possibility of seeing the value of their slave property decline. These slavocrats combined with other groups to pass the new law. Along with immigrationists who wanted Europeans to make up the future influx of laborers

59. *Annaes da Assembléa Legislativa Provincial de São Paulo* (1878), March 27, pp. 474, 478–79.

60. *Província de São Paulo,* January 19, 1881, p. 1.

61. *O Cruzeiro,* December 16, 1880, p. 3.

and abolitionists who saw the act as an attack on slavery, planters voted to terminate the traffic through heavy taxation.[62]

The legislation did not silence proponents of the interprovincial trade. In São Paulo, for example, some spokesmen for "small planters" and "western planters" criticized the act as favorable to special interests. Labor-hungry *fazendeiros* engaged in westward expansion were especially successful in devising tricks to evade the new taxes on slaves brought in from other provinces. They falsified records, listing slaves from other areas as residents of São Paulo. Some simply tried to slip bondsmen into the province without notice. As late as 1887, abolitionists were still busy trying to check the illegal traffic.[63]

Efforts to invoke the Anglo-Brazilian treaty of November 7, 1831, also attracted considerable attention from the abolitionists in the early years of the campaign. This agreement with the British had stated that any Africans transported into Brazil after the treaty would be declared free. As the majority of the slaves in the coffee lands had blood ties with the Africans illegally imported after 1831 (they were either Africans themselves or partial or full descendants of the post-1831 African slaves), abolitionists sought to prove the "illegality" of their slave status. They believed that implementation of the 1831 agreement could bring freedom to the majority of slaves in the Central-South region.[64] Whenever records could be found to prove the illegality of a Negro's bondage, abolitionists took the cases to court. Eminent lawyers such as Antônio Joaquim Macedo Soares de Azevedo and magistrates such as Antonio Rodrigues Monteiro made the 1831 law the basis of their arguments in legal cases involving the freedom of individual

62. *Rio News,* May 24, 1882, pp. 4–5.

63. *Annaes da Assembléa Legislativa Provincial de São Paulo* (1881), June 18, pp. 318–20; *Relatório* of the president of São Paulo, João Alfredo Corrêa de Oliveira, April 26, 1886, p. 6; *Província de São Paulo,* January 18, 1881, p. 2; *Rio News,* January 24, 1882, p. 4; *A Redempção,* November 30, 1887, p. 2.

64. *O Abolicionista,* January 1, 1881, p. 3; *O Paíz,* October 9, 1887, p. 1; *Manifesto da Confederação Abolicionista do Rio de Janeiro* (Rio de Janeiro, 1883), pp. 8–9; Joaquim Nabuco, *O abolicionismo* (São Paulo, 1938), p. 221.

slaves.[65] The total number of slaves freed by reason of the 1831 law was not great. Legal cases were costly, and records had to be found to supply proof. Many of the most important decisions in favor of slaves came after 1885, in the last years of slavery.

As abolitionists continued their work to halt the interprovincial slave traffic, win legal cases for the freedom of individual slaves, and pass other legislative reforms to eat away at the abuses of slavery and improve the opportunities for emancipation, they increasingly realized that their multifaceted goals could best be achieved through political action on the national level rather than through local ordinances. Most important, if the progress of abolition was to be improved greatly, Parliament would have to take the provisions of the Rio Branco Law into account and decide if they offered satisfactory solutions to the slavery problem. As abolitionists examined the effects of the 1871 law, they found the legislation grossly inadequate for several reasons. More and more, they became determined to expose its shortcomings.[66]

First, abolitionists expressed concern for the status of the *ingenuos,* the children affected by the law. For all practical purposes, slaveholders treated *ingenuos* in the same manner as they dealt with their slaves. *Fazendeiros* often worked the *ingenuos* in the fields and sold them in the market place. Planters openly discussed the need to drive as much labor out of them as possible before they would become free at the age of twenty-one.[67] Very few masters chose to redeem eight-year-

65. *Obras completas do Conselheiro Macedo Soares (Antônio Joaquim),* Vol. I, *Campanha jurídica pela libertação dos escravos: 1867–1888* (Rio de Janeiro, 1938), pp. 29–72; *O Paíz,* February 4, 1881, p. 1; February 10, 1881, p. 1; *Província de São Paulo,* July 19, 1887, p. 1.

66. Abolitionists had no quarrel with the venerable Viscount of Rio Branco. They made him an honorary member of their abolitionist societies, praised him at the time of his death, and honored his name every year on September 28 (the anniversary of the Rio Branco Law). *O Abolicionista,* December 1, 1880, p. 1; *Gazeta da Tarde,* September 28, 1882, p. 1.

67. *Congresso Agricola,* p. 72; *Brasil Agricola,* March 15, 1881, p. 98; Herbert H. Smith, *Brazil: The Amazons and the Coast* (New York, 1879), pp. 516–17. Smith illustrated the cruel irony of the *ingenuos'*

old *ingenuos* for financial remuneration as provided in the 1871 law. As late as 1884 the government reported that in all of the empire only 113 *ingenuos* had been freed by this option.[68] Moreover, the *ingenuos* were being raised in the social conditions of slavery, an environment which the abolitionists deemed detrimental to their personal development. They would learn the habits of the other slaves, and true education would not be possible until the age of twenty-one. Essentially, abolitionists asked the question: What kind of free man would come out of twenty-one years of slavery? [69]

Second, the abolitionists were concerned about the one million slaves who would probably die in captivity under the provisions of the 1871 law. Emancipation funds would not touch most of them; their fate would be "emancipation by death," as Rui Barbosa described it.[70]

Third, slavery would continue to exist in Brazil for a long time under the arrangements of the law. Conceivably, said Senator Christiano Ottoni, a slave could be born on September 27, 1871 (one day before passage of the law), and still be a slave at the age of eighty—in the year 1951! At the time when Parliament passed the Rio Branco Law, it was generally calculated that fifty to sixty more years would pass before slavery would completely disappear in Brazil, but even that prediction was simply conjecture because it involved speculation about

---

condition: Masters worked the *ingenuos* especially hard because, eventually, they would have to free them. Also, see the broadsides "*Piracicaba: avaliação de uma ingenua*" and "*Câmara dos Deputados, 15 de Julho de 1885—Joaquim Nabuco*" in the Instituto Joaquim Nabuco.

68. *Relatório* of the Minister of Agriculture, Commerce and Public Works, Affonso Augusto Moreira Penna, 1884, p. 184.

69. *Emancipação dos escravos—discurso proferido no Senado por C. B. Ottoni, 30 de Junho de 1883* (Rio de Janeiro, 1883). Ottoni was not an abolitionist at the time he made the speech, but he well expressed the abolitionist criticisms of the Rio Branco Law. *O Paíz,* October 18, 1887, p. 1; Fonseca, *A escravidão, o clero e o abolicionismo,* pp. 587–88; Octávio Ianni, *As metamorfoses do escravo* (São Paulo, 1962), p. 215; Stanley Stein, *Vassouras: A Brazilian Coffee County, 1850–1900* (Cambridge, 1957), p. 231.

70. Furtado, *Estudos sôbre a libertação dos escravos no Brasil,* pp. 77–82; Ruy Barbosa, *Emancipação dos escravos,* in *Obras completas de Ruy Barbosa* (Rio de Janeiro, 1945), XL, 8.

the date when diminution in the slave population would make it possible for the emancipation fund to free the last bondsmen. Such a prospect seemed appalling to the people who viewed chattel labor as a great moral and economic blot upon the country.[71]

Fourth, abolitionists complained that slaveholders had greatly abused the provisions of the law. Officials misused the emancipation funds.[72] In some cases they paid masters three times over for redemption of the same slaves who remained in their possession.[73] Often, officials selected their friends as beneficiaries of the emancipation funds in order to reward them for political favors.[74] *Senhores* committed many other abuses such as lying about their slaves' ages to obtain higher compensation, selling slaves who could not legally be sold, and breaking up slave families. Furthermore, in 1876 control over allocations of the funds passed from the provincial assemblies to the municipal chambers. The "municipal" districts, which in reality included much rural area within their boundaries, could be controlled more closely by the *senhores* than the provincial assemblies.[75] Until abolitionists began to apply new pressure, allocation of emancipation funds almost came to a standstill. The government actually used some of the money for other purposes, such as educating *ingenuos,* and by 1880 about 4,000 *contos* of untouched funds had accumulated in the treasury.[76] Disgusted with these conditions, Joaquim Nabuco called the 1871 law a "monstrous lie" and declared:

71. Caio Prado Junior, *História econômica do Brasil* (São Paulo, 1949), p. 183; *Annaes do Senado* (1884), June 1, p. 30; *Rio News,* October 15, 1880, p. 4.

72. André Rebouças, *Abolição immediata e sem indemnisação* (Rio de Janeiro, 1883), pp. 4, 12–16.

73. *Gazeta da Tarde,* November 11, 1884, p. 1.

74. *Annaes da Câmara* (1885), I, 143.

75. *"80 Anos de abolição,"* p. 122.

76. *Relatório* of the Minister of Agriculture, Commerce and Public Works, José Antônio Saraiva, 1881, p. 3; Moraes, *A campanha abolicionista,* p. 2; *Rio News,* April 15, 1880, p. 2. As late as 1887, some municipalities in the province of Rio de Janeiro reported that they had not used their full quota of funds available for emancipation. See the *Relatório* of the president of Rio de Janeiro province, Antônio da Rocha Fernandes Leão, September 12, 1887, p. 41.

> The truth is that in our country it is useless to vote for laws to favor the slave, because the masters do not fulfill them, and there is not organized justice to obligate them to fulfill them.[77]

Finally, abolitionists pointed to the meager achievements of the emancipation fund as an example of the clear deficiency of the 1871 law. It freed a disappointingly small number of slaves. For example, the total slave population of Brazil declined "officially" by 329,873 in the 1874–1883 period, but only 18,900 of this decline was accounted for by the emancipation fund. The bulk of the total was represented by deaths (195,348) and manumissions (115,625).[78] The government's last official report on the slave population, made in 1888, indicated that a total of only 32,436 had been freed by the fund since its inception.[79] In the light of such statistics, Senator Christiano Ottoni declared that the emancipation fund "is not a serious thing." [80] Even the Minister of Agriculture, Commerce, and Public Works admitted that the fund's record was far from the expectations of its creators, and its over-all contribution to the emancipation process was "virtually insignificant." [81]

The general statistics on slavery seemed very disappointing to the abolitionists. Many had believed the nation was making substantial progress toward diminishing its slave population, but once the government released new data on the registration figures, abolitionists became shocked by the results of their own calculations. The number of slaves freed gratuitously by their

77. Moraes, *A campanha abolicionista,* pp. 6–7; *O Paíz,* October 18, 1887, p. 1.

78. Monteiro, *Pesquisas e depoimentos para a história,* pp. 71–72.

79. *Relatório* of the Minister of Agriculture, Commerce and Public Works, Rodrigo Augusto da Silva, 1888, p. 25.

80. Ottoni, *Emancipação dos escravos,* p. 42.

81. *Relatório* of the Minister of Agriculture, Commerce and Public Works, Henrique d' Avila, 1883, p. 32. Even the slavocrat newspaper *Brazil* admitted the results of the emancipation fund had little significance (April 1, 1884, p. 1). Reviewing the statistical record in 1880, the editor of the *Rio News* said, "As the case now stands, gradual emancipation is a failure and a fraud; it deceives the world with fair promises and deceptive protestations" (July 15, 1880, p. 1).

masters and by the emancipation fund did not seem to be very significant. For example, the total of 134,525 emancipations by manumission and the emancipation fund in the 1874–1883 period may appear large, but when compared with the base total of about 1,500,000 slaves in 1874, it represents a relatively small decline by emancipation of about 9 percent in nine years or 1 percent per year. Including the "emancipations by death," this would bring the total decline to roughly 2 percent per year.[82] Realizing that significant reduction of the slave population would be a slow process if left to the emancipation spirit of the slaveowners and the emancipation fund, abolitionists became determined in the 1883–1884 period to pass new legislation to hasten and increase the liberation of slaves. This new drive to pass reforms culminated in the ascendancy in 1884 of Senator Manoel Pinto de Souza Dantas to the position of chief minister of the empire.

Before considering the tremendous controversy over the program of Senator Dantas, it is important to point out that he took office at a time when a general wave of antislavery agitation rose across the empire, enabling abolitionists to make significant progress in particular areas. Several major cities in Rio Grande do Sul and Paraná were freed entirely of slavery, and sections of the cities of São Paulo and Rio de Janeiro also became liberated. In the north the entire provinces of Amazonas and Ceará abolished slavery.[83] These developments created strong new currents of political pressure which convinced many sensitive politicians of the need to release some of the emotional steam, alleviate tensions, and placate abolitionists before the situation got out of hand. The case of Ceará particularly excited abolitionists and frightened slavocrats. Abolitionists cheered the news from Ceará because the action

82. Using figures for different years, the *Rio News* estimated that the total yearly decline was 1½ percent and that it would take more than fifty years to emancipate all of the slaves in Brazil (September 24, 1885, p. 3).

83. *Gazeta do Porto Alegre,* April 26, 1884, p. 1; *Brazil,* May 25, 1884, p. 1; Teodureto Carlos de Faria Souto to Visconde de Paranaguá, July 1, 1884, Arquivo do Museu Imperial, 1. 7. 884, Sou-cl.

involved the liberation of many slaves and set a precedent for provincial abolition. They hailed the decision as an important victory, and José do Patrocínio christened Ceará the "Land of Light." On the other hand, slavocrats condemned the act as "illegal" and shuddered at the thought that the pattern of antislavery activity in Ceará might spread to other areas.[84]

Actually, severe economic difficulties had done much to precipitate the change in attitudes in Ceará. In the 1870s fierce winds began to blow into the province from the west, sweeping away the few rain clouds. After years of extreme heat, the land became parched and fine white dust covered the soil, sometimes blowing up into huge, ugly clouds. The drought of 1877–1880 killed thousands of people and left the economy in ruins. Thousands emigrated and many desperate slaveholders quickly began to free their bondsmen. In fact, a large proportion of the liberated slaves were old or sick; the slave proprietors had already sold their best workers to the Central-South.[85] Some Ceará slaveholders still hoped to sell groups of slaves to the southern market, but Negro *jangadeiros* (raftsmen) frustrated their efforts by refusing to allow the slaves to be taken to boats that were waiting off the harbor of Fortaleza. Eventually, several thousand citizens of the city joined the *jangadeiros* by gathering on the beaches to shout, "No more slaves will leave the port of Ceará [Fortaleza]!"[86] A short time later the major slave-purchasing provinces of the coffee region passed laws against the interprovincial slave traffic, thus closing the safety valve of the hard-pressed Ceará slaveowners. A powerful antislavery campaign under the leadership of many of the most respected commercial and professional members of Ceará society gathered force in the

84. Hermes Vieira, *A Princesa Isabel no cenário abolicionista do Brasil* (São Paulo, 1941), p. 244.

85. *Rio News,* February 24, 1880, p. 2; *Brazil,* April 1, 1884, p. 1; May 8, 1884, p. 1.

86. *Gazeta da Tarde,* February 15, 1883, p. 1; *O Libertador,* February 7, 1881, p. 1; February 17, 1881, p. 3; Broadsides printed by the *Sociedade Cearense Libertadora: Alerta! Alerta!; Corra Sange!; Rio News,* April 5, 1881, p. 3.

province. These leaders succeeded in passing high taxes on slave property. With outside markets closed, proprietors found the economic value of their bondsmen to be less than the tax. The records showed as many as 24,648 slaves registered in Ceará in 1882, but, in the next two years, individual municipalities quickly declared their areas free territory. By March 1884 the last sections fell into line, giving the *coup de grâce* to servile labor in Ceará.[87]

From the point of view of other slaveholders in the empire, the experience in Ceará seemed ominous, not only because it raised the danger of further campaigns for provincial emancipation but because it showed the repercussions of creating areas of refuge in the midst of slaveholding communities. Once abolitionists had gained support from the magistrates and the chief of police in the city of Fortaleza, they were not hesitant to shelter fugitive slaves in their homes. Some members of the prestigious Liberator Society of Ceará went to trial on charges of inciting slaves to escape, but judges acquitted them without trouble. As the city and, eventually, the entire province became liberated, abolitionists from other northern provinces organized "underground railroads," making free Ceará the terminus. In Pernambuco these clandestine activities proved especially successful through the leadership of three popular abolitionists: João Cordeiro, João Ramos, and José Mariano. In October 1884 many of the antislavery leaders in Recife decided to coordinate their work through the highly secret Termite Club. It was so named because the organizers intended to eat away silently at the institution of slavery. Working under fictitious names, club members concealed fugitives in two rented buildings and cooperated with barge workers to guide slaves to ships that would take them to Ceará. Hence, Ceará became the soft underbelly in the northern plantation littoral of Brazil. The presence of an asylum for fugitives exposed *senhores* in neighboring provinces to a new and disturbing problem. Moreover, it provided a frightening lesson to the

87. *Gazeta da Tarde,* February 8, 1883, p. 2; *Brazil,* April 24, 1884, p. 1.

fazendeiros of the Central-South. What would happen if the major cities in their own regions became asylums for fugitive slaves? Already urban areas like Rio de Janeiro and São Paulo were centers of strong, organized abolitionist activity. Did the events in the Northeast signal the beginning of a new wave of extralegal agitation that would spread through the empire? [88]

Indeed, abolitionists in the city of Rio de Janeiro tried similar tactics but with less success. While the *Gazeta da Tarde* featured an instructive series of articles on the Underground Railroad in the United States, the Abolitionist Confederation, under the leadership of João Clapp, worked to bring fugitive slaves to the city of Rio de Janeiro. The machinery of intrigue included secret agents, passwords, and falsified freedom papers. But the underground movement in Rio, operating near the hub of slavocrat power, met stiff resistance. Slaveholders succeeded in suppressing many of the extralegal activities in 1884.[89]

It was in the environment of strong abolitionist agitation in Ceará, Amazonas, and several cities throughout the empire that Dom Pedro chose Senator Manoel Pinto de Souza Dantas to form a new ministry in June 1884. Dantas, a Liberal party leader from Bahia, had served for many years in high government posts. He had traveled widely through Europe, where he was inspired by English civilization and liberal ideas.[90] The choice of Dantas was interpreted as a progressive turn for the Emperor, for the Bahian had long been an advocate of new reforms to supplement the emancipation apparatus of the Rio Branco Law. Dantas' elevation marked the beginning of a long period of intense debates in Parliament as well as excited

88. Duque-Estrada, *A abolição,* pp. 96–113; Moraes, *A campanha abolicionista,* p. 230; *Brazil,* May 15, 1884; "Livro: Livro I," notes of Joaquim Nabuco in the Instituto Joaquim Nabuco; *Cincocentenário da abolição em Pernambuco,* p. 17.

89. Dent, *A Year in Brazil,* p. 287; Carolina Nabuco, *The Life of Joaquim Nabuco,* p. 103; *Gazeta da Tarde,* May 21, 1883, p. 1; Orico, *Patrocínio,* pp. 85–87.

90. Dantas, a devoutly religious man, was characterized by his black attire, because he often entered Parliament after attending Mass in the morning. Carolina Nabuco, *The Life of Joaquim Nabuco,* pp. 66–67.

activity outside the halls of government. Representatives of diverse interests clashed angrily in the midst of a mounting political crisis.

Slavocrats viewed the selection of Dantas with hostility and directed their invective directly at the Emperor. Antônio Coelho Rodrigues of Piauí, an eloquent defender of the rural aristocracy, was particularly biting in a book he published anonymously in 1884. He warned Dom Pedro that "slavery in Brazil is the twin sister of monarchy in America; they are both supported by the same arguments: tradition, custom and the law." Rodrigues admitted that he, personally, was losing his enthusiasm for the monarchy because of disturbing political developments. Actually, Rodrigues spoke for the concerns of many slaveholders who believed the Emperor betrayed them.[91]

For the most part, Dom Pedro never had been very bold in regard to the abolition issue. A well-educated man of liberal inclinations, he personally disapproved of Negro slavery and wished to see its termination in Brazil. Yet the close connection between the Imperial Government and the rural aristocracy forced the Emperor to temper overt expressions of his attitude. The strength of the monarchy rested on the support of slaveholders, and Dom Pedro could not afford to risk estrangement from his power base.[92] Abolitionists and slavocrats recognized the Emperor's dilemma and criticized him accordingly. While abolitionists scolded Dom Pedro for protecting slavery, slaveholders constantly reminded him of his dependent status. As emancipation of the slaves became a major political issue in the 1870s and 1880s, Dom Pedro reacted to the transformations in public opinion by issuing moderate statements on

91. Antônio Coelho Rodrigues, *Manual do subdito fiel ou cartas de um lavrador a sua magestage o Imperador sôbre a questão do elemento servil* (Rio de Janeiro, 1884), p. 108. Also see *O erro do Joaquim Nabuco* (Rio de Janeiro, 1886), pp. 6, 15; *Cartas do imperador D. Pedro II ao Barão de Cotegipe ordenadas e annotadas por Wanderley Pinho* (São Paulo, 1933), pp. 286–87.

92. *Gazeta da Tarde,* December 1, 1882; September 26, 1885; *A Redempção,* February 27, 1887, p. 2; Prado Junior, *In Memoriam,* p. 185; Emília Viotti da Costa, *"Sôbre as origens da república," Anais do Museu Paulista,* XVIII (1964), 95.

the subject. During the times of greatest agitation for reform, he presented his *Falas do Trono* (Speeches from the Throne) favorable to "free labor" and "gradual" emancipation through "legal" means and in a "tranquil" political environment. At no time did these speeches radically depart from the state of public opinion, and they always showed respect for the interest of the slaveholders.[93]

In 1884 the political heat became so intense that the Emperor could not avoid being scorched. National sentiment pressed for meaningful reform legislation. The Emperor's decision to choose Dantas was based on the great popularity of the statesman and the impact of the widespread and popular movement for significant reform in the emancipation process.[94] When Dantas assumed authority, he declared, "I am not an abolitionist as already they wish to portray me." Instead, Dantas defined himself as an "emancipationist." [95] But no matter; abolitionists adopted him as the personification of their hopes. Even Joaquim Nabuco, who only a year before had called Dantas' suggestions "inadequate," now gave the Bahian full support and declared that the terms "abolitionist" and "emancipationist" were synonymous.[96] The enormous enthusiasm for Dantas, despite his reluctance to embrace radical programs, can best be explained by the fact that he represented the abolitionists' best hope at that time for a political solution to emancipation, and the great wrath of the slavocrats that Dantas quickly incurred stirred the abolitionists to identify with his cause.[97]

93. See *Falas do trono* (Rio de Janeiro, 1889); Duque-Estrada, *A abolição*, pp. 299–301.

94. For the first few months of Dantas' leadership, abolitionist agitation in the streets subsided as antislavery leaders waited to see the reactions of Parliament to Dantas' proposals. See *Annaes da Câmara* (1885), I, 181.

95. Monteiro, *Pesquisas e depoimentos para a história*, p. 70.

96. Nabuco, *O abolicionismo*, p. 229; Carolina Nabuco, *Life of Joaquim Nabuco*, p. 108.

97. Moraes, *A campanha abolicionista*, p. 59. *The Gazeta da Tarde* explained its support for the Dantas program in the following way: "What is to be done is not all, but at least it is something" (June 19, 1884, p. 1).

The program of the Dantas ministry, as presented in Parliament by Dantas' son, included immediate liberation for all slaves over sixty years of age (the sexagenarians), an increase in the emancipation fund through new taxes, a total end to the interprovincial slave trade, immediate liberation of slaves not properly registered, and an official table for the progressive amortization of slave values.[98] The majority in the Chamber of Deputies was amenable to accepting at least some of these reforms, since under the existing conditions it appeared that far too many slaves would experience "emancipation by death" —an assessment which had been given much unpleasant publicity.

This concern provided a rationale for one of the most important elements in the Dantas proposal: liberation of the sexagenarians. Although abolitionists admitted that the plan represented a very moderate reform measure, at least it would relieve slaves of the horrible anticipation of a lifetime in bondage.[99] In addition, abolitionists could construe the act as indirect recognition that many of the sexagenarians were natives of Africa who had been illegally imported after 1831.[100] But Dantas' proposal called for *unconditional* liberation of the sexagenarians, and this created a major stumbling block. The supporters of Dantas wanted emancipation without indemnification. Slaveholders found the approach unacceptable, fearing that it would establish a dangerous precedent. At stake was the whole question of the legality of slave property. The Dantas plan would destroy the slaveholder's right to remuneration for his "property."[101] Many slaveholders also opposed the proposal to free sexagenarians because of another twist in interpretation. Approval could make slave proprietors victims of their own machinations. For years planters had officially registered their

98. *Rio News,* July 24, 1884, p. 2.

99. *Rio News,* October 15, 1880, p. 3.

100. *Conferência do Sr. Joaquim Nabuco a 22 de junho de 1884 no Theatro Polytheama* (Rio de Janeiro, 1884), p. 13.

101. Monteiro, *Pesquisas e depoimentos para a história,* pp. 72–73. During the 1884 debates, many "emancipators" supported slaveholders on the indemnification issue.

slaves as older than they really were in order to hide their African origins, thus avoiding litigation for freedom on the basis of the 1831 law. Now they would suffer, as the slaves could be declared sixty or older and, therefore, free.[102]

Abolitionists rallied around Dantas and gave his project their full support. They warned the opposition that resistance to his plan would only make the antislavery movement more radical. In a speech in the Chamber of Deputies on July 24, 1884, Rui Barbosa said:

> Every battle on the slave issue that the liberals lose in the political arena, every reverse that you inflict by crushing with your votes the Cabinet that personified this proposed enactment, shall constitute no advantage whatever to the vested interests concerned but rather a step toward unconditional emancipation.[103]

Others warned that opposition could lead to violence. For example, a letter signed by "A Farmer," which appeared in the newspaper *O Paíz,* declared that "the rejection of the Dantas project would be a calamity. . . . Fortunately, until now abolitionist propaganda has been maintained on legal terrain with extreme moderation." The writer said that the campaign could turn to criminal acts that would directly provoke the liberty of the 1,200,000 slaves—actions that would bring grave disturbances.[104]

For months the bitter debates continued in Parliament with the proceedings marred by ugly incidents. Deputies slapped each other in the face, political opponents exchanged disparaging remarks, and crowds in the galleries interrupted the discussions with angry shouts. After protracted parliamentary battles which failed to change the tide of thought significantly in one direction or the other, the deputies adjourned, turning their attention to the election campaign that would choose

102. *Rio News,* December 5, 1884, p. 2.

103. Charles W. Turner, *Ruy Barbosa: Brazilian Crusader for Essential Freedoms* (New York and Nashville, 1945), p. 77.

104. *O Paíz,* April 19, 1885, p. 2.

the men to return to Rio for the session of 1885. The campaign proceeded under extremely tense conditions, with many of the candidates polarized into a pro or con position on the Dantas plan.[105] In Pernambuco fierce competition led to violence as abolitionists and slavocrats vied for a victory. In the city of São José a huge crowd joined the popular abolitionist José Mariano to march on the building where the votes were to be counted. Mariano was aware that slavocrats had already falsified election data in other areas, and he wanted to prevent the same problem from occurring in his own district. As officials began to tally the results, they closed the door on the crowd, but the enraged throng forced the doors open and poured into the lobby. Amid shouting and confusion, a major standing at the top of a staircase discharged a warning shot from his revolver. Then one of the excited intruders mistakenly screamed, "José Mariano is wounded!" and the crowd surged up the steps and brutally murdered the major and his nephew.[106]

The incidence of violence embarrassed the abolitionists and generated charges that debates over Dantas' program had a dangerously unsettling effect. When the Chamber of Deputies reopened in Rio in 1885, the division between pro- and anti-Dantas forces remained very close, but a deputy representing the opposition soon tipped the delicate balance by capitalizing on the fear of disruption. After being hissed by a crowd of Dantas' partisans while entering Parliament from the street, the deputy presented the following motion to the assembly: "The House of Deputies, convinced that the ministry cannot guar-

105. Manoel Pinto de Souza Dantas to Dom Pedro II, 3-VIII-84; 15–7–84; João da Cruz e Santos to Visconde de Paranaguá, October 30, 1884, 30.10.884: San. C1–3, Arquivo do Museu Imperial; *Documentos do próprio punho do Cons. Luiz Felippe de Souza Leão relatando conferências políticas com o Sr. Sancho de Barros Pimentel, Presidente de Pernambuco e com o Cons. Gasper da Silveira Martins: eleição de Joaquim Nabuco,* 1, 2, 4–9–1884, Lata 456, D-136, Arquivo do Instituto Histórico e Geográfico Brasileiro.

106. Nabuco, *Conferências e discursos abolicionistas,* pp. 394–96; Joaquim Nabuco, *Eleições liberaes e eleições conservadores* (Rio de Janeiro, 1886), pp. 48–49.

antee order and public security, which are necessary for the resolution of the slavery question, negates its confidence." The motion passed by a narrow margin of 52–50 with the help of some Liberal party leaders who deserted Dantas. The vote precipitated the fall of the ministry. Dantas said he was falling "in the hands of the people." [107]

Dom Pedro then turned to a new Prime Minister to address the slavery controversy, José Antônio Saraiva, a Bahian. Saraiva had been in and out of the top echelons of government for many years and he was widely respected for his skills of leadership. Although a Liberal, Saraiva wished to be more accommodating to the interests of the slaveholders than Dantas, and he was acceptable to many members of the Conservative party. Saraiva presented a new, complicated project. It sought to resolve the question of the sexagenarians by declaring them free but with the obligation of serving their masters for three more years. Slaves over sixty-five years of age would be totally free. The plan officially described the three-year term of service as "indemnification" for the masters; thus Saraiva's project recognized the "legality" of slavery. The plan called for a new registration of slaves and determination of the value of bondsmen by a table based on ages (the older the slave, the lower the value; also, values would decline with increasing rapidity each year). It also included an increase in the emancipation fund through new taxes and government bonds, a stipulation that slaves could not be transferred from the municipality where registered unless they would remain with the same master, and a fine of 500 to 1,000 milreis for enticing or sheltering fugitive slaves.[108]

When the designers of the Saraiva project first presented their program, they calculated that it would end slavery in about seventeen years; this was later whittled down to thirteen

107. Carolina Nabuco, *Life of Joaquim Nabuco,* pp. 133–35; *Rio News,* May 15, 1885, p. 2; *Moraes, A campanha abolicionista,* pp. 84–85; C. B. Ottoni, *Autobiographia de C. B. Ottoni* (Rio de Janeiro, 1908), pp. 278–81.

108. *O Paíz,* May 9, 1885, p. 1.

years. However, Antônio Prado, the planter-capitalist from São Paulo, succeeded in making the plan much more conservative than it appeared at first glance. He engineered a series of amendments through Parliament which raised the official redemption prices of slaves to a very high level—in fact, to the point where the government price for redeeming a slave would, in many cases, be greater than the current market price. In particular, the table listed high values for young slaves. The purpose behind this arrangement was clear: Young bondsmen were considered the best workers, and slaveholders wanted to hold on to them as long as possible. High values could effectively preclude early liberation. Moreover, Prado's new table offered only a very slow depreciation rate for values of all slaves during the early years of the law. Under this system, liberations through the emancipation fund would largely be delayed until the latter part of the thirteen-year period. Finally, Prado would subsequently find a subtle means of adding one and one half years to the projected thirteen-year period. Through later implementation of the law while serving as Minister of Agriculture, he decided to begin marking the depreciation of values upon completion of the government's official registration campaign rather than on the date when the law was passed. Because Imperial agents needed many months to obtain figures from numerous isolated plantations, Prado's decision significantly altered the timetable for liberation.[109]

Once antislavery leaders scrutinized the diverse provisions of the plan, numerous other loopholes came to light. A projection of the sum total of the emancipation fund over the next thirteen years revealed that these monies would suffice to liberate only a small percentage of the slave population—10 to 12 percent, according to the calculations of one discriminating senator. In fact, over the span of thirteen years about one-third

109. Duque-Estrada, *A abolição,* pp. 165–68; Moraes, *A campanha abolicionista,* pp. 96–118, 146; Nazareth Prado (ed.), *Antônio Prado no império e na república* (Rio de Janeiro, 1929), pp. 104–106; *Gazeta da Tarde,* August 14, 1885, p. 2; Ottoni, *Autobiographia de C. B. Ottoni,* p. 281.

of the emancipation fund would be scheduled to service loans rather than directly redeem slaves.[110] The plan also dodged the sensitive issue of registering the nationality of bondsmen by stating that such information was necessary only "when it is known." Abolitionists had hoped to guarantee the freedom of slaves in cases where proprietors could not prove that they were born in Brazil. This procedure would free thousands of Africans who had arrived in Brazil after 1831. Interpretation of the meaning of "when it is known" became an issue of great debate in the years to follow.[111]

Only a few of the keenest minds immediately grasped the significance of the most basic potential loophole in the Saraiva plan—that it lacked a coercive sanction to effectuate the definitive abolition of slavery at the end of the projected term. The prolonged discussions about tables of values proceeded, for the most part, under the assumption that declining values would lead to emancipation. Yet the fact remained that even the complete disappearance of a slave's value did not necessarily guarantee his freedom. "The elimination of value is not a declaration of liberty," said Rui Barbosa; "it is not the extinction of property." The extremely complicated provisions of the Saraiva plan left this essential issue obscure—a bridge to be crossed when society would come to it in the following decade. When Barbosa joked about the diverse ramifications of the proposal, saying they had been explained and re-explained with no observable improvement in understanding, his audiences greeted the comment with bursts of laughter. Yet Barbosa's point was well taken, for the extensive provisions of the new plan bewildered many.[112]

José Antônio Saraiva, whose name became most closely

110. Ottoni, *Autobiographia de C. B. Ottoni,* pp. 282–83.

111. Duque-Estrada, *A abolição,* p. 165.

112. Rui Barbosa, *Conferência abolicionista realisada a 7 de junho de 1885 no Theatro Polytheama da Côrte* (Bahia, 1885), pp. 27–37; Ottoni, *Autobiographia de C. B. Ottoni,* pp. 282–83; Affonso Celso, *Oita anos de parlamento. Poder pessoal de D. Pedro II, reminiscências e notas* (São Paulo, n.d.), p. 130; *Annaes da Câmara* (1886), September 4; September 11, 110; *Jornal do Commércio,* June 2, 1886.

identified with the proposal, was not really as much a proslavery figure as many abolitionists portrayed him. Saraiva hoped to give some degree of satisfaction to all parties in the controversy. To avoid accusations of personal bias, he liberated all of his own slaves—more than seventy—before submitting the project.[113] Arch-slavocrat Andrade Figueira warned Saraiva that he was deceiving himself if he believed the program would destroy abolitionist agitation. In spite of some sincere attempts to assuage the hurt feelings of abolitionists, he could not escape from the central meaning of his elevation in the wake of Dantas' defeat. Saraiva had been called to duty to break the stalemate and calm the deepest fears of the planter class. His plan could be described as "emancipationist," but, most important, it offered slaveholders many of the provisions they requested to stave off the threat of early abolition.[114]

After completing his work of campaigning for the project, Saraiva submitted his resignation and, for the first time since the 1870s, the Emperor handed the reins of government to a Conservative minister. Under the leadership of the Baron of Cotegipe, Parliament quickly passed the proposals of Saraiva in slightly altered form, and they became known as the Saraiva-Cotegipe Law. It was voted into effect on September 28, 1885, the fourteenth anniversary of the Rio Branco Law.[115]

113. *O erro do Joaquim Nabuco,* p. 13.

114. Moraes, *A campanha abolicionista,* pp. 94–96; *Gazeta da Tarde,* September 4, 1885, p. 1; José Antônio Saraiva to Dom Pedro II, August, 1885, Lata 456–103, Arquivo do Instituto Histórico e Geográfico Brasileiro.

115. A complete text of the law, along with examples of the kind of slave registration it provided, can be found in José Maria Vaz Pinto Coelho, *Legislação Servil-Lei N.3270 de 28 de Setembro de 1885* (Rio de Janeiro, n.d.). This registration material makes up one of the principal sources of information that has been lost to historians because of the Brazilian government's decision in 1890 to burn the official records of slavery.

A total of 90,923 slaves were freed because of age in the first year of administration of the Saraiva-Cotegipe Law (*Correio Paulistano,* September 16, 1887, p. 1). Many slaveholders later evaded the law passed by Parliament. They did not follow the contract provisions or

Abolitionists burst out with indignation against the new legislation. They declared it reactionary, a "black law" in the words of José do Patrocínio, a "capitulation to the slavocrats" according to Rui Barbosa.[116] It is likely that antislavery leaders would have accepted many provisions of the plan a year before, but their goals had evolved rapidly in the 1884–1885 period while Dantas was under attack from the slaveholders. What was acceptable to the abolitionists in 1884 was no longer satisfactory only a year later. "It is as if in a year we have traveled a century," exclaimed Barbosa. Slaveholders would later admit that they should have accepted the original Dantas project because it could have placated the abolitionists and prevented their turn toward immediatism.[117]

In the short run, however, passage of the Saraiva-Cotegipe Law did have a quieting effect on the political scene. For many months public agitation died down, and the lull in activity seemed to indicate that the "emancipatory" appearances of the legislation either confused or satisfied the public. Abolitionists continued their work, but many of their earlier supporters appeared willing to wait temporarily to see how the law would be implemented. In the quiet of early 1886, Joaquim Nabuco wrote of "The Eclipse of Abolitionism" and the editors

---

make use of the emancipation fund. Some sold sexagenarians between the ages of sixty-one and sixty-four for the value of their services. Especially important, masters changed the ages of their old slaves in the new registration to make them appear younger. In 1887 the Imperial Government reported the number of sexagenarians freed to be only about one-fourth the total that would be expected on the basis of earlier registration figures. *Relatório* of the Minister of Agriculture, Commerce and Public Works, Rodrigo Augusto da Silva, 1887, pp. 40–41; *Relatório* of the president of Rio de Janeiro province, Antônio da Rocha Fernandes Leão, September 12, 1887, p. 40; C. B. Ottoni, *O advento da república no Brasil* (Rio de Janeiro, 1890), p. 58; *Gazeta da Tarde,* September 21, 1886, p. 1; *Revista Illustrada,* November 6, 1886, p. 2.

116. *Gazeta da Tarde,* May 3, 1886, p. 1; Barbosa, *Conferência abolicionista,* p. 42.

117. Monteiro, *Pesquisas e depoimentos para a história,* p. 181; Duque-Estrada, *A abolição,* pp. 236–37; *Gazeta da Tarde,* June 7, 1886, p. 1; Ottoni, *O advento da república,* p. 66; *Cincoentenário da abolição em Pernambuco,* p. 43.

of the *Gazeta da Tarde* sadly announced that "abolitionism is dead." [118]

The conservative slaveholding interests were now back in power, represented by the Baron of Cotegipe, his cabinet and a Chamber of Deputies dominated by the Conservative party. Slave proprietors and their political spokesmen stood determined to make the Saraiva-Cotegipe Law the last word on emancipation reform; they would adamantly resist all further proposals of the abolitionists. On the other side of the controversy, a new abolitionist profile was emerging that boded trouble for the future. Many antislavery activists, now frustrated and embittered by their legislative failures, were ready to look outside of politics to achieve their goals.

118. *Gazeta da Tarde,* May 8, 1886, p. 2; Joaquim Nabuco, *O eclipse do abolicionismo* (Rio de Janeiro, 1886).

II

Abolitionists and Planters Confront the Issue

4: The Abolitionist Perspective

THROUGH A VAST outpouring of literature and speeches in the 1880s, abolitionists constructed a broad-based, multifaceted, comprehensive view of slavery and its place in Brazilian life. Leaders of the movement extended the connection between the system of slavery and the problems of the economy and society so far that sometimes they appeared to elevate abolition to the level of a panacea. Through incisive criticism of slavery's multifarious influences, they interpreted abolition as the fundamental step necessary to turn Brazil into a modern, "civilized" nation. Three salient arguments appear in the documents of the campaign: that slavery was illegal, that it was immoral and that it was a detriment to the material development of the country. Individual abolitionists placed greater emphasis on one or another criticism, but, over-all, they tended to give all three ideas considerable attention in their literature and speeches.

The tendency of abolitionists to question the legality of slavery was especially evident in the early years of the campaign, when most of them stressed the need to work in the system and make their appeal moderate and respectable. An attack on slavery's institutional sanctions seemed a logical way to unnerve slaveholders about the constitutional weaknesses in their argument while keeping antislavery polemics philosophically acceptable to the moderate citizenry.

In the search for legal ammunition to fight their case, abolitionists found, for example, that slavery had never been legitimized by civil legislation. No laws had sanctioned slavery officially, they argued, and, therefore, it had "no right to be."[1]

1. See the argument of J. Simoes in *Gazeta da Tarde,* December 5, 1882, p. 2.

As the Lawyer's Anti-Slavery Club explained in its 1884 manifesto, slavery was never authorized by express law; in fact, "the law found itself in constant protest against the violent fact and repugnant usurpation." [2] Viewing the legal question from a different perspective, abolitionists could also find specific legislation to bolster their argument. Often they based their case on the 1831 law against the African slave trade which declared that all slaves entering Brazil after its promulgation would be *ipso facto* free. Recognizing that thousands of Brazilian slaves were illegally imported Africans or their descendants, abolitionists branded slavery in Brazil "a theft," "illegitimate," and "illegal." [3] Carrying their reasoning a step farther, some leaders emphasized the historic origins of the slave traffic. All of Brazilian slavery, they said, resulted from the piracy of reducing free people in Africa to slaves. It was, declared Luiz Gama, the work of robbers and brigands. As an anonymous writer in the *Gazeta da Tarde* reasoned, "If slavery in our country was born with the traffic, if the traffic was a theft, and if the theft constitutes among us legitimate property, then slavery is palpably a crime." [4] Although abolitionists had good legal precedent to support their case against enslavement of Africans imported after 1831, the law was difficult to implement. Slave proprietors refused to reveal information that would prejudice their interests, and judges feared political reprisals for delivering decisions in favor of the slaves.[5] Abolitionists began to make significant headway on the basis of this legislation only in the last years of the campaign.

All of these legal arguments rested on shaky ground, however, because of a more basic constitutional question. Slavocrats could easily retort that abundant legislation in the books related to slavery essentially gave the institution legal recognition. The slavocrat position posed a weighty problem, because

2. Hélio Vianna, *Estudos de história imperial* (São Paulo, 1950), p. 299. See the Manifesto-Program of the Lawyers' Anti-Slavery Club, written by Tristão de Alencar Araripe.

3. See the comments of Gomes de Castro and José Mariano in *Annaes da Câmara* (1885), I, 149, 189.

4. February 5, 1883, p. 2.

5. *Gazeta da Tarde,* June 4, 1881, p. 2.

abolitionists had to deny centuries of lawmaking in stressing the illegality of slavery. Many Brazilians stood in the middle of the debate, believing there were two sides to the question, each position being, in a certain sense, "right." For example, one anonymous author declared slavery illegal in moral terms but, at the same time, accepted it as a legal form of property because it had been authorized by the constitutional powers of the country.[6] As another writer in the *Província de São Paulo* saw the situation in 1880, the issue forced a confrontation between two legitimate schools of thought: those who argued in terms of "natural right" versus those who defended "positive right." [7]

As abolitionists probed the intellectual problem more and more deeply, they recognized the need for criticisms that transcended the matter of written laws. The formidable barrier of property rights could not easily be surmounted by confining arguments to legal questions; they needed to direct the attack toward more fundamental issues. Abolitionists took up the challenge by underscoring the moral aspects of the question, asking if one man had the right to own another. Was not the property of man over himself the most sacred right of all? As some described it, this was a concept of "natural law" which placed the human personality outside the realm of private ownership. In the environment of nineteenth-century liberal ideas, the thought of one individual possessing another appeared glaringly wrong. Moral issues had to be considered paramount to the legal and property considerations propounded by the slaveholders.[8]

Abolitionist propaganda featured abundant condemnations of human bondage based on moral precepts. Writers labeled slavery a "moribund and nefarious institution," "shameful," "criminal," and "immoral"—"an injustice and a horrible viola-

6. Cincinnatus, *O elemento escravo e as questões econômicas do Brasil* (Bahia, 1886), p. 2.

7. November 19, 1880, p. 1.

8. *Vinte e Cinco de Março,* May 8, 1884, p. 1; *Gazeta da Tarde,* December 11, 1882, p. 2; December 12, 1883, p. 2; July 2, 1884, p. 2; Rui Barbosa, *Emancipação dos escravos: Parecer formulado pelo deputado Rui Barbosa (Projecto N. 48)* (Rio de Janeiro, 1884), p. 53.

tion of rights."[9] Joaquim Nabuco, who attributed his antislavery sentiment to his "own moral nature," declared that the abolitionists sought to create "a new moral conscience for the Brazilian nation."[10]

In stressing the immorality of slavery, abolitionists tackled the old, thorny legal question of whether a slave should be considered a person or a thing.[11] By judging the issue in terms of morality rather than formal law, abolitionists were able to remove the doubts associated with a web of legal complications. They said that the servile institution stripped men of their individual personality and reduced them to the level of animals. A master could trade off his slave just as he could dispose of a horse, a piece of furniture, or any other form of property. When would it be prohibited to buy, sell, and exchange men, women, and children? asked abolitionists.[12] And how could a man in slavery achieve true human dignity?[13] The editors of the newspaper *O Libertador* complained that "the slave, without the recognition of his individual self, without the conscience of his force, without the right of his dignity, is the festering wound in the regular functions of social life."[14] Pointing directly to the person-thing controversy, abolitionist Silva Jardim stated that by common practice bondsmen were treated as things, a condition which revealed the moral bankruptcy of the institution. Men could not be things and could not be property.[15] Laws might try to mitigate the slave's condi-

9. See, for example, *Gazeta da Tarde,* July 6, 1882, p. 1; April 18, 1887, p. 1; L. Anselmo Fonseca, *A escravidão, o clero e o abolicionismo* (Bahia, 1887), pp. 84–88.

10. Carolina Nabuco, *The Life of Joaquim Nabuco* (Stanford, 1950), p. 90; Joaquim Nabuco, *Campanha abolicionista no Recife* (Rio de Janeiro, 1885), p. 2.

11. Dr. J. Baptista Pereira, *Da condição actual dos escravos, especialmente após a promulgação do Lei N.3270 de 28 de Setembro de 1885* (Rio de Janeiro, 1887), p. 16.

12. Joaquim Nabuco, *O abolicionismo* (São Paulo, 1938), p. 39.

13. André Rebouças, *A agricultura nacional* (Rio de Janeiro, 1883), pp. 164–66; Barbosa, *Emancipaçao dos escravos,* p. 60.

14. July 2, 1881.

15. Silva Jardim, *A patria em perigo—conferência "meeting" sôbre a actual situação brasileira, realisada na cidade de Santos, em a noite de 28 de janeiro de 1888,* p. 14.

tion, giving him certain "rights" as a bondsman, but the principal and effective approach to erasing this ambiguity lay in abolition. Only complete liberation could transform the Negro slave into a dignified citizen. André Reboucas, particularly, emphasized this point, arguing that emancipation would bring the Negro into civil status on the basis of "Liberty, Equality, and Fraternity." [16]

In attempting to gather support for their moral attack on slavery, abolitionists were disturbed by the indifference of the Church. The clergy had long been tied to both slavery and the slaveowners. Slaves owned by the religious authorities served friars, monks and bishops.[17] These practices continued far into the years of the antislavery campaign; for example, as late as July 1887, religious orders in the province of Maranhão owned 203 slaves.[18] Some padres even advertised rewards in the newspapers for return of their fugitive slaves! [19] The clergymen's deferential treatment of the powerful rural landlords was also disturbing. Religious leaders almost never made offensive remarks about slavery, and, when they preached to the slaves, they encouraged obedience to the plantation managers. In effect, they fulfilled a task of psychological pacification for the *senhores.*[20]

Abolitionists condemned the silence of the Church. An editorial in the São Paulo abolitionist organ *A Redempção* blasted the padres for not remembering the "mission" which they were duty-bound to fulfill, and added that "the Church cannot be indifferent to the fate of millions of Brazilian unfortunates only so not to offend the rich and powerful." [21] Joaquim Nabuco

16. *O Libertador,* January 1, 1881, pp. 1–6; January 15, 1881, p. 1; Evaristo de Moraes, *A campanha abolicionista: 1879–1888* (Rio de Janeiro, 1924), p. 22; *Gazeta da Tarde,* November 30 1882, p. 2.

17. *Gazeta da Tarde,* May 28, 1883, p. 1; Fonseca, *A escravidão o clero e o abolicionismo,* pp. 27–29; Nabuco, *O abolicionismo,* pp. 186–87.

18. *Correio Paulistano,* September 24, 1887, p. 2.

19. Fonseca, *A escravidão, o clero e o abolicionismo,* p. 400.

20. Moraes, *A campanha abolicionista,* p. 281; Leôncio Basbaum, *História sincera da república, das origens até 1889* (Rio de Janeiro, 1957), pp. 175–76, 316–17.

21. February 27, 1887, p. 3.

charged that "no padre ever tried to impede the auction of slaves or condemn the religious regimen of the *senzalas.*" [22] He concluded that the abolitionist movement owed nothing to the Church. Luís Anselmo Fonseca presented the most thorough censure of the Church's indifference in his book *A escravidão, o clero e o abolicionismo* (*Slavery, the Clergy and Abolitionism*), published in Bahia in 1887. Fonseca claimed that the Church did not have an important traditional role in Brazilian society and that very few religious leaders made significant contributions to the development of the nation. The Brazilian Church displayed moral indifference on the great social questions, particularly on the issue of slavery. Unlike the clergymen in Britain and the United States, Brazilian religious leaders kept silent during most of the abolition campaign. In fact, said Fonesca, only one padre stood out in the slavery controversy from 1879 to 1887—João Manoel, who gave his services to the slaveholders! [23]

In the absence of an active campaign from the pulpit, some abolitionists took the initiative and stressed religious doctrines. They interpreted slavery and Christianity to be incompatible and said that the servile institution was ignominious to Christian civilization and condemned in the Bible. A Catholic could not be a slavocrat, they insisted, because a slavocrat was necessarily an aetheist.[24] A. Pereira d'Araujo denounced slav-

22. Nabuco, *O abolicionismo,* p. 18.

23. Fonseca, *A escravidão, o clero e o abolicionismo,* pp. 1–12, 26. Fonseca did overlook some minor contributions by men of the Church, but it should be noted that these actions were taken at times when the particular local communities were already strongly moving against slavery. In Rio Grande do Sul, for example, the Vicar of Pelotas, Father Canabarro, was an outspoken abolitionist, and in 1884 he led a mob that freed slaves from the city jailhouse. Also, the newly appointed Bishop of Ceará was critical of slavery when he took power in January of 1884—when abolition was almost complete in that province.

24. *Gazeta da Tarde,* January 17, 1881, p. 1. Also, see the same newspaper, May 15, 1883, p. 2; *Manifesto da Confederação Abolicionista do Rio de Janeiro* (Rio de Janeiro, 1883), p. 4; *Discurso que tinha de ser proferido por occasião da primeira sessão magna da sociedade—Libertarora Cearense—No dia 27 de Setembro de 1882, em um dos saloes do palácio da presidência por Diogo Cavalcanti de Albequerque* (Pernambuco, 1882), p. 8.

ery as contradictory to all civil, constitutional, and ecclesiastical rights and incompatible with justice and humanity. A slave without religion, just as a free man without religion, was capable of committing dangerous acts. The person who worked for liberty worked for the coming of Jesus.[25]

Despite references made to a Christian approach to the problem, religion never did become a major theme in the antislavery campaign. As Joaquim Nabuco noted, Brazil did not experience the strong religious currents that had awakened clergymen in the northern United States.[26] Because of the Brazilian Church's close association with the rural landholders, clergymen did not speak out against slavery until the last year of the antislavery campaign. Confronted with an indifferent ecclesiastical establishment, abolitionists did not choose to make the work of the Church a pillar of their campaign. The antislavery movement remained primarily secular.

In addition to legal and moral undertones, Brazilian antislavery leaders placed great emphasis on the concrete problems engendered by slavery, a perspective which apparently achieved a more fundamental position in their approach to the problem than in the case of their counterparts in North America. Abolitionists in the United States attacked an institution with which, in most cases, they had little personal, daily contact. With servile labor concentrated in the South, debates frequently focused on moral questions. As individuals, the institution did not usually affect their lives in a direct way —at least not until Free Soilers and other groups connected the issue to the question of territorial settlement. In Brazil the situation was strikingly different. Slavery was a national experience rather than a sectional one. It touched the life of every Brazilian. As one observer described it, the empire was one big Georgia. Abolitionists responded accordingly. Besides charging

25. Pereira d'Araujo, *A incoherência da escravidão n'um paíz christão, obra religiosa, moral, e política* (Bahia, 1885); A Pereira d'Araujo, *A monarchia brasileira se agarrando a taboa da escravidão* (Bahia, 1885).

26. Joaquim Nabuco, *Minha formação* (São Paulo, 1934), p. 212.

that slavery did violence to the individual rights of men, they also called the entire system into question, finding it detrimental to their own interests and, in a related way, a pervasive problem that hindered national development. Economically, socially, and politically, the servile institution seemed to be the main cause of Brazil's backwardness. To destroy the cancer of slavery would be to open the door to a new era of modernization. Most Brazilian abolitionists considered slavery in its totality; more than just an injustice to the slaves or an offense to their moral sensitivities, it was a problem of material concern for themselves and the society.

Joaquim Nabuco made the most eloquent statement of the totality theme in his classic study of Brazilian slavery, *O Abolicionismo.* After many months of research in the libraries of London, Nabuco published his penetrating investigation in 1883. The importance of the book lies in the fact that it summarized many of the major ideas that became popular in the abolitionist literature of the 1880s. In one of the key statements Nabuco explained that the word slavery had to be understood in the broad sense: "It does not only signify the relationship between the slave and the master; it signifies much more: the sum of the power, influence, capital and clientele of all the slaveholders, the feudalism established in the interior; the dependency of commerce, religion, the poor, industry, Parliament, the Crown and the State, in the presence of the aggregate power of the aristocratic nobility. . . ." [27] Nabuco saw abolition as central to progress in other matters and indicated this clearly in describing his plans to write additional books. He intended *O Abolicionismo* to be the first work in a series that would also deal with economic and financial reform, public education, administrative decentralization, religious equality, foreign relations, political representation, and European immigration.[28] The purpose of abolitionism, said Nabuco, was that of "reconstituting Brazil on the basis of free labor and the union of the races in liberty." [29] It would be the first major step

27. Nabuco, *O Abolicionismo,* pp. 5–6.
28. *Gazeta da Tarde,* March 6, 1884, p. 1.
29. Nabuco, *O Abolicionismo,* p. 19.

in the effort "to elevate Brazil to the category of useful member in the human community." [30]

Most abolitionists agreed with Nabuco's critical assessment of the tremendous power of the slaveholding class. They disputed the slavocrats' assertion that the system of slaveholder leadership and slave labor had made Brazil rich. Abolitionists contended that slavery had created an illusory appearance of order and well-being and that under the surface the institution had wrought grave problems which abolitionism brought into focus. The power of the slaveholders was paralyzing the national economy, claimed the abolitionists. It kept Brazil dependent upon single crops and hindered the development of cities and industry. In rural areas, the land monopoly of slave proprietors left the majority of the people landless and poor. Small-property owners seemed nonexistent in many areas, and there was almost no middle class—only the masters on one side and the slaves and the poor proletariat on the other.[31] Moreover, the institution left unfortunate psychological repercussions on diverse classes. Servile labor degraded free labor and made the population slothful and apathetic. Toil was dishonored; free men disdained manual work.[32] Slavery seemed to affect *fazendeiros* in a similar way, making them lazy and inefficient plantation managers. Planters exploited the land and left the soil dissipated. "The primitive fertility of the soil is left so exhausted and without care that fertile valleys are transformed into lagoons," reported an abolitionist newspaper.[33] The basis of the problem, said the abolitionists, was

30. *Gazeta da Tarde,* March 6, 1884, p. 1. Also see Joaquim Nabuco, *Conferências e discursos abolicionistas* (São Paulo, n.d.), pp. 229–31, 387.

31. *Manifesto da Confederação Abolicionista do Rio de Janeiro,* pp. 17–19; *Diário de Santos,* August 23, 1887, p. 1; Nabuco, *O abolicionismo,* pp. 145–59; *Gazeta da Tarde,* June 27, 1884, p. 2. *The Gazeta da Tarde* bemoaned the plight of those "who not being the slaves of any master, nor masters of any slave, are all enslaved in their ignorance and misery . . . they are pariahs in their own land" (December 1, 1882, p. 2).

32. See the letter of Affonso d'Escragnolle Taunay in *O Paíz,* December 25, 1887, p. 2; Nabuco, *O abolicionismo,* pp. 173–75; Rebouças, *Agricultura national,* p. 173.

33. Quoted in *O abolicionismo,* November 1, 1880, p. 4.

that *fazendeiros* had become so accustomed to working with a servile labor force that they were reluctant to use fertilizers and machinery and to learn about modern techniques of farming. Consequently, neither free laborers nor their managers were very industrious.[34]

The continuation of slavery also appeared to preclude an effective program of land reform. André Rebouças, one of the most vehement proponents of the idea of agrarian reform, saw small property as the key to progress in agriculture. He outlined Brazil's problems in a series of articles on such subjects as "Latifundio" (large landed estates), "Landocracy," "Territorial Monopoly," and "Territorial Aristocracy." His solution, which he titled "Rural Democracy," depended on the division of extensive unused land areas into sections that could be given to freedmen and immigrants. The specific areas to be affected would be chosen from numerous documents of mortgaged *fazendas* that were in the charge of Brazilian banks. Rebouças believed that small farmers would become industrious and productive citizens if they could be given their own land as well as some seeds and equipment. He tried to implement his ideas by creating a Territorial Association for the division of mortgaged *fazendas,* but the proposal never received strong support in Parliament.[35] Joaquim Nabuco, a close friend of Rebouças, also stressed the motif of "Rural Democracy." In a campaign speech in Recife, for example, Nabuco declared that emancipation of the slaves and democratization of the land would be complementary. The abolition law would also be an agrarian law, because it would lead to

34. *A Redempção,* March 3, 1887, p. 1; June 5, 1887, p. 3.

35. André Rebouças, *Diário e notas autobiográficas,* ed. Ana Flora e Inácio José Veríssimo (Rio de Janeiro, 1938), p. 292; Inácio José Veríssimo, *André Rebouças através de sua auto-biografia* (Rio de Janeiro, 1939), pp. 208–220; André Rebouças, *Abolição immediata e sem indemnisação* (Rio de Janeiro, 1883), p. 34; André Rebouças, *"O Ypiranga da abolição"* in *Homagem da Sociedade Emancipadora Academica,* p. 4. Rebouças developed some of his ideas from the writings of Henrique de Beaurepaire Rohan, an early advocate of abolition and land reform. See *"O futuro da grande lavoura e da grande propriedade no Brasil: Memória apresentada ao Ministério da Agricultura, Commércio e Obras Publicas"* in *Congresso Agricola: Colleção de documementos* (Rio de Janeiro, 1878), pp. 243–51.

the development of small property, providing the poor people with a route of escape from their congestion and suffering. Nabuco suggested that the state institute a territorial tax in order to raise funds to help the poor to acquire land.[36]

This view connecting the issues of slavery and land monopoly represented a serious threat to the rural proprietors: It revealed a way in which the impact of the abolitionist movement could extend beyond the matter of emancipation to incorporate other structural reforms. As an editor of the newspaper *O Paíz* explained his position on January 1, 1887:

> The battle is far from finished; abolitionism is at once a revolution concerning both labor and the land, and it can finish with the democratization of the land and with the definitive constitution of the Brazilian nation. . . . The year 1887 ought to see the first attempt at the organization of an abolitionist party, not only for the abolition of slavery, but for the abolition of all of its related problems, beginning with territorial monopoly.[37]

Abolitionists also tied the issue of political reform to the slavery question. The disproportionate power of the slaveholders seemed to preclude the possibility of true political change. "Only after slavery is abolished and the aristocracy is weakened by the enlargement of the vote can we have regular parties in São Paulo with discrimination of ideas," wrote the São Paulo abolitionist Fernandes Coelho, who felt that both

36. See *"Formação moral e intellectual de Joaquim Nabuco"* in *Revista do Instituto Histórico e Geográfico Brasileiro,* CCIV (Julho-Setembro, 1949), 145; Nabuco, *Campanha abolicionista no Recife,* pp. 47–49. Nabuco displayed interest in the ideas of Henry George but declared them unsatisfactory because they did not provide indemnification for property taken from landowners. See Joaquim Nabuco, *Nacionalisação do solo. Apreciação da propaganda para a abolicão do monopólio territorial na Inglaterra* (Rio de Janeiro, 1884), pp. 3–12.

37. *O Paíz,* January 1, 1887; *Jornal do Commércio,* January 4, 1887, p. 2. The *Jornal do Commércio,* which was cautiously wavering in the debate over abolition, labeled the *O Paíz* editorial as "nihilism."

The Liberal ministry of the Viscount of Ouro Prêto, with the support of many ex-abolitionists, proposed land reform in 1889. But, before Parliament was to convene to consider the matter in November of that year, the revolution occurred which overthrew the monarchy.

major political parties represented almost the same interests.[38] Many critics of slavery believed that the success of political reforms such as the extension of suffrage and greater autonomy for the provinces was dependent upon abolition.[39] The indefinite prolongation of slavery meant, in the words of abolitionist J. I. Arnizaut Furtado, "the continuation of a political system that, if it has precedents in history, does not have any present parallel in the world." [40]

Abolitionist protestations against both the land and the political systems naturally alarmed *fazendeiros*. The association of abolitionism with these other issues made the movement an ever more serious threat to the interests of the slaveholding planters. To allay these fears, as well as to expand the economic perspective of their argument, abolitionists sought to show that emancipation would serve the interests of the planters too; that abolition would benefit the *senhor* as well as the slave.[41] As Araripe Junior explained this idea:

> What the abolitionists desire, without distinction of color, is to liberate the country from an obstacle, perhaps the most real of the many that today hinder our economic development. It is not a question of affection, nor of piety for an unprotected class. The interest is not only for the slave: it is also for the master of the slave.[42]

Abolitionists tried to convince slave proprietors that free labor was more profitable than slave labor. Their propaganda included numerous calculations aimed at demonstrating the

38. *Ibid.*, September 8, 1887, p. 1.

39. *Gazeta da Tarde*, January 7, 1881, p. 3; June 2, 1886, p. 1; April 4, 1887, p. 1.

40. J. I. Arnizaut Furtado, *Estudos sôbre a libertação dos escravos no Brazil* (Pelotas, 1883), p. 79.

41. *A Terra da Redempção: Orgão dos Cearenses Abolicionistas*, May 24, 1883, p. 3; Joaquim Ignácio Ramalho, *"O direito da escravidão e contra a natureza," Homagem da Sociedade Emancipadora Academica*, p. 3.

42. *Gazeta da Tarde*, July 1, 1882, p. 1. For similar arguments, see Nabuco, *O abolicionismo*, pp. 24–25, 266; *Discurso proferido na sessão de 17 de Julho de 1884 pelo deputado Dr. Affonso Celso Junior* (Rio de Janeiro, 1884), p. 13.

superiority of the wage system. Sources of the calculations ranged from the writings of Alexis de Tocqueville, the Frenchman who traveled through the United States in the 1830s, to the works of Louis Couty, a French professor in the Polytechnic School in Rio de Janeiro.[43] Abolitionists argued that a free labor system would provide an intelligent and industrious labor force that would be capable of learning how to operate complex machinery.[44] Production would increase tremendously because a free man could do twice the work of a slave.[45] In addition, the *fazendeiro* would have fewer responsibilities under the free labor system; he would not be responsible for feeding and clothing the workers and caring for the old and sick. And, of course, the planter would no longer suffer from his common economic problem: the loss resulting from the escape or death of his slaves.[46]

Frequently abolitionists referred to the experience in the United States to illustrate and support the idea that emancipation would benefit the *fazendeiro* rather than harm him. They claimed that the historical record proved Southern slavocrats were wrong in predicting that abolition would bring economic ruin. Before the Civil War, they said, the American South was noticeably backward compared with the North. Southern agriculture was inefficient, and the region lagged far behind in the statistics of population growth and industrial and commercial development.[47] Apparently borrowing a famous description

43. *Annaes do Senado* (1887), p. 16; Rebouças, *Agricultura national,* pp. 175, 187, 189; Louis Couty, *L'esclavage au Brésil* (Paris, 1881); Louis Couty, *Pequena Propriedade e imigração européia* (Rio de Janeiro, 1887; *Brasil Agricola,* January 31, 1881, pp. 74–75; Rebouças, *"O Ypiranga da abolição,"* p. 4; Domingo Maria Gonçalves, *A intrucção agricola e o trabalho livre* (Rio de Janeiro, 1880), p. 59. Affonso d'Escragnolle Taunay told his colleagues in the Chamber of Deputies of a factory in Ipanema which increased production after exchanging a work force of 500 slaves for 66 free men. See *Brazil,* June 11, 1884, p. 2.

44. *Gazeta da Tarde,* January 3, 1881, p. 2.

45. *A Redempção,* January 27, 1887, p. 2.

46. *O Libertador,* February 7, 1881, p. 4.

47. *O Abolicionista,* November 1, 1880, p. 3; January 1, 1881, p. 7; Barbosa, *Emancipação dos escravos,* pp. 83–86.

from Alexis de Tocqueville, Affonso Celso Junior highlighted these differences by contrasting the antebellum conditions of the free state of Ohio with the neighboring slave state of Kentucky. This comparison revealed, he said, that "in one the white transmits his intelligence to the land; in the other the land is exploited without zeal, without light, without discernment." [48] Then the situation changed. Abolition introduced the American South to modern development. Manufacturing, almost impossible with slavery, rose and flourished in the Southern states. New industrial population centers appeared, such as Birmingham, and the South began to attract immigrants. Production of staples increased; figures showed that cotton sales in the late 1870s exceeded prewar figures.[49]

In the broadest sense, then, abolitionists foresaw a new age dawning for Brazil after the eradication of slavery. Upon removing the principal barrier to progress, the country could achieve greatness through improvement in education, purification of religion, flourishing of arts and letters, increased immigration, development of new industries and the rise of new cities. All of this progress would advance rapidly in an environment of free institutions. In short, Brazil would become a truly modern nation.[50]

It was precisely in this area of thought—that of Brazil's position in the modern world—that the moral and economic arguments of the abolitionists converged. The post-abolition era in Brazil would be one of human dignity and material progress. Upon wiping out the stain of slavery, Brazil could take its place in the world of truly civilized countries. It

48. *Discurso proferido . . . pelo deputado Dr. Affonso Celso Junior,* pp. 14–15.

49. Nabuco, *O Abolicionismo,* pp. 216–18; *O Abolicionista,* February 1, 1881, p. 6; *Gazeta da Tarde,* December 19, 1883, p. 1; *Correio Paulistano,* September 10, 1887, p. 1. Abolitionists presented the case of the American South as a shining example of the economic benefits that could accrue from the abolition of slavery. Of course, the antislavery literature rarely reflected on the loss of planters' fortunes in the American South and the difficulties that came with Reconstruction. These problems were emphasized in slavocrat propaganda.

50. See, for example, the manifesto presented by abolitionists in Porto Alegre reported in *O País,* October 10, 1887, p. 1; Nabuco, *O abolicionismo,* pp. 243–44.

would be a day of moral and economic emancipation—as much as a moment of national liberation as the independence day of September 7, 1822.[51]

Significantly, the abolitionists' drive to place Brazil in the mainstream of modern civilization developed concurrently with the establishment of new and improved communications with the Western world. The development of steamboat travel, railroads, the telegraph, the book and newspaper industries, and increased contact with foreign businessmen put Brazilians in touch with the latest ideas and fashions of Europe and the United States. Rio de Janeiro became known as "Paris in America." Brazil's urban citizens admired the culture of the French, the progressive liberalism of the English, and the practical success of the Americans. They discussed the popular actions of individual liberty and material progress and quoted from Victor Hugo, Auguste Comte, Walter Bagehot, and Herbert Spencer in efforts to point out the relevance of nineteenth-century literature and philosophy to their own institutions.

Abolitionists were disturbed by Brazil's position in relation to the "modern" civilizations of the time. How did their institutions appear in the age of "the Press, the Steamship and the Electric Telegraph," and in a world that accepted as fundamental the equality of all men?[52] It was "the pressure of all the atmosphere of modern civilization, that pressure of censure from the civilized world" that worried the abolitionists, said Rui Barbosa, who declared that slavery could not exist in an enlightened society.[53] How did foreigners view Brazil? asked the abolitionists. Isolated in the Americas as the only slave society? As the world's second Sudan? Only the destruction of slavery could elevate the nation to dignity before America and the whole civilized world.[54]

A strong flavor of nationalism pervaded this popular de-

51. Nabuco, *O abolicionismo;* see the Preface.

52. Periera d'Araujo, *A incoherência da escravidão,* preface; *Gazeta da Tarde,* January 14, 1881, p. 1.

53. Osório Duque-Estrada, *A abolição:* 1881–1888 (Rio de Janeiro, 1918), pp. 141–42; Barbosa, *Emancipação dos escravos,* pp. 57–58.

54. *O Libertador,* July 29, 1881, p. 3; Nabuco, *O abolicionismo,* p. 231; *Gazeta da Tarde,* September 1, 1886, p. 1.

scription of the blessings of abolition. To liberate the captive would be to liberate Brazil. "Under the name of the abolitionist party, the true and radical emancipation of the Brazilian people is being realized," declared a writer working under the pseudonym of "Franklin." [55] Emancipation would open the doors to diverse forms of moral and material progress. As Rui Barbosa explained this point, "Abolitionism is reform over reform; abolition is fundamental reconstruction of the country; abolition is radical organization of the future; abolition is national rebirth." [56] Emancipation would give Brazil force and power in the community of nations.[57] It would "pay a debt to national dignity, to serve the most important interests of Brazil," said Senator Souza Dantas.[58] Abolition would "redeem and glorify the country before the universe," declared an abolitionist group in Porto Alegre. This much repeated appeal to nationalism was a call to the diverse elements in Brazilian society to join in a common cause and recognize that they all had something to gain by building a new, progressive country that would be free from the stigma and the retarding effects of chattel slavery.[59] As a poem in the Fortaleza newspaper *O Libertador* reflected this nationalistic hope:

> Fatherland! People of Ceará! Welcome us into your heart!
> The battle is ours but the glory is yours,
> Here, then, is our opportunity.
> *Allons, enfants de la patrie!*
> *Le jour de la gloire est arrivé!* [60]

Assessment of this emotional rhetoric requires restraint and caution. Often abolitionists couched their ideas in patriotic phrases which obscured their personal interests. Many ex-

55. *A Redempção,* January 27, 1887, p. 1.
56. *Diário de Santos,* May 15, 1888, p. 1.
57. *Gazeta da Tarde,* July 19, 1882, p. 1.
58. Fonseca, *A escravidão, o clero e o abolicionismo,* p. 297.
59. Charles W. Turner, *Rui Barbosa: Crusader for Essential Freedoms* (New York and Nashville, 1945), p. 79; *Gazeta da Tarde,* July 19, 1882, p. 1; Nelson Werneck Sodré, *Panorama do segundo império* (São Paulo, 1939), p. 183.
60. January 1, 1881, p. 3.

pected to make individual gains from abolition. Merchants, commercial agents, lawyers, doctors, teachers, engineers, and others could well see the opportunities that a modern economic system would open to them. Moreover, those with political aspirations could ride the wave of abolition to break onto the beachheads which so long had been monopolized by the planter class. In this way, self-interest concerns wedded to nationalistic goals provided a broad-based attack on slavery. By identifying the obstacles to their own advancement, abolitionists called the entire system into question. They saw diverse groups—masters, slaves, the free rural masses, and urban classes—all victimized by an institution considered repulsive by the "civilized" world.

Also, emphasis on the diverse liabilities of slavery could have its drawbacks. The broad-based attack appealed to many individuals who felt little sympathy for the Negro but were excited by the prospect of using abolition as an instrument for removing the stain of slavery and turning Brazil into a modern country. In their list of priorities the gains abolition would bring to themselves and the nation ranked high, while the benefits given to the slaves would be largely incidental. They viewed freedom in the abstract, as liberty from formal bondage, but failed to see that, if unaccompanied by complementary assistance and protection, such "freedom" could be very tenuous. Indeed, many who joined the antislavery movement as it gained in popularity lost sight of the important humane concern behind the campaign: sympathy for the slave. On the other hand, hard-core abolitionists like José do Patrocínio, André Rebouças, and Joaquim Nabuco understood this problem. They recognized the need to balance a general demand for change with stress on the basic moral issue.

In sum, the scope of antislavery arguments made abolitionism in Brazil more than just a battle for the redemption of the slave. It was also a battle for the redemption of the nation. Abolitionists were concerned not only about the plight of the captive but also about the effects of slavery on all the citizens. They viewed slavery as an economic as well as moral problem, a political as well as an individual problem. Almost all of the abolitionists believed slavery was the principal barrier to the nation's progress, and many of them boldly identified the hegemony of the slaveholding class as the key to this retardation. In short, Brazilian abolitionists extended their view of slavery well beyond the moral issue, giving much attention to political, economic, and social considerations. They viewed the problem in its totality.

The slaveholders' reaction to these arguments reveal that they did not find the multifaceted character of abolitionist thought any more palatable than an ideology that rested squarely on moral considerations. When, in the twentieth century, historians looked back on the antislavery controversy, many of them criticized the abolitionist agitators for giving too much emphasis to arguments of the heart. By stressing sympathy for the slave and the immorality of bondage to the point of extremes, said the historians, abolitionists lost touch with reality and laid the foundations for a naïve and dangerous approach to reform. To be sure, a similar viewpoint also found a place in the historical treatment of abolitionism in the United States. With specific regard to the Brazilian case, however, it is clear that antislavery propaganda actually contained much practical appeal—arguments suggesting that liberation would serve the interests of the slaveholder as well as the slave. It is also clear that slaveholders were convinced that abolition would not be the blessing its advocates described it to be.

While proprietors were ever ready to dispute the abolitionist perspective, they had to be cautious in forming a counter-argument. Abolitionism put them under attack at an historical juncture when they could not reject the emancipation idea outright. If they attacked all of the abolitionist themes, they would sound like tyrants and enemies of economic progress. For most slaveholders, it seemed that the late nineteenth century was not the time to argue that slavery was moral and the key to prosperity and happiness in the future. The servile institution would have to be defended in practical terms rather than in view of a morality of its own.

5: The Defense of Slavery

THE MAJOR ARGUMENTS expressed to support slavery in Brazil in the era of the abolitionist campaign aimed not to defend the institution as a positive good but to extend its life. Unlike slavocrats in the American South, the Brazilian slave proprietors usually did not justify slavery as more humane than liberty or more beneficial to the over-all society than a free labor economy. With the exception of a few extreme statements by spokesmen for the Hard-Core Slaveholders, most pro-slavery thought was couched in deceptively flexible terms. Historical circumstances established the milieu for this situation. Slavery stood condemned in the world of the 1880s; major philosophers of the day loudly repudiated human bondage. Brazilian slaveholders had been jolted by the Civil War in the United States, the consequent Thirteenth Amendment, and the Cuban declaration of 1880 in favor of an early settlement of the emancipation question. By 1886, after the definitive abolition of slavery in Cuba, Brazil stood alone and embarrassed as the only country in the Americas that maintained the institution censured by the nations of the Western world. Moreover, Brazilian legislators had already condemned slavery in a mild fashion by the passage of the Rio Branco Law in 1871. The law of the nation after 1871 committed the planters to a policy of long-range emancipation. By announcing the eventual extinction of the servile institution, as long delayed as it might be, political leaders left little opportunity for a successful development of the "positive good" argument.

Actually, the slave proprietors did not need a sophisticated "positive good" rationale to support their case, because, from their perspective, the 1871 law proved to be a blessing in disguise. They could subscribe to the legislation already in the books—supposedly progressive legislation—and proclaim themselves enlightened supporters of a moderate emancipation policy. Under the pretense of advocating gradualism, they tightened their forces in defense of the *status quo*. When abolitionists began demanding further reforms in the 1880s, slaveholders, especially the hard-core and progressive groups, reaffirmed their confidence in the Rio Branco Law as the definitive solution to the problem. "In Brazil we are all emancipators, there are no more slavocrats," boasted the slave proprietors. When conditions moved them to adopt new legislation in 1885, similarly they embraced it as the final answer to the question. Again they called themselves "emanicpationists" and invoked the Saraiva-Cotegipe Law when abolitionists tried to expedite abolition.[1]

In reality, slaveholders were not the emancipationists they claimed to be. They were willing to condemn slavery mildly, but at the same time they defended their interests by insisting that abolition should be postponed until conditions were acceptable to them. No one "reputes slavery to be a good and virtuous institution," said slavocrat Martinho Campos of Minas Gerais, but emancipation schemes had to respect property rights.[2] "Slavery is a terrible evil," asserted the pro-slaveholder newspaper *O Cruzeiro,* but the slaves should not be freed without indemnification to the masters.[3] "Slavery is a cancer," admitted the Bahian slaveholder-politician José Antônio Saraiva, but abolition was a matter of time and patience.[4] "Slavery is condemned by law, morality, and religion," ac-

1. Antônio Coelho Rodrigues, *Manual do subdito fiel ou cartas de um lavrador a sua magestade o Imperador sôbré a questão do elemento servil* (Rio de Janeiro, 1884), p. 6; *Rio News,* July 5, 1884, p. 3; *O Cruzeiro,* December 20, 1880, p. 3; Fernando Henrique Cardoso, *Capitalismo e Escravidão* (São Paulo, 1962), p. 239; *Rio News,* October 15, 1880, pp. 3–4; Luiz Monteiro Caminhoá, *Canna de assucar e café—relatório apresentado ao governo* (Rio de Janeiro, 1880), p. 104; Baron of Cotegipe to J. Arthur de Sousa Corrêa, March 9, 1888, Instituto Joaquim Nabuco; *Diário do Brazil,* May 10, 1884, p. 1.

2. *Annaes da Câmara* (1880), IV, 445.

3. November 22, 1880, p. 3.

4. *Annaes da Câmara* (1880), IV, 502.

knowledged the Paulista planter Antônio Prado, but it should not be dealt with emotionally or precipitously because it was a complex economic and social problem.[5] Naturally, these slaveholders realized that full recognition of such "conditions" would delay abolition for several decades.

The campaign in support of slavery was, therefore, a true "defense" of the institution. It did not usually show the strikingly offensive pattern of argument presented by slavocrats in the American South, such as the assertions of J. C. Calhoun and George Fitzhugh that slavery provided the best way of life for both whites and blacks, but it was, nevertheless, a serious attempt by the Brazilian slaveholders to extend the life of their institution with all the forces that they could muster. Fighting boldly to protect their economic, social, and political interests, the master class and their political spokesmen developed a complex series of arguments to justify their position and counteract the abolitionist offensive.

While granting that the servile institution rested on questionable moral principles, slave proprietors insisted that another matter of principle deserved very serious consideration: the issue of property rights. This "right" had to be guaranteed; laws required respect for legally sanctioned ownership.[6] Viewing the slave as property, slaveocrats declared that chattel labor could not be taken away from the owners without indemnification. Anything to the contrary would be "robbery." It did not seem fair to penalize only the slaveholders for the presence of the institution.[7] "The present slave proprietors did not invent slavery," explained a writer in the newspaper *O*

5. Nazareth Prado (ed.), *Antônio Prado no império e na república* (Rio de Janeiro, 1929), p. 102. Also see the comments of other slaveholders in *Congresso Agricola: Colleção de documentos* (Rio de Janeiro, 1878), p. 241; Barão do Paty do Alferes, *Memória sôbre a fundação e costeio de uma fazenda na província de Rio de Janeiro* (Rio de Janeiro, 1860), p. 22.

6. *Annaes da Câmara* (1884), I, 245; Luis Anselmo Fonseca, *A Escravidão, o clero e o abolicionismo* (Bahia, 1887), p. 295; *Associação Commercial do Rio de Janeiro: Elemento servil* (Rio de Janeiro, 1884), p. 5.

7. *Brazil,* April 25, 1884, p. 1.

Cruzeiro; "they found that institution in the country, sanctioned by the laws and by the secular customs, and they accepted it in good faith." [8] The Baron of Cotegipe insisted that the ownership of a slave, like the ownership of inanimate objects, was recognized by the Constitution and the laws.[9] In this manner, slaveholders claimed that they were amenable to emancipation measures that would not annul the value of the capital they had tied up in slavery.[10] Indemnification would have to complement emancipation.

To a large extent, however, the indemnification argument served as a decoy. It placed a thorny legal question and expensive economic proposition in the path of the opponents of slavery, challenging them to provide answers under difficult conditions. Actually, indemnification was not the central issue. Although some planters would accept compensation, most important spokesmen for the slave proprietors made remuneration an important factor only when threatened by abolitionist legislation. The Hard-Core Slaveholders, particularly, were too attached to the servile institution as a way of life to consider its extinction simply as a matter of financial remuneration. Only after they lost the battle—that is, after the abolition law of 1888—did the planters mount a well-organized campaign for indemnification.[11]

Hard-Core Slaveholders sometimes stretched their defense beyond the issue of property rights to describe the quality of the lives of masters and slaves in glowing terms. These were the exceptional cases of vehemently pro-slavery thought which, in many ways, resembled the explanations of slavocrats in the United States. Slaveholders were the finest class in society, contended Brazil's Hard-Core Slaveholders, pointing to the proprietors' "admirable" record of leadership and paternalistic concern for the masses. Slaveholders had become the na-

8. November 22, 1880.
9. *Annaes do Senado* (1888), I, 35.
10. *Associação Commercial do Rio de Janeiro,* p. 5.
11. *Annaes do Senado* (1880), p. 521; *Annaes da Câmara* (1880), IV, 172–73; *Cidade do Rio,* May 10, 1888, p. 3.

tion's most distinguished elite.[12] "The most respectable men in the country are such because they possess slaves," said Lacerda Werneck of Rio de Janeiro, and the witty and eloquent Andrade Figueira, also of Rio and a tenacious defender of slavery in Parliament who once boasted that he was the John C. Calhoun of Brazil, declared that all the great civilizations of the world had been erected on the foundations of slavery.[13] Perhaps the most frankly slavocrat politician in Parliament during the period of abolition was Martinho Campos of Minas Gerais. He proudly announced his intention of defending the property of the elite class in the spirit of John C. Calhoun, and, when he assumed leadership of the government in 1881, unabashedly declared himself a "slavocrat to the core." [14]

Slaveholders also expressed displeasure over the abolitionists' descriptions of cruel masters and poor treatment of slaves on the plantations. Not true! they exclaimed. Under the paternalistic care of the *senhores,* slaves received adequate food, clothing, and shelter, while the proletariat in Europe might be left to starve, isolated in a society that would not look after them.[15] Atrocity stories about the death of slaves from excessive flogging were "exaggerations and lies." [16] Brazilian slaveholders were humane and kind masters who, by their generosity, often took the initiative to liberate their bondsmen.[17] "Slaves are treated as in no other country in the world,"

12. *Annaes da Câmara* (1884), I, 88–89; II, 67.
13. *Ibid.* (1887), V, 72.
14. *Ibid.* (1880), IV, 445–46.
15. Rodrigues, *Manual do subdito fiel,* pp. 9–10; *Novidades,* January 26, 1888, p. 2; Manuel Rodrigues Peixoto, *A crise do assucar: Os pequenos engenhos centraes, a colonização e o problema servil* (Rio de Janeiro, 1885), p. 128; Richard M. Morse: *From Community to Metropolis: A Biography of São Paulo* (Gainesville, 1958), p. 141. Responding to such descriptions, Joaquim Nabuco said, "If they persist in this propaganda in favor of slavery, it is possible that, in the future, many will want to be slaves." See *Sociedade Brasileira Contra a Escravidão, banquete offerecido ao Exm. Sr. Ministro Americano Henry Washington Hilliard a 20 de novembro de 1880* (Rio de Janeiro, 1880), p. 7.
16. Peixote de Brito, *Considerações geraes sôbre a emancipação dos escravos no império do Brasil. Indicação dos meios próprios para realisal-a* (Lisbon, 1870), pp. 5, 11–13.
17. *O Cruzeiro,* December 20, 1880, p. 3.

said Martinho Campos. Besides, argued Campos, by virtue of his condition as slave, the Negro did not necessarily lose his quality as a human being. Campos even suggested that "slavery ought to be maintained by the love of the slaves themselves!" [18]

The principal argument employed in defense of slavery, however, was that more time was needed for a satisfactory transition to free labor. Neither the planters nor the Negro slaves were prepared for revolutionary change, insisted the slaveholders. Counseling the nation to "go slow" on abolition, they warned that precipitous action would shock the country and bring ruin to the agricultural interests.[19] Slavery had been the dominant labor system in Brazil for over 300 years, they said, and abolitionists should not expect to dispose of it in one swift act.[20] "Slavery is the corner-stone of our civilization!" cried deputy Belfort Duarte.[21] Since the booming coffee economy depended heavily on servile labor, bondsmen were considered the indispensable source of national riches. "Brazil is coffee, and coffee is the Negro," said Senator Casper Silveira Martins in an oft-quoted statement.[22] If Negro slavery was the instrument of wealth, reasoned an anonymous slavocrat pamphleteer, then abolition had to be the instrument of poverty.[23] Throughout the antislavery campaign, slaveholders continued to predict disorder, bankruptcy, and misery if a program of rapid abolition were adopted. As late as 1884, the *Rio News* noted: "The belief that the abolition of slavery will necessarily bring ruin upon the country is so widespread and so deeply implanted in the minds of the Brazilian planters that there is probably little use in trying to prove the contrary." [24]

18. *Annaes da Câmara* (1880), IV, 445–46; V, 39; *Revista Illustrada,* 1884, n. 385, p. 8.

19. *Brazil,* April 3, 1884; *Falla* of the president of the province of Bahia, João Capistrano Bandeira de Mello, October 4, 1887, p. 155.

20. *Annaes da Câmara* (1880), IV, 446; Associação Commercial do *Rio de Janeiro: Elemento servil,* p. 4.

21. *Rio News,* April 15, 1881, p. 2.

22. *Vinte e Cinco de Março,* May 11, 1884, p. 3.

23. *O abolicionismo perante a história ou o dialogo das três províncias* (Rio de Janeiro, 1888), p. 87.

24. *Rio News,* March 24, 1884, p. 2.

Most slaveholders did not believe that freedmen could be trusted to take the positions on the plantations so long dominated by slaves. It was senseless to argue that the Negroes would continue working on the *fazendas* as freedmen, said the slavocrats. "This is romance. I do not believe in it. They [the planters] will be without workers and without credit," argued Andrade Figueira.[25] He believed that "there is no patriotic heart that does not long for the extinction of slavery; but we must first accomplish the substitution of the free worker for the slave worker. Until then, all efforts for abolition will be criminal." [26] Slaveholders showed little trust in the Negro freedmen's ability to labor without coercion. As one pro-slaveholder commentator explained it, the planters needed free workers, not simply free men.[27]

Slaveholders claimed they favored emancipation but were determined not to repeat the experience of the United States —abolition of slavery by a violent blow. "No one aspires for abolition more than I," declared the Rio de Janeiro *fazendeiro* Paulino de Souza, "but I desire the reform in the conservative spirit." Paulino de Souza said he would compare himself more with Andrew Johnson than with Abraham Lincoln, because Johnson sought to mitigate the effect of the social revolution.[28] Paulino's political ally, the Baron of Cotegipe, echoed the same concerns. Emancipation projects would have to guarantee order in agricultural activities and a reliable source of work hands. Emancipation was a social, political, and economic question as well as a humanitarian one.[29] Cotegipe, Paulino, and other slavocrats insisted that considerable time

25. *Annaes da Câmara* (1885), I, 241.
26. *Ibid.* (1884), II, 50.
27. Alcindro Sodré, *O elemento servil, a abolição* (Rio de Janeiro, 1942), pp. 102–103.
28. *Annaes do Senado* (1888), I, 38–42.
29. Baron of Cotegipe to Francisco Belisario Soares de Souza, April 6, 1887, Lata 277, D–56, Arquivo do Instituto Histórico e Geográfico Brasileiro; Baron of Cotegipe to J. Arthur de Sousa Corrêa, March 9, 1888, Instituto Joaquim Nabuco; Almeia de Rezende Martins, *Um idealista realizador: Barão Geraldo de Rezende* (Campinas, n.d.), p. 361.

was necessary to work out a gradual transition to a free labor system and the assimilation of the Negro masses into the body politic.[30] They were not going to be "romantics" like the Americans, whose radical approach to abolition led to the ruin of the plantation owners.[31] History revealed that all immediate, unconditional emancipation was followed by economic disasters, decline of production, reduction of land values, and decadence in the agricultural industries. Abolition in the United States, explained the slavocrats, brought anarchy, disorder, terror, vagabondage, and racial hostility to the Southern states.[32]

The situation called for an evolutionary approach, one that would avoid social upheaval and economic calamity. Finding a satisfactory solution was a question of "time," "opportunity," "prudence," and "convenience."[33] Were slavery not an economic necessity, the proprietors would gladly liberate all of their bondsmen, suggested a Rio de Janeiro planter.[34] In this context, the term "slavocrat" seemed improper.[35] By the 1880s most slaveholders rejected the title although the extremist Martinho Campos accepted it proudly. They preferred to be called "emancipationists," understanding the negative connotations of the slavocrat label. As they explained the difference, an emancipationist sought to bring change without upsetting the economy and society—an approach markedly different from the intransigence of a slavocrat or the impatient radicalism of an abolitionist. For example, members of the

30. Rodrigues, *Manuel do subdito fiel,* pp. 79, 90–91; Stanley Stein, *Vassouras: A Brazilian Coffee County, 1850–1900* (Cambridge, 1957), p. 254.

31. *Associação Commercial do Rio de Janeiro,* p. 6; *Annaes da Câmara* (1885), I, 174–76.

32. *O Cruzeiro,* November 6, 1880, p. 1; December 20, 1880, p. 3.

33. Rui Barbosa, *Emancipação dos escravos; Obras completas de Rui Barbosa* (Rio de Janeiro, 1945), p. xvi.

34. *Congresso Agricola,* p. 142.

35. The editor of *Brazil* said defenders of the slaveholders were "patriots," not slavocrats (May 25, 1884, p. 2). An anonymous author of an anti-abolitionist book, who identified himself only as "A Patriot," declared it was libelous to call the slaveholders "slavocrats." See *O eclypse do patriotismo* (Rio de Janeiro, 1886), pp. 13–14.

Planters' Club of Vassouras (Rio de Janeiro) announced their sympathy for the idea of emancipation, but vehemently opposed the "ultra-abolitionism" of many of the antislavery leaders.[36] In the same vein, Luís Pereira Barreto, the Positivist planter-philosopher from São Paulo, pleaded for patience by stressing "two aphorisms of positive politics: 1) All radical and immediate reform is absurd; 2) One should not destroy that which one cannot substitute." Reforms were necessary, he admitted, but they could achieve practical success only after a long period of preparation. All-important in Positivist terms was the proper conciliation between progress and order. To Pereira Barreto, the Rio Branco Law provided the right combination.[37]

Almost all spokesmen for the slaveholders touched on variations of the same theme, but the Progressive Planters gave particular emphasis to their supposed flexibility on the emancipation question. They wished to distinguish themselves from the *fazendeiros* of the Paraíba Valley whose attachment to the institution, they said, was much deeper than their own. For example, the wealthy Paulista planter Antônio Prado identified his group's attitude as a middle position between the extreme abolitionism of Joaquin Nabuco and the retrograde antiabolitionism of Andrade Figueira.[38] Given sufficient time and propitious conditions, said the Progressive Planters, they were willing to change. Prudente de Morais, another influential Paulista planter and a leading figure in the Republican party, claimed a sincere interest in turning to free labor, but also demanded assurances that change would be accompanied by a peaceful transformation of many able laborers into the new plantation work routine. Since resolution of the "complex" problem still appeared remote and he had a good deal of capital tied up in slavery, Prudente de Morais rejected abolitionist programs. His

36. *Brazil,* May 25, 1884, p. 2.

37. Articles in the *Província de São Paulo,* November 20 to 30, 1880. Pereira Barreto announced in 1881 that he would try to liberate all of his slaves within five or six years. See Sodré, *O elemento servil,* p. 102.

38. Prado, *Antônio Prado no império e na república,* pp. 86–87.

statements and those of his fellow planter-Republicans in the early 1880s represent eloquent examples of equivocation in the face of the slavery question.[39]

Judging that the slaves were not ready for liberty and that the plantation society was not prepared for the shock of a sweeping change in the labor system, the defenders of slavery condemned the ideas and tactics of the abolitionists and labeled the antislavery leaders idealistic, fanatic, and dangerous. Slaveholders charged that the abolitionists' sentimental, impassioned idealism threatened the social order.[40] Brazil should not be carried to ruin by arguments of the heart, they insisted.[41] Abolitionists were basing their opinions on abstractions, said Luís Pereira Barreto—the rhetoric of metaphysics that had little relationship to reality.[42] As Almeida Nogueira explained, "the problem . . . cannot be considered on the terrain of abstraction, but on the practical terrain." [43] Slaveholders blasted the abolitionists for "wearing the cloak of philanthropy at the expense of others." [44] Abolitionists, they said, could feel free to make all the idealistic appeals they wanted and not lose anything at all, but the family that depended on the work of many slaves would suffer greatly.[45] "Humanitarianism for the slaves, persecution for the proprietors!" charged the editor of a slavocrat newspaper.[46] Moreover, abolitionist motivation concerned more than just irresponsible idealism. Some antislavery agitators derived personal profits from their activities by exploiting the Negroes, said the slavocrats. They deceived manumitted slaves and fugitives by taking their savings and obligating them to ac-

39. José Maria dos Santos, *Política geral do Brasil* (São Paulo, 1930), pp. 189, 218, 225; Leôncio Basbaum, *História sincera da república, das origens até 1889* (Rio de Janeiro, 1957), p. 264.

40. Rodrigues, *Manual de um subdito fiel,* p. 68; *Annaes da Câmara* (1884), II, 68.

41. *Annaes da Câmara* (1884), I, 80.

42. *"Os abolicionistas e a situação do país,"* in *Província de São Paulo,* November 20, 1880, p. 1.

43. *Annaes da Câmara* (1884), II, 177.

44. See the speech by Martinho Campos in Carolina Nabuco, *The Life of Joaquim Nabuco* (Stanford, 1950), p. 77.

45. *Novidades,* April 9, 1888, p. 2.

46. *O Cruzeiro,* November 22, 1880, p. 3.

cept unfair labor contracts which demanded arduous and excessive work. Such knavery brought handsome returns to the employers while leaving the poor blacks in a miserable state, making them slaves in the worst sense of the term.[47]

Name-calling went beyond accusations of irresponsible idealism and personal exploitation. Critics frequently compared abolitionists with the radicals of Europe, conjuring up the specter of revolution. It was not a new idea. Similar charges had been made during the debates over the Rio Branco Law.[48] Now, however, allusions to radicalism were much more frequent. Spokesmen for the slaveholders described abolitionists as nihilists, anarchists, Socialists, and Communists and referred to the popular antislavery magazine *Revista Illustrada* as the "Red Review." [49] Antislavery propaganda and agitation could easily lead to great tumult, they warned. When one excited member of Parliament shouted, "They want to shock!" in a session in 1884, another added, "They want to liberate with a movement in the streets!" [50] A writer in the newspaper *Gazeta de Notícias* feared that these popular demonstrations could arouse the great "horde" of vagabonds, unemployed, and rowdy elements into action, unleashing their destructive potential.[51] The Brazilian form of government was too fragile a mechanism to avert the crises that abolitionism could precipitate, said Almeida Nogueira. The dangerous propaganda was not aiming at the abolition of slavery but at the abolition of order and legality. Nogueira and others sug-

47. *Brazil,* April 29, 1884, p. 1; *Diário do Brazil,* May 11, 1884, p. 1; *Relatório do Dr. Chefe de Polícia Interino, Dr. Luiz Lopes Baptista dos Anjos Junior* (São Paulo, 1887), p. 4.

48. Rui Barbosa, *Emancipação dos Escravos: Parecer formulado pelo Deputado Rui Barbosa* (*Projecto N.48*) (Rio de Janeiro, 1884), pp. 47–48.

49. Dent, *A Year in Brazil,* p. 287; Alceu Marinho Rego, *Nabuco* (Rio de Janeiro and São Paulo, 1951), p. 50; *A Redempção,* January 27, 1887, p. 2; *Annaes da Câmara* (1885), I, 143; *O Cruzeiro,* December 18, 1880, p. 3; *O Paíz,* April 1, 1885, p. 1; Joaquim Nabuco, *Conferências e discursos abolicionistas* (São Paulo, n.d.), p. 349.

50. Affonso Celso Junior, *Discurso proferido na sessão de 17 de julho de 1884 pelo deputado Dr. Affonso Celso Junior* (Rio de Janeiro, 1884), pp. 7–8.

51. Reported in *Brazil,* April 1, 1884, p. 1; April 3, 1884, p. 1.

gested that abolitionism could well set off a social revolution.[52] If fanatics had their way, a true program of communism would follow abolition: war against property and the lives of the planters.[53] Today the abolition of slavery, tomorrow the abolition of the *senhores*.[54] What guarantee did *fazendeiros* have that the antislavery campaign would not soon evolve into an effort to defeat the conservative classes in society? [55] And might the campaign also ignite a revolution against religion and the Church? [56] In the face of such grave threats, planters' organizations were necessary to fight communism.[57]

Especially ominous was the possibility that antislavery agitation would incite the bondsmen to violence, awakening "the ferocious instincts of the slaves against the peaceful class of planters." [58] It was with this fear in mind that José Antônio Saraiva rejected Nabuco's proposal in 1880 to set a ten-year term for abolition because "the radical solution would immediately establish the battle between the slave and the master, anarchy on all the *fazendas,* the extermination of the master and the slaves." [59] Expressing similar concern, a planters' club in Minas Gerais issued a formal statement in 1880 warning that the abolitionist proposals could force Brazil to face the horror that had ravaged Haiti.[60]

52. *Annaes da Câmara* (1884), II, 177; *O abolicionismo perante a história,* p. 123.

53. *Brazil,* May 3, 1884, p. 1.

54. Coelho Rodrigues, *Manual do subdito fiel,* p. 131; *Novidades,* May 7, 1888, p. 1. The word *senhor* meant much more than "master" when used in this context; it connoted the seignorial vision of the world. Abolition appeared as a threat not only to their positions as slaveholders but to the special privileges that they held as the traditional *fazendeiro* class.

55. Reported in the *Gazeta da Tarde,* November 23, 1882. Also see Nilo Odalia, *"A abolição da escravatura," Anais do Museu Paulista,* XVIII (1964), 126, 133–34; *Annaes do Senado* (1888), I, 35–36.

56. The warning was mentioned in the manifesto of the Planters' Club of Conceição da Boa Vista. See *Brazil,* May 20, 1884, pp. 2–3.

57. *Diário do Brazil,* May 10, 1884, p. 1.

58. *Diário do Brazil,* July 25, 1884.

59. *Annaes da Câmara* (1880), IV, 501–502.

60. The statement of the Club Agricola da Leopoldina was reported in *O Cruzeiro,* November 12, 1880, p. 1.

If slavocrats scorned antislavery literature and speeches as the propaganda of anarchy, neither did they approve of institutional approaches to the problem of abolition.[61] Whatever ideas or methods abolitionists proposed to work within the political system to effectuate emancipation, most slavocrats reacted by showing a strikingly negative posture, rejecting the approaches as unacceptable. When abolitionists appealed to the people to vote against pro-slavery representatives in Parliament, slavocrats accused them of making vicious attacks against the statesmen of the empire.[62] Furthermore, slavocrats declared that abolition was not the business of government. Neither the members of Parliament, nor the ministers of state, nor the Emperor should interfere in the matter of emancipation.[63] The same applied to local government; abolitionists had no right to seek help from provincial and municipal authorities. Slaveholders considered the liberation of Amazonas a "scandal" and a "shame" because the campaign there received the protection of the police.[64] Judges too were criticized for declaring slaves free in cases won by abolitionist lawyers. In effect, none of the campaign methods employed by the abolitionists was wholly acceptable to the slavocrats of the Hard-Core Slaveholder and Progressive Planter groups. The emancipation problem should be left to the *fazendeiros,* said the slaveholders. Indeed, the planters had liberated more slaves by their own volition than all the emancipation associations and government programs combined. This was the proper kind of action: manumission by individual initiative rather than by the coercion of governmental legislation. As for emancipation laws already on the books, slaveholders would try to honor them in good faith. After all, they were "emancipators," not "slavocrats." [65]

61. *Gazeta da Tarde,* May 15, 1883, p. 2.
62. *Annaes da Câmara* (1884), I, 90.
63. *Ibid.* (1884), I, 76.
64. See the comments of the Baron of Leopoldina in *Annaes da Camâra* (1884), II, 66–67.
65. "The Necessities of Agriculture," written by the Baron of Rio Bonito, a planter from Rio de Janeiro province, *Rio News,* November

This attitude prompted sardonic comment from Christiano Ottoni. In a Senate speech in 1884 he said he was becoming accustomed to hearing slave proprietors say, "I too am an emancipator." But who was not? asked Ottoni. "We all are emancipators." The real problems arose when someone recommended an effective measure to help free the slaves. To this the slaveholders would quickly respond, "Sorry, no. The planter cannot do it." If this was the approach of the emancipators, complete liberation was a long way off. "By the middle of the twentieth century," suggested Ottoni, "death will do its work." [66]

In the process of insisting on delays in the emancipation process and pleading for sufficient time to work out a satisfactory transition to free labor, slaveholders frequently expressed attitudes about race which revealed some of the fundamental reasons for their dogged resistance to abolition. The effort to stave off emancipation involved more than just a fear of economic, social, and political loss; it also concerned a fear of having to deal with free Negroes in the post-abolition period. During the time of abolitionist agitation, all groups caught in the growing slavery controversy would have to come to terms with their own attitudes about the future of the black man in Brazilian society.

5, 1882, p. 3; Malvino da Silva Reis, *Situação econômica do Brasil: Exposição apresentada a commissão especial nomeada pela assembléa geral da Associação Commercial em 2 de maio de 1884* (Rio de Janeiro, 1884), pp. 22–23; *Brazil,* April 1, 1884, p. 1.

66. *Annaes do Senado* (1884), June 9, p. 29.

6: Race and the Manpower Issue

DURING THE LAST months of slavery in Brazil, when thousands of bondsmen fled from their masters, leaving proprietors without work hands to tend the crops, Paula Souza, a well-known planter-politician from São Paulo sent a letter to a friend offering a solution to the *fazendeiros'* manpower problems. Souza tried to assuage the apprehensive planters by noting that many of the fugitives were beginning to return to work. He then urged his colleagues to reconsider their attitude toward Negro labor. Why should so many *fazendeiros* insist on working either with slaves or European immigrants? he asked. In order to cushion the shock of the impending abolition of slavery, why not consider a third alternative—the black freedman? "We have an enormous body of workers upon which we were not counting," he explained. "I do not allude to the immigrant who today is seeking us in abundance; I refer to the Brazilian, a sluggard yesterday. . . . This Brazilian today devotes himself to labor, either because this has become more respectable through liberty, or because his former resources have failed him. This is what we are seeking here." [1]

The appeal of Paula Souza highlights one of the central issues in the debate over the abolition of slavery—the reluctance of planters, particularly the Hard-Core Slaveholders and Progressive Planters, to change their labor force of Negro slaves for Negro freedmen. By expressing faith in the potential

1. *Rio News,* April 15, 1888, p. 3. Paula Souza's letter drew considerable attention throughout the empire. See, for example: *Província de Minas,* April 14, 1888, p. 3; *Diário da Bahia,* April 20, 1888, p. 2; *Gazeta Mineira,* April 19, 1888, p. 1; *Revista Illustrada,* April 14, 1888, p. 2.

of free black labor, Paula Souza sounded like one of Brazil's radical abolitionists rather than a typical *fazendeiro* of the Central-South. Most other *senhores* showed little enthusiasm for recruiting ex-slaves, despite the fact that the ranks of the freed blacks could easily supply one of the largest and most immediately available sources of labor after abolition. Even the Progressive Planters immersed in rhetoric celebrating the superiority of free labor over slave labor, dragged their feet on the emancipation question. In an age when planters identified "manpower shortage" as a major economic problem, their hesitancy in welcoming the employment of freedmen appears ironic. At the source of this contradiction was the whole question of the planters' concept of the character of free blacks and the role they could play in society as citizens and workers. It was an attitude toward free labor which left slaveholders skeptical about abolition schemes and stirred them into efforts to delay the process of emancipation. In fine, during the 1880s, the problems of manpower recruitment, abolition, and attitudes toward the Negroes remained closely related.

As the abolitionist movement gained momentum, Brazilian planters increasingly invoked the "manpower problem" in efforts to silence their critics. This became true especially of the Hard-Core and Progressive Planters groups. While Hard-Core Slaveholders responded to abolitionist proposals by attempting to maintain chattel labor as long as possible or by trying to import semi-servile Chinese coolie laborers, Progressive Planters insisted that full emancipation could not take place until sufficient numbers of European immigrants could be found to replace the slave workers. Both groups continued to deny that the potentially large population of black freedmen could serve as a viable solution to their labor needs, arguing that emancipated slaves would not be good workers. Though Progressive Planters were more flexible on the long-range question of emancipation—a factor which could eventually cause a split in the slaveholders' ranks—their fetish for foreign labor boded ill for the Negroes. To Progressive Planters, "free labor" usually meant free white labor. As for abolitionists, opinions about the manpower issue varied. Like the Progressive Planters, antislavery leaders supported programs to increase European immigration, especially because abolitionists believed foreigners would help to modernize Brazil. Some abolitionists stressed the value of white labor over black labor. But the most ardent abolitionists emphasized the need to use both Europeans and free Negroes in meeting the labor needs of post-emancipation Brazil. In fact, leaders in the vanguard of the movement showed genuine concern that the great interest in immigrants might unjustly prejudice the position of liberated blacks. Thus, in their perspectives on the "manpower problem," slaveholders and abolitionists expressed crucial disagreements in assessing the Negro's future role in the Brazilian economy and society.

Worried discussions about the "manpower problem" were common among all three types of planter groups in nineteenth-century Brazil. Especially after the close of the African trade and later, following termination of the interprovincial slave trade, planters discussed the question of labor supply with a sense of urgency.[2] They echoed an old cry with greater intensity: "Laborers, we must have laborers!"[3] "We are walking toward an abyss," warned Manuel Rodrigues Peixoto of Rio de Janeiro province. "We do not have work hands and in the meantime the solution to a terrible problem presses upon us—the slavery question. It is the shadow of Banquo at the banquet of Macbeth!"[4] Even in the Northeast, where the sluggish economy provided large pools of unemployed laborers, Traditional Planters expressed concern over the manpower issue. The presidents of the provinces of Maranhão and Bahia worried about labor shortages in 1887, and the latter

2. Joaquim Caetano da Silva Guimaraes, *A agricultura em Minas* (Rio de Janeiro, 1965), p. 8.

3. Herbert H. Smith, *Brazil: The Amazons and the Coast* (New York, 1879), p. 467.

4. Manuel Rodrigues Peixoto, *A crise de assucar: Os pequenos engenhos centraes, a colonisação e o problema servil* (Rio de Janeiro, 1885), p. 25.

went so far as to announce "We have before us the specter of an absolute deficiency of agricultural workers." [5] In general, however, Traditional Planters had much more experience in employing ex-slaves as free workers than the coffee *fazendeiros*. The manpower issue received much more consideration in the Central-South, where slaves made up a greater proportion of the work forces on the plantations.[6] Most Hard-Core Slaveholders had an adequate supply of bondsmen in the 1880s, the Paraíba group having acquired them from the African and interprovincial slave trade, while the Minas planters secured servile laborers from the depressed mineral regions of their province. For the most part, their labor needs could be satisfied as long as slavery was maintained, but once the abolitionist movement became a threat, they again raised the bugaboo of a manpower crisis. Progressive Planters from São Paulo addressed the issue from a different perspective. They did not have sufficient bondsmen available to them during their tremendous westward expansion into new coffee areas in the 1880s. With the market of slaves from other provinces now closed, they focused on the European immigrants as the answer to their manpower needs. Until foreign workers would be available in sufficient quantity to allow a complete transformation to a wage economy, they would cast a critical eye on plans for immediate and total emancipation of the slaves.

By rejecting the freedmen as an important source of manpower, the proprietors unwittingly provided a profound condemnation of the institution of slavery. Black slaves knew only the authority of the master and the power of the whip, said the slaveholders. As free individuals, they could not be

5. *Falla* of the president of Maranhão, José Bento de Araujo, March 18, 1887, p. 28; *Falla* of the president of Bahia, João Capistrano Bandeira de Mello, October 4, 1887, p. 136.

6. The "labor shortage" theme appears throughout the speeches presented at the Agricultural Congress of the South in 1878. See *Congresso Agricola: Colleção de documentos* (Rio de Janeiro, 1878). Also see the *Relatório* of the vice president of São Paulo, Conde de Três Rios, 1882, p. 56.

trusted. Bondsmen were a crude, lazy, and ignorant lot, they believed, and the bad habits learned through their servile condition could not easily be reformed. With these concerns in mind, slaveholders worried that abolition would force them suddenly to face the backfire of years of exploiting their captives. They feared that the coercive nature of slavery would prove a distinct liability to the planters and that the ex-bondsmen, who had been forced to labor all of their lives, would abuse the new opportunities of freedom by evading their work.[7]

Black slaves were not sufficiently educated to become respectful citizens and had not learned to accept liberty responsibly, insisted the *fazendeiros*.[8] What guarantees did the society have that freedmen would not abandon their agricultural employment and cluster in the cities as paupers, vagabonds, and criminals? Citing examples from the history of the English Antilles, Cuba, and the United States, slaveholders argued that other countries suffered from great economic dislocation in the wake of mass emancipation.[9] Production declined because the labor of inactive, shiftless people became almost worthless. And already Brazil too was heavily burdened with a large class of such aimless "parasites." In 1878 a *fazendeiro* conjectured that the idle element represented 3½ million in the empire of 11 million people.[10] A decade later a journalist provided statistics indicating that vagabonds accounted for 42 percent of Brazil's population.[11] It seemed that emancipation of the slaves would only inflate

7. Peixoto de Brito, *Considerações geraes sôbre a emancipação dos escravos no império do Brasil. Indicação dos meios próprias para realisal-a* (Lisbon, 1870); *Brazil,* April 4, 1884, p. 1; Peixoto, *A crise de assucar,* pp. 126–30; Fernando Henrique Cardoso, *Capitalismo e escravidão: O negro na sociedade do Rio Grande do Sul* (São Paulo, 1962), p. 275; Stanley J. Stein, *The Brazilian Cotton Manufacture: Textile Enterprise in an Underdeveloped Area, 1850–1950* (Cambridge, 1957), p. 54.

8. *Annaes da Câmara* (1884), I, 246; *Annaes do Senado* (1888), I, 42.

9. *Brazil,* June 3, 1884, p. 3; *Rio News,* July 15, 1882, p. 2; Louis Couty, *L'esclavage au Brésil* (Paris, 1881), p. 64.

10. *Congresso Agricola,* p. 58.

11. *Província de São Paulo,* April 10, 1888, p. 1.

these figures, plaguing the state with monumental responsibilities. Abolition would require new laws to compel freedmen to remain at their jobs, punish delinquents, and augment the police forces to guarantee the security of individuals and property.[12] Without this protection, suggested the *fazendeiros,* blacks were likely to run away from the plantations or create civil disorders.[13]

Throughout the period of the abolitionist movement, slaveholders worked, sometimes successfully, to pass laws regulating the labor contracts of freedmen.[14] The legislation aimed at forcing the liberated to fulfill all obligations of new contract agreements or face severe penalties. Provisions in the Saraiva-Cotegipe Law, for example, contained restrictions designed to hamper the movement of *libertos.* According to the law, freedmen who absented themselves from the plantations could be considered "vagrants," subject to apprehension by the police and detention in "agricultural colonies" organized on the basis of "military discipline." In the more refractory cases, freedmen could be subjected to long compulsory contracts or prison terms.[15] In letter and spirit many of these regulations resembled the Black Codes which proscribed the activities of free Negroes in the southern United States. The framers of both the Black Codes and the Brazilian regulations were motivated by similar purposes: to create a system of controls which, though not formally defined as slavery, approximated the traditional patterns of authority over servile labor.

Slaveholders criticized the abolitionists for not recognizing the seriousness of the problems. Antônio Coelho Rodrigues explained that "there are two main problems in the slavery

12. *Gazeta da Tarde,* January 24, 1884, p. 1; *Annaes da Câmara* (1884), II, 68; (1885), I, 139; *O Cruzeiro,* November 6, 1880, p. 1.

13. *Associação Commercial do Rio de Janeiro: Elemento servil* (Rio de Janeiro, 1884), p. 6.

14. *Congresso Agricola,* p. 56; *Relatório* of the Minister of Agriculture, Commerce and Public Works, João Ferreira de Moura, 1885, p. 376; *Província de São Paulo,* May 1, 1888, p. 2.

15. Luiz Maria Vidal, *Repertório de legislação servil: lei n.3270 de 28 de setembro* (Rio de Janeiro, 1886), pp. 10, 35, 46; Edison Carneiro, *Antologia do negro brasileiro* (Rio de Janeiro, n.d.), pp. 122, 131–36.

question: to free the slave from captivity and to incorporate the freedmen into civil society." He suggested that the abolitionists had shown themselves incapable of providing a solution for the second problem. "If they had more prudence in their plans, and more probity in their means, they would be a party of the future, and not limit their views to simple liberation of the Negroes." [16] Other pro-slavery literature contained similar arguments. Slaveholders alluded to stories about freedmen who dissipated their energies and engaged in antisocial behavior—the "realities" to which they said the abolitionists were blinding themselves.[17]

Many contemporaries contended that the Negroes were unprepared for freedom because of the environmental influence of slavery. Peixoto de Brito, for example, warned of the danger of liberating the Negroes who, he said, viewed labor as a condition of slavery rather than a universal human responsibility. With this negative attitude nurtured by the system, many bondsmen would equate freedom with the right to be idle.[18] Others offered similar assessments of the difficulty, tracing unattractive behavioral characteristics to the subculture of slavery.[19] They observed a society of sullen, despondent captives as well as a large element of ignorant and desperately poor black and mulatto freedmen. The presence of so many dark-skinned people in the lowest stations of society tended to reinforce whatever prejudices they already held. Perdigão Malheiro accepted this interpretation in his classic book *A Escravidão no Brasil* (*Slavery in Brazil*), published in 1866–1867. Malheiro believed the slave was despised not particularly because of his race but because of his low, degraded

16. Antônio Coelho Rodrigues, *Manual do subdito fiel ou cartas de um lavrador a sua magestade o Imperador sôbre a questão do elemento servil* (Rio de Janeiro, 1884), p. 92.

17. *O abolicionismo perante a história ou o diologo das três províncias* (Rio de Janeiro, 1888), pp. 20–21.

18. Brito, *Considerações geraes sôbre a emancipação dos escravos no império do Brasil,* p. 20.

19. Francisco Antônio Brandão Junior, *A escravatura no Brasil* (Brussels, 1865), p. 53.

position.[20] Yet even Malheiro had to admit that the average white man usually did not take caution to describe behavioral characteristics principally as a product of the milieu in which a person lived. Instead, white Brazilians adopted racial stereotypes, identifying Negroes as an "inferior race, to the white above all, an intermediary between men and irrational beings." [21] Shortly before Malheiro wrote his book, a Frenchman traveling through the empire heard a Brazilian describe Africans as an intermediary race between the white man and the gorilla.[22] Many people popularly characterized Negroes for traits of "sensuality," "stupidity," "weakness," and "indolence." With regard to the planters' interests, however, they ascribed some endearing features to the "African race," such as the ability to work long hours under a hot sun. Europeans, it seemed, were too fragile to work effectively under severe conditions.[23]

As the abolitionist movement gathered momentum and defenders of slavery mustered their arguments to oppose emancipation, the condescending views toward Negroes and references to race became increasingly manifest. In a series of articles featured in the *Província de São Paulo,* the Positivist Luís Pereira Barreto was direct and frank in expressing his low regard for blacks and their potential role in society. Barreto, a slaveowner, asserted it was a scientific fact that the "Aryans" were superior to the Negroes as evidenced by the "Aryans" greater intelligence and progress in human evolution toward civilization. It was senseless to offer im-

20. Agostinho Marques Perdigão Malheiro, *A escravidão no Brasil: Ensaio histórico-jurídico-social* (Rio de Janeiro, 1866–1867), II, p. 27. For modern commentary on the problem, see Charles Granville Hamilton, "English-speaking Travelers in Brazil, 1851–1887," *Hispanic American Historical Review* (November 1960), p. 544; Eugene D. Genovese, *The World the Slaveholders Made: Two Essays in Interpretation* (New York, 1969), pp. 103–113; J. H. Plumb, "Slavery, Race, and the Poor," *New York Review of Books,* March 13, 1969, pp. 3–5.

21. Malheiro, *A escravidão no Brasil,* II, p. 87.

22. Emília Viotti da Costa, *Da senzala à colônia* (São Paulo, 1966).

23. Peixoto, *A crise do assucar,* pp. 126–29; Luiz Monteiro Caminhoá, *Canna de assucar e café—relatório apresentado ao governo imperial* (Rio de Janeiro, 1880), p. 106; Couty, *L'esclavage au Brésil,* p. 46.

mediate liberty to the Negroes, he declared, because freedom would be useless in their hands and would only increase their impatience. Barreto cautioned the abolitionists against "dumping in the center of the society a horde of semi-barbaric men, without direction, without a social goal, without savings, and what is more distressing yet, in an age that does not permit them to reconstruct their education." He believed that liberating thousands of dangerous slaves could bring a conservative reaction that would make the Negroes' condition even worse than under slavery.[24] Arguing in the same vein, the editors of the pro-slaveholder newspaper *O Cruzeiro* charged that abolitionists did not understand the unreliable nature of the slave. When not obligated to work, the Negro would turn to crime and vagabondage "like a savage animal of the African deserts." "The animal instinct in them is superior to reason," added the editors.[25] Similarly, a propaganda pamphlet disseminated by the Commercial Association of Rio de Janeiro expressed apprehension about making the Negroes freedmen. The truth is, claimed the association, "that in Brazil, as all over, the freedman is incompatible with any regime of economy, order, labor and morality." It described the free Negroes as "miserable" individuals who were ignorant of their rights and duties and without a proper notion of morality. Abolition would have to wait until some adequate plan could be arranged to provide for "the adaptation of an inferior and uneducated race to the precepts of the civilization and the social state of the other races." [26]

Most claims of racial inferiority were offered as personal assessments of Negro character, unsupported by the supposedly sophisticated evidence of the "scientific" schools of racism emerging at the time in Europe and the United States. Only a few people in the academies and intellectual circles

24. See the *Província de São Paulo,* November 20 to November 30, 1880.

25. *O Cruzeiro,* December 20, 1880, p. 3.

26. *Associação Commercial do Rio de Janeiro: Elemento servil,* pp. 8–10.

had much exposure to the ideas of Houston Stewart Chamberlain, Joseph Arthur Gobineau or the Social Darwinists.[27] Louis Couty, a Frenchman and professor in the Polytechnic School in Rio de Janeiro, probably came closest to espousing the new interpretations reaching popularity in other countries. Couty wrote several books and articles on slavery, immigration, and politics in Brazil, which attracted considerable attention from all groups—slavocrats, emancipationists, and abolitionists. He described slavery as an inefficient and antiquated system which had to be abandoned, but argued that immediate abolition would be disastrous because slaves could not be expected to handle freedom responsibly. The basis of the problem was the Negro's innate inferiority, said Couty. He rejected outright the environmentalists' view that the culture of slavery alone had fostered apathetic attitudes among the bondsmen. Liberty would not bring reformation in the blacks' behavior, asserted Couty, because "biological and sociological conditions" made lazy work habits immutable. To understand the depths of the problem of racial differences, Couty suggested study of the shape of the Negro's cranium and his record of difficulty in learning the ways of "civilized" people. Couty believed the evidence would support his contention that the Negro was less intelligent than the white man—that is, an inferior being. Consequently, he called for mass immigration of Europeans to replace the slave workers, a process that eventually would permit the complete abolition of slavery.[28]

During the era of the antislavery campaign, many people resorted to racial slurs in identifying individuals and groups. The English traveler Frank Bennett recalled the common way in which Brazilians referred to each other as "white" or "black" in obviously hostile context.[29] Similarly, in a book of reminiscences, Brazilian writer Dunshee de Abranches de-

27. I am indebted to Professor Thomas E. Skidmore for allowing me to see an early draft of his paper on the subject, "Brazilian Intellectuals and the Problem of Race, 1870–1930."

28. Couty, *L'esclavage au Brésil,* pp. 63–74.

29. Frank Bennett, *Forty Years in Brazil* (London, 1914), pp. 9–10.

scribed the last years of slavery in the province of Maranhão, admitting the presence of a pervasive attitude of prejudice against Negro bondsmen.[30] Words became especially harsh when defenders of the slave proprietors were provoked into responding to abolitionist attacks. Senator Silveira Martins of Rio Grande do Sul once barked, "I love the country more than the Negro" when irritated by oratory sympathetic to the slaves.[31] Even more blatant was the notorious slavocrat Martinho Campos, who countered a proposal by Joaquim Nabuco by asking if the abolitionist wished "to sacrifice the population of the empire for a half dozen brutal and savage Africans." [32] Sometimes opponents of the antislavery movement employed *ad hominem* remarks and racial innuendoes in their invective against abolitionists. They called abolitionists "Negrophiles," claimed that the white antislavery leader Rui Barbosa was a descendant of Africans and identified Negro journalists writing for the *Gazeta da Tarde* as troublemaking "mestizos." [33]

The prominent black abolitionist José do Patrocínio frequently became the target of racial slurs. Hecklers interrupted his speeches, shouting offensive words about his color. During one tense moment, an antagonist in the crowd shouted, "Shut up, Negro!" but Patrocínio earned cheers from the audience after his tart reply: "God gave me the color of Othello so that I would be the envy of my country!" When Patrocínio traveled to Europe to solicit support for the Brazilian antislavery movement, he incurred much more criticism than any white abolitionist who made the Atlantic crossing for similar pur-

30. João Dunshee de Abranches Moura, *O captiveiro, memórias* (Rio de Janeiro, 1941), pp. 50–51.

31. Moraes, *A campanha abolicionista,* p. 149.

32. *Annaes da Câmara* (1880), November 11, p. 258.

33. Luiz Luna, *O negro na luta contra a escravidão* (Rio de Janeiro, 1968), p. 214; *O Cruzeiro,* November 22, 1880, p. 2; December 16, 1880, p. 3. André Rebouças, a mulatto, was sometimes the victim of racial discrimination. In the most famous incident, white ladies at a formal ball refused to dance with him. Disgusted by their behavior, Princess Isabel approached Rebouças and asked if he would lead her in the next dance.

poses. His enemies implied the trip was really a pleasure excursion financed by questionable means. As one slavocrat phrased the complaint, Patrocínio "enjoys using the money of the Negroes of Rio de Janeiro to take trips to Europe, land of the whites."[34] It is not surprising, then, that Patrocínio surveyed the situation in Brazil in 1885 with a feeling of frustration, lamenting that "prejudice against men of color can prolong slavery indefinitely."[35]

Anti-Negro prejudice did show some subtle flexibility, however. Individuals of mixed racial background generally received better treatment than those of pure African ancestry. Brazilian society put a premium on whiteness, a situation that clearly gave advantages to the mulatto over his black brothers. The propensity of masters to manumit mulatto slaves rather than black slaves reflected this attitude. Of course, some cases involved the liberation of the proprietor's own illegitimate children, but often the acts simply gave evidence of the *senhor*'s differential treatment of the two groups. To see a fair-skinned mulatto in bondage seemed much more distasteful than to see a dark-skinned Negro in bondage. Perdigão Malheiro even conjectured that if all the slaves in Brazil were mulattoes, the servile institution would fast disappear.[36]

The heightened attention to racial origin in the midst of the growing slavery controversy left many mulattoes insecure. Some had attained positions of social and economic respect and did not wish to forfeit hard-earned accomplishments by identifying with the cause of Negro slaves. Many had a direct stake in the system; the planter class included a large complement of mulatto slave proprietors.[37] In fact, one of Brazil's

34. *O abolicionismo perante a história ou o dialogo das três províncias,* p. 12; Gazeta da Tarde, September 27, 1884, p. 1; João Guimaraes, *Patrocínio: O abolicionista* (São Paulo, 1956), p. 29; *Rio News,* January 24, 1882, p. 2.

35. *Gazeta da Tarde,* September 18, 1885, p. 1. Also see the *Vinte e Cinco de Março,* No. 1, May 1884.

36. Malheiro, *A escravidão no Brasil,* II, p. 117.

37. André Rebouças' father revealed his own sensitivities about color when he announced in Parliament that he was proud to be a mulatto.

leading slavocrats, the Baron of Cotegipe, was himself a very light-skinned mulatto.[38] In São Paulo prominent mulatto lawyers and republicans allied with antiabolitionist groups; in other areas, too, many mulattoes did the same or remained cautiously indifferent to the movement against slavery. Recently manumitted mulatto freedmen who were struggling to raise their economic level shied away from employment that would associate them with black slaves. They preferred to leave the plantation areas, seeking urban occupations as artisans, small shopkeepers, and office boys.[39] These attitudes frustrated the abolitionists. Joaquim Nabuco complained that people were "indifferent to their own color." [40] Unstable, insecure, and working carefully to appear more white than black, many mulattoes were slow to respond to the abolitionist challenge.

The importance of attitudes toward race in the controversy over manpower recruitment and abolition is also evidenced by the way groups opposed the idea of using Chinese coolies as substitutes for slaves. Many Hard-Core Slaveholders advocated mass employment of Chinese immigrants in the 1870s and 1880s as a means of easing the transition from slave labor to free labor. They viewed the Orientals as docile and obedient, yet efficient laborers. Especially important, the coolies could be expected to work for very low wages, probably less than one-half those of the European immigrants.

Brito, *Considerações geraes sôbre a emancipação dos escravos no império do Brasil,* p. 16; Dorothy B. Porter, "The Negro in the Brazilian Abolition Movement," *Journal of Negro History,* 1952, p. 72.

38. Other leading Brazilian politicians of the era described as having partial African ancestry are the Viscount of Rio Branco, Zacharias de Goes, Salles Torres Homen, Tobias Barretto, and Marshal Deodoro da Fonseca. See Santos, *Política geral do Brasil,* pp. 176–77; Orlando de Almeida Prado, *Em defenza da raça negra: O preconceito de raça não existe no Brasil* (São Paulo, n.d.), p. 9.

39. Couty, *L'esclavage au Brésil,* pp. 64–65; *A Redempção,* May 13, 1899, p. 1; Raymond S. Sayers, *The Negro in Brazilian Literature* (New York, 1956), pp. 201–19.

40. Joaquim Nabuco, *O eclypso do abolicionismo* (Rio de Janeiro, 1886), p. 32.

Reports indicated that cheap coolie labor in the United States, Cuba, Peru, and the Philippines proved very successful. Moreover, the presence of many coolies in Brazil could help maintain keen competition in the job market, forcing free Negroes to settle for low-paying contracts. If Hard-Core Slaveholders were to be forced into accepting a system of wage labor, employment of coolies appeared to be the best alternative at a time when they were hard pressed for liquid capital.[41]

When *fazendeiros* of the Central-South held an Agricultural Congress in Rio de Janeiro in 1878, Hard-Core Slaveholders gave the strongest appeals for government assistance in recruiting Chinese immigrants. The Prime Minister at the time, the Viscount of Sinimbú, approved of the idea and sent an emissary to China to negotiate a treaty of commerce and win support for emigration to Brazil. But the plans proved abortive. On the diplomatic front the program met opposition from British officials, who became suspicious of the intentions of the Brazilian government and ordered agents in Hong Kong to counsel against emigration. On the home front the movement was thwarted by proponents of European immigration and abolitionists.[42]

The immigrationists' reservations about Chinese labor concentrated on matters of race. "They are a 'degenerate race,' " asserted the Campos planter Manoel Rodrigues Peixoto. "To introduce them into Brazil would be like introducing all the Africans and present slaves all over again."[43] Paulistas were particularly disturbed by the prospect of Chinese immigration, viewing Orientals greatly inferior to Europeans. The basis of the inferiority, suggested one *fazendeiro,* could be traced to race, indolent habits, and the debilitating effects of opium.[44] The possibility of assimilation and miscegenation seemed

41. *Demonstração das conveniências e vantagens a lavoura ao Brasil pela introducção dos trabalhadores asiáticos* (*da China*) (Rio de Janeiro, 1877), pp. viii, 14–15, 101; Quintino Ferreira de Souza Bocayuva, *A crise da lavoura* (Rio de Janeiro, 1868), pp. 29–40; *Rio News,* July 5, 1881, p. 1.

42. *Rio News,* November 15, 1881, p. 1; May 24, 1882, pp. 4–5.

43. Peixoto, *A crise de assucar,* pp. 123–24.

44. See the speech of Eduardo A. Pereira de Abreu in *Congresso Agricola,* pp. 38–39.

frightening too. "One can imagine the physionomic aspect, the configuration and conditions of the organs that the hybrid product of so detestable a union will offer for view and study!" exclaimed João Menezes de Souza in a popular tract favoring European immigration.[45] Abolitionists used similar arguments. They opposed a new influx of a "degenerate race," and Joaquim Nabuco described the Chinese as "decadent" and "effeminate," warning of the danger of mixing blood with the Orientals. "The history of the world proves," said Nabuco, "that when the most intelligent and brilliant races are placed in contact with inferior races, the former are usually overcome by the latter."[46] But abolitionists like Nabuco also criticized coolie labor because it would substitute only nominal freedom for legal slavery. Contracts forced upon weak and naïve Asiatics would undermine the whole principle of free market labor agreements. In essence, the yellow "slave" would replace the black slave on the plantations and the white laborers in the cities.[47]

Spokesmen for the Hard-Core Slaveholders tried to present a strong rebuttal to the detractors of Chinese immigration, but they had difficulty establishing agreement on the race issue. Indeed, some claimed there was nothing to fear, insisting that the Orientals represented one of the most intelligent and civilized "races" in the world. Brazil had always been a tolerant country, they said, opening the doors to diverse groups and providing for their assimilation. Opponents of the Chinese were acting like racists in the United States.[48] Others

45. João Cardoso de Menezes de Souza, *Theses sôbre colonização do Brazil: Projecto de solução as questões sociaes, que se prendem a este dificil problema—relatório apresentado ao Ministério da Agricultura, Commércio e Obras Públicas em 1873* (Rio de Janeiro, 1875), p. 420.

46. Joaquim Nabuco, *Discursos parlamentares: 1879–1889* (São Paulo, n.d.), pp. 25, 63; *Revista Illustrada,* October 13, 1888, p. 6; November 17, 1888.

47. Souza, *Theses sôbre colonização do Brasil,* pp. 414–15; Miguel Lemos, *Immigração chineza* (Rio de Janeiro, 1881), p. 13; *Rio News,* April 24, 1880, p. 1; Nabuco, *Discursos parlamentares,* p. 67. The editor of the *Gazeta de Porto Alegre* called Chinese immigration "a *surrogate* of slavery." See the *Rio News,* September 5, 1881, p. 4.

48. *Congresso Agricola,* pp. 228–29; *Província de Minas,* April 27, 1888, p. 1; *Importação de trabalhadores chins. Memória apresentada*

from the Hard-Core Slaveholders group, however, shared the apprehensions about Chinese racial characteristics. To defend their advocacy of Oriental immigration they emphasized the vital necessities of agriculture and pointed out that most coolies probably would not intend to remain in Brazil. After saving their wages for a few years, most could be expected to return to their native land. Proponents of Chinese immigration were not trying to be apologists for the coolies, explained a planter from Rio de Janeiro, but this form of labor had to be considered as a last resort.[49]

The Hard-Core Slaveholders' plans to attract cheap, semiservile Chinese labor on a large scale never materialized. Their appeal coincided with both the campaign for the abolition of slavery and the campaign in favor of European immigration, two movements which worked successfully in opposition to coolie immigration. Most Brazilians never had any contact with Oriental civilization or the Chinese people. In an environment of ignorance and fear, racist views prevailed, and the abolitionists were able to check the threat of coolie "bondage."

Many *fazendeiros* as well as urban immigrationists showed much greater enthusiasm for encouraging Europeans to settle in Brazil. The white immigrants, they thought, would prove to be more reliable and productive laborers and more socially acceptable than either the Chinese coolies or the black freedmen. They also believed that the Europeans offered superior intelligence to the other groups.[50] This had been a major concern during the days of the African slave trade when some Brazilians opposed the traffic because it only increased the population of "stupid slaves," perpetuating ignorance in

ao Ministro da Agricultura, Commércio e Obras Públicas e impressa por sua ordem (Rio de Janeiro, 1869), p. 20; *Demonstração das conveniênias e vantagens a lavoura ao Brasil pela introducção dos trabalhadores asiáticos (da China)*, pp. v–viii, 45. Also see the article from *O Cruzeiro* reprinted in the *Rio News*, August 5, 1881, p. 1.

49. *Congresso Agricola*, pp. 64–65, 228–29, 253.

50. *Ibid.*, pp. 70, 147; *Relatório* of the president of Rio de Janeiro province, Antônio da Rocha Fernandes Leão, September 12, 1887, pp. 40–41; *1st Centenário do Conselheiro Antônio da Silva Prado* (São Paulo, 1946), p. 169.

the empire. One writer at the time suggested that liberated blacks who did not work should be shipped back to Africa.[51] After the close of the Atlantic slave trade, Positivist Francisco Antônio Brandão, Jr., rejoiced, claiming it would work to the "advantage of the white race, which, being the more intelligent, will eventually triumph over the Negro race by exclusive dominance or by complete fusion, as is now happening." [52] As Brazilians addressed the manpower issue in the last quarter of the nineteenth century, they spoke of the good and poor "blood" in the nation's racial and ethnic stock and the need, as a prominent slaveholder from Rio de Janeiro described it, of "inoculating new blood into our veins." [53] Almost all believed that an increase in white "blood" would improve the national character. The immigration of Italians and Germans would help "to populate this vast land, instituting a new crossing from which will emerge the New-Brazilian, much better than the present one," reported the governor of Pernambuco.[54]

Progressive Planters and other representatives from São Paulo and the Deep South showed more reluctance to consider assimilation as an answer. They intended to recruit Europeans with the expectation that immigrants would work to the exclusion of other groups and avoid racial intermixture. The country was already terribly debilitated from the "impure blood" of Africans, they thought, and there was no need further to "bastardize" the population.[55]

The interest in immigration was not new, for there had been considerable discussion in earlier years about transporting Europeans to Brazil for plantation labor. Most notable were the projects of Senator Nicolau Vergueiro of São Paulo, who received a subsidy for immigration in 1842 and in 1847

51. Augusto de Carvalho, *O Brazil: Colonização e emigração* (Porto, 1876), pp. 130–34.
52. Brandão, *A escravatura no Brasil,* p. 155.
53. See *"A nossa lavoura"* by Pedro D. G. Paes Leme in *Demonstração das conveniências e vantagens a lavoura ao Brasil pela introducção dos trabalhadores asiáticos (da China)*, p. 117.
54. *Mensagem* of the governor of Pernambuco, Alexandre José Barbosa Lima, March 6, 1893, pp. 28–29.
55. *Congresso Agricola,* pp. 38–39.

began settling Europeans on his *fazenda* through a partnership arrangement. Others followed his example in the 1850s and 1860s, but many of these projects were not very successful. Conflicts between the proprietors and immigrants multiplied. The planters desired to control the Europeans as they dominated their slaves, but the immigrants rose up in protest against the poor treatment. Immigrants also had difficulty adjusting to the tropical climate and plantation work. Eventually many of the foreign settlers abandoned the *fazendas* and moved to the cities to seek employment in commerce and artisan trades. The system of colonization and partnerships with immigrants gradually lost prestige in this period.[56]

In the 1880s new factors converged to increase the flux of immigration into Brazil. With the prospect of the abolition of slavery appearing more imminent at the very time that the São Paulo coffee economy was rapidly expanding, Progressive Planters sought new ways to satisfy their labor demands. They began to look to Europe for help. Meanwhile, the upheaval that accompanied the political unification of Italy provided a new source of foreign labor for Brazil. Unification accentuated the backwardness of the primitive agricultural economy of southern Italy. Unable to compete with their more efficient northern countrymen, the southern Italians suffered from severe economic depression. Also, many northern Italians found the competition keen and their opportunities limited in the Old World. These individuals looked to the Western Hemisphere for new opportunities. Along with sizable migrations to the United States and Argentina, many Italians went to Brazil. Of the 803,000 immigrants who entered Brazil in the last quarter of the nineteenth century, 557,000 were from Italy. Second highest in immigration to Brazil in the period were the Portuguese; Spanish, Germans, and Poles also entered in large numbers.[57]

56. Costa, *Da senzala à colônia,* pp. 65–124; Brandão, *A escravatura no Brasil,* pp. 158–59; Luiz Francisco da Camara Leal, *Considerações e projecto de lei para a emancipação dos escravos sem prejuizo de seus senhores, nem grave onus para o estado* (Rio de Janeiro, 1866), p. 3.

57. Celso Furtado, *The Economic Growth of Brazil* (Berkeley and Los Angeles, 1963), pp. 134, 140, 153; Emília Viotti da Costa, "O

São Paulo was most successful in attracting Europeans. The Paulistas were fortunate in being able to offer more fertile soil, a more attractive climate, higher wages, and better employment opportunities than in other provinces of the empire. Also, they took concerted action to attract foreigners, especially through the leadership of important political figures such as Antônio Prado, Rodrigues Alves, Martinho Prado Junior and the Baron of Parnaiba. The provincial government of São Paulo aided immigration in the 1880s through taxing slavery to raise funds for recruitment, issuing government grants to private immigration societies, supplying funds for the transportation of Europeans, providing food and lodging for settlers in Brazil, and arranging other forms of subsidization. Consequently, the province received the bulk of the immigrants. Of 55,965 Europeans who settled in Brazil in 1887, 34,306 went to São Paulo.[58]

The immigration fetish also excited leaders in other parts of Brazil. Provinces to the south of São Paulo were successful in attracting Europeans. Numerous Germans moved to Rio Grande do Sul and Santa Catarina, and many Poles settled in Paraná.[59] Leaders in other sections tried to attract immigrants, too, but with less success. Interest in the subject intensified in Bahia, for example, when the abolition of slavery appeared

---

escravo na grande lavoura" in Sérgio Buarque de Holanda (ed.), *História geral da civilisação brasileira* (São Paulo, 1966), V, pp. 176–78; T. Lynn Smith, *Brazil: People and Institutions* (Baton Rouge, 1954), pp. 62, 119–25; *Rio News*, February 15, 1884.

58. *Jornal do Commércio*, January 9, 1888, p. 1; *Relatório* of the president of São Paulo, Francisco de Paula Rodrigues Alves, April 27, 1888, p. 64; Joaquim Nabuco, *O abolicionismo* (São Paulo, 1938), p. 206; *Rio News*, January 24, 1884; February 15, 1884; Nazareth Prado (ed.), *Antônio Prado no império e na república* (Rio de Janeiro, 1929), pp. 53–57; Roberto C. Simonsen, *Aspectos da história econômica do café* (Rio de Janeiro, 1938), p. 54; Pierre Monbeig, *Pionniers et planteurs de l'etat de São Paulo* (Paris, 1952), p. 92; Paula Beiguelman, *Formação Política do Brasil:* Vol. I: *Teoria e ação no pensamento abolicionista* (São Paulo, 1967), p. 30; *Dados para a história de immigração e da colonização em São Paulo* (São Paulo, 1916), p. 8; P. Pereira dos Reis, "Algumas considerações sôbre a imigração em São Paulo," *Revista Sociologia* (March 1961), p. 83.

59. Sérgio Milliet, *Roteiro do café e outros ensaios* (São Paulo, 1946), p. 145.

imminent. Citizens formed the Bahian Immigration Society to sponsor subsidized programs similar to those of the Paulistas. They hoped the new efforts would facilitate "the transition from the boorish labor of the slave to the intelligent labor of the European. . . ."[60] *Fazendeiros* in Minas Gerais and Rio de Janeiro also advocated immigration, particularly the recruitment of Portuguese and Germans. They found the Portuguese attractive for the language and customs they shared with Brazilians, while Germans appeared to offer the special qualities of the "Anglo-Saxon Race." The Minas and Rio planters were less inclined to appeal to the Italians than their counterparts in São Paulo. In part this was due to the behavior of the newcomers. Italians enjoyed the company of their fellow countrymen and preferred not to disperse into the isolation of the countryside. Many who settled in Minas Gerais, for example, quickly left the plantations to take jobs in the cities or join the larger Italian community in São Paulo.[61]

Immigration to Brazil increased immensely in the 1880s.[62] During this period, it became clear that the area from São Paulo to Rio Grande do Sul was experiencing extraordinary

60. *Falla* of the president of Bahia, João Capistrano Bandeira de Mello, October 4, 1887, pp. 135, 140–54; *Falla* of the president of Bahia, Manuel do Nascimento Machado Portella, April 3, 1888, pp. 12–14, 30–35; *Falla* of the vice president of Bahia, Aurelio Ferreira Espinheira, April 3, 1889, p. 98.

61. Couty, *L'esclavage au Brésil,* p. 48; Peixoto, *A crise de assucar,* pp. 123–24; *Jornal do Recife,* March 24, 1888; *Congresso Agricola,* pp. 69–71; Pierre Denis, *O Brasil no século XX* (Lisbon, n.d.), pp. 334–37.

62. The following figures appear in Roberto Simonsen, "*As econômicas consequências da abolição,*" *Revista do Arquivo Municipal de São Paulo* (May 1938), pp. 257–68.

Immigration to Brazil

Year	*Total*
1884	24,890
1885	35,440
1886	33,486
1887	55,965
1888	133,253
1889	65,246
1890	107,474
1891	216,760

success in recruiting Europeans in comparison with most other sections of the empire. The presence of many slaves, weaknesses in the economy, and climatic conditions all operated to the disfavor of other regions. Much to the distress of provincial leaders, it seemed that the new immigrant wave was bypassing them. Immigrationist Carlos von Kosseritz highlighted the disparity, for example, when he estimated that scarcely 200 foreigners went to the northern provinces of approximately 25,000 who entered Brazil in 1882.[63] The success of São Paulo's efforts especially alarmed the Hard-Core Slaveholders of Rio de Janeiro and Minas Gerais. Once they became fully aware of their inability to attract large numbers of Europeans, they began to oppose immigration programs, viewing foreign labor in other provinces as unwanted competition. With heavy indebtedness, they could hardly afford to pay the immigrants attractive wages. Other *fazendeiros* might easily outstrip their production of coffee by using free European labor, and eventually the competition would place their own slave-based economy in serious jeopardy.[64] Consequently, ministries that represented Hard-Core Slaveholders opinion in the 1880s avoided using the power of the government to aid immigration. Even when legislation was enacted on the local level, the slaveholders often ignored it. For example, the provincial government of Minas Gerais voted for a subsidy for the introduction of foreign tenants on the *fazendas,* but the law had little effect. Minas planters chose to remain tied to slave labor until the eve of abolition.[65]

Abolitionists joined the Progressive Planters in appealing for Europeans. Through newspapers, pamphlets, and public speeches, abolitionists described the interest in foreigners as consistent with their general goals of establishing a society

63. Prado, *Antônio Prado no império e na república,* pp. 122–46; Anyda Marchant, *Viscount Mauá and the Empire in Brazil* (Berkeley and Los Angeles, 1965), p. 269.

64. Cardoso, *Capitalismo e escravidão,* p. 214; Furtado, *Economic Growth of Brazil,* p. 137; *Gazeta de Notícias,* April 7, 1884, p. 1.

65. Alcindro Sodré, *O elemento servil, a abolição* (Rio de Janeiro, 1942), p. 143.

based on free labor and regenerating the nation's institutions. Immigrants, with their special skills and repugnance for slavery, would play a central role in making Brazil a modern country.[66] Indeed, some abolitionists emphasized the matter more than others, but almost all of them agreed that the issues of immigration and abolition were closely connected —that foreigners would not want to settle in a country where slave labor was prevalent. Abolitionists and Progressive Planters formed societies to promote their ideas. The two most important such organizations were the Sociedade Central de Imigração (Central Immigration Society) and the Sociedade Promotadora de Imigração (Immigration Promotion Society). While the former included many urban abolitionists, the composition of the latter largely represented planter membership.

As the Progressive Planters still possessed many slaves in the 1880s, they were often cautious about acknowledging the incompatibility of slavery and immigration. But abolitionists showed no such reserve. They loudly condemned slavery as a deterrent to immigration. "The slave demoralizes the immigrant," declared José do Patrocínio.[67] "It is slavery that impedes spontaneous immigration to Brazil. Slavery is the first argument of the European governments against colonization in Brazil," insisted André Rebouças.[68] Abolitionists were disturbed by Argentina's greater success in attracting Europeans and attributed the presence of slavery in Brazil as the reason for this. As long as slavery existed, the European would feel that he would be treated like a white slave alongside the black slave.[69] Abolitionists warned that planters who worked the immigrants like bondsmen would only discourage other

66. Letter from André Rebouças in *Diário da Bahia,* April 18, 1888, p. 1; *Gazeta do Povo,* May 13, 1888, p. 1; Joaquim Nabuco, *Circular aos eleitores do segundo districto do Corte* (n.p., 1884), August 18, 1884, p. 6; *Gazeta de Notícias,* March 29, 1884, p. 1.

67. *Gazeta da Tarde,* April 30, 1884, p. 1.

68. André Rebouças, *A agricultura nacional* (Rio de Janeiro, 1883), p. 290.

69. *Annaes da Camara* (1884), II, 13; *Discurso proferido na sessão de 17 de julho de 1884 pelo deputado Dr. Affonso Celso Junior* (Rio de Janeiro, 1884), p. 18; Nabuco, *O abolicionismo,* pp. 232–33.

foreigners from coming to Brazil. Immigrants had left Europe to escape the tyranny of feudal barons, explained the abolitionists. The Europeans wanted to own their own land; they expected life on the *fazendas* to be only a transitional stage before they would achieve their ultimate goal of becoming individual proprietors. In this sense, the abolitionists were more direct and critical in drawing the connection between abolition and immigration than the planters.[70]

In pointing to the poor treatment of immigrants in the presence of slavery, abolitionists had a good case. Many *fazendeiros* tried to manage their foreign workers as they managed their slaves. Immigrants complained that they were treated with contempt, left without adequate food and shelter, deceived about their land, and paid low wages. The best land was monopolized by the great *fazendeiros,* who desired to see the immigrants settled as sharecroppers. Disillusioned and angry, many of the new settlers abandoned the plantations and relocated on small farms or in the cities. The problems eventually became so acute that São Paulo authorities had to pass laws to protect the foreigners from exploitation at the hands of their employers. The governments of Europe were aware of these difficulties; at various times, for example, the authorities in Germany and Italy either gave warnings against immigration to Brazil or expressly prohibited it.[71]

Progressive Planters displayed much warmer interest in immigration than in abolition. They wanted to spur immigration first while delaying emancipation of the slaves. These planters believed that pro-immigration policies would augment the labor force, while abolition would only diminish it. In fact, *fazendeiros* frequently asked that half of the government's emancipation funds be applied to attracting immigrants. As one planter explained the logic of such a plan, "In furnish-

70. *Gazeta da Tarde,* January 25, 1881, p. 1.

71. *Gazeta da Tarde,* June 4, 1881; Caio Prado Junior, *História econômica do Brasil* (São Paulo, 1949), pp. 191–95; 218–19; *Rio News,* July 3, 1886, p. 2; *Correio Paulistano,* September 22, 1887, p. 1; October 20, 1887, p. 1; Couty, *L'esclavage au Brésil,* p. 48; Denis, *O Brasil no século XX,* pp. 161–63; *Congresso Agricola,* pp. 63–66.

ing laborers to agriculture there ought to be expended at least the same quantity which is expended in taking them away." Once abolition was imminent, these planters wanted to see all the money in the emancipation funds transferred to immigration projects.[72]

A clear difference in stress developed between the abolitionists' and the Progressive Planters' views on labor supply. While abolitionists saw immigration as desirable and necessary, they viewed the abolition of slavery as the primary question. After that, immigration would naturally follow. Progressive Planters, on the other hand, viewed immigration as the more important matter. They needed work hands and felt that European settlers would perform much more efficiently and effectively than black freedmen. To maintain an adequate labor force, these planters would work immigrants and slaves together until abolition would gradually take place and immigrants would fill the openings in the labor force. Some abolitionists shared this preference for free white laborers over free black laborers, such as Affonso d'Escragnolle Taunay, but most abolitionists displayed more interest than Progressive Planters in the economic role that free blacks would play after abolition. In short, abolitionists pointed to the Brazilian Negro as the first answer to the manpower problem while Progressive Planters focused on the European immigrant.

Joaquim Nabuco well expressed the attitude of many of the most vocal abolitionists when he directed attention to the masses who already were "Brazilians" and desired a more important role in the national economy:

> The recourse to immigration is very important, but it is secondary to . . . another: that of transforming and linking all of our population to labor. If the people do not toil it is because they *cannot* or *do not wish* to do

72. Cardoso, *Capitalismo e escravidão,* p. 210; *Rio News,* October 5, 1883, p. 2; June 24, 1886, p. 2; *Annaes do Senado* (1888), I, 26; Almelia de Rezende Martins, *Um idealista realizador: Barão Geraldo de Rezende* (Campinas, n.d.), p. 325; Florestan Fernandes, *A integração do negro na sociedade de classes* (São Paulo, 1965), I, p. 11.

> so, and our task is to make sure that they are able and that they desire to work, creating the competitive spirit that they lack if they are short on initiative, destroying the obstacles—*whatever they are*—that obstruct them, if it is because they are unable to work.[73]

Abolitionists stressed the central role of freedmen in the future labor market, but they also showed awareness of attendant difficulties. They readily conceded that slaves were not fully prepared for freedom. But abolitionists saw this condition as a result of slavery and, therefore, another reason for extinguishing human bondage. Even Nabuco spoke of the slaves' animal-like passions and the problems in working with older bondsmen whose servile habits were already deeply ingrained. He saw greater potential in the younger, more corrigible generation that could learn new approaches to life and labor.[74] Similarly, Henrique du Beaurepaire Rohan, an early proponent of abolition and agricultural education, acknowledged the liability of indolent work habits.[75] Another abolitionist, J. Simoes, agreed that the blacks had been kept ignorant under slavery, and Luís Anselmo Fonseca believed they had to be carefully protected and guided. "The slave is a little more than a brute and a little less than a child," said Fonseca.[76] Yet abolitionists differed from most slaveholders in that they proposed to do something about the black's social and economic deficiencies. Throughout the antislavery campaign, abolitionists discussed and presented

73. Nabuco, *Conferências e discursos abolicionistas,* pp. 253, 254. For similar views on the difficulties of changing habits developed under conditions of slavery, see Domingo Maria Gonçalves, *A instrucçao agricola e o trabalho livre* (Rio de Janeiro, 1880), pp. 61–62; *Cartas de Miguel Lemos a R. Teixeira Mendes* (Rio de Janeiro, 1965), p. 178.

74. *Conferência do Sr. Joaquim Nabuco a 22 de 1884 no Theatro Polytheama* (Rio de Janeiro, 1884), pp. 33, 37–38; Joaquim Nabuco, O abolicionismo (São Paulo, 1938), pp. 23–24.

75. *Congresso Agricola,* pp. 243–51; André Rebouças, *Abolição immediata e sem indemnisação* (Rio de Janeiro, 1883), pp. 18–19.

76. *Gazeta da Tarde,* December 11, 1882, p. 2; Luis Anselmo Fonseca, *A escravidão, o clero e o abolicionismo* (Bahia, 1887), p. 590.

numerous projects to help the freedmen make new adjustments.

Antislavery leaders said that their goal had to be more than just simple liberation; they needed to prepare the blacks for civic and economic life through moral and vocational instruction. They claimed that in the United States abolitionists had done excellent work in educating the freedmen and, consequently, the blacks there acted like civilized men, not "barbarians." [77]

The means that abolitionists suggested to help the emancipated blacks adjust to freedom varied according to the personal orientations of the particular individuals. Many of the abolitionists' suggestions were designed to keep the blacks involved in agriculture. André Rebouças, with his deep interest in agrarian reform, wished to see the government give the freedmen land. He thought that if the blacks could become individual proprietors, they would have a stake in society and become more industrious.[78] Joaquim Nabuco sought to link the freedmen to the land through arrangements similar to the immigration colonization programs.[79] Many proposals involved providing special supplies and training for the liberated slaves. The projects of Rebouças and J. Simoes called for the establishment of special schools to educate the freedmen, while a plan by Souza Dantas suggested that the government establish agriculture colonies to educate the *ingenuos* and to provide employment for freedmen.[80] The Sociedade Cearense Libertadora (Liberator Society of Ceará) wanted special care and training for the women and children who were freed from

77. Fonseca, *A escrãvidao, o clero e o abolicionismo,* p. 658; Gonçalves, *A instrucção agricola e o trabalho livre,* pp. 46–53.

78. Rebouças, *A agricultura nacional,* p. 126; Inácio José Veríssimo, *André Rebouças através a sua auto-biografia* (Rio de Janeiro, 1939), p. 214; André Rebouças, *Diário e notas autobiográficas,* ed. Ana Flora and Inácio Veríssimo (Rio de Janeiro, 1938), p. 315; *Diário da Bahia,* April 18, 1888, p. 1.

79. Carolina Nabuco, *The Life of Joaquim Nabuco* (Stanford, 1950), p. 55.

80. *Gazeta da Tarde,* December 11, 1882, p. 2; *Annaes do Senado* (1887), June 3, pp. 16–18.

slavery, while a multifaceted project presented in the *Gazeta da Tarde* asked that the liberated be guaranteed a minimum wage and be given primary-school instruction as well as food, clothing, and shelter.[81] Francisco Maria Duprat, editor of a magazine for planters in Pernambuco, called for creation of a school of agriculture and an apprenticeship program of three years.[82] Some educational projects were carried out by the abolitionists' own initiative. For example, João Clapp, the president of the Abolitionist Confederation, and Luiz Gama, the black abolitionist leader in São Paulo, operated night classes for slaves and freedmen.[83]

While slaveholders echoed recurrent complaints about the slaves' apathy, ignorance, and lack of education, abolitionists offered the most concrete remedies for the problems. They emphasized that the slave proprietors themselves should show interest in constructive improvement if emancipation was to be a success. Joaquim Nabuco questioned the propriety of excessive talk about teaching slaves the responsibilities of liberty when it appeared that *fazendeiros* needed education regarding *their* responsibilities.[84] With adequate experimentation through incentive programs, it seemed that planters could work out a profitable transition to the free labor system.[85]

Abolitionists enjoyed referring to specific examples which supported their argument about the value of incentives. In one situation, for example, a planter promised his 70 slaves freedom in five years if they produced a specified amount

81. *O Libertador,* January 1, 1881, p. 5; *Gazeta da Tarde,* October 6, 1882, p. 2.

82. *Brasil Agricola,* August 30 and 31, 1881. Duprat described his ideas as projects for "peaceful social reconstruction."

83. *Gazeta da Tarde,* August 1, 1882, p. 1; April 17, 1883, p. 1. In 1886 the Sociedade Libertadora Alagoana founded a school for *ingenuos* in the city of Maceió, registering 216 students in its first year. See the *Falla* of the president of Alagoas, José Moreira Alves da Silva, April 15, 1887, p. 5.

84. Nabuco, *Conferências e discursos abolicionistas,* pp. 285–86.

85. Antônio Cesario de Faria Alvim of Minas Gerais told his fellow *fazendeiros* that they would have few problems if they would liberate the Negroes and pay them what they would intend to pay European immigrants. *Congresso Agricola,* p. 132.

of sugar in the allotted time. The bondsmen met their quota, then remained on the plantation, working effectively through a partnership arrangement. A Bahian planter made a similar promise, offering freedom in three years if his slaves could meet a production target. The bondsmen worked energetically, reached the mark, and brought large returns to the proprietor. In other cases cited, *fazendeiros* offered the liberated parcels of land, clothing, medical supplies, and advances in food and money before harvest time. All of these incentives worked successfully to instill a positive attitude toward labor and encourage the manumitted to remain on the plantations.[86]

Other *fazendeiros* would do well to heed these examples, suggested the abolitionists. The day of national emancipation was fast arriving, an event which could only prove shocking to masters who did not anticipate the change and try to win the allegiance of their workers. For favorable employer-employee relationships in the years to follow, it would behoove planters to begin treating their slaves as men rather than as "dogs."[87]

Some abolitionists worried about the labor contracts consummated with freedmen because provisions often shackled the employee's freedom of movement and interfered with his opportunity to bargain for wages. They understood the concern for encouraging free blacks to work in agriculture and the efforts to discourage vagabondage but felt that many of the unilateral stipulations written by *fazendeiros* were grossly unjust. After the Paulista planter Paula Souza turned abolitionist, he admonished his fellow proprietors for making deceptive agreements and warned that workers would soon show

86. *Congresso Agricola,* pp. 247–48; *Revista Illustrada,* March 15, 1887, p. 3; *Brazil,* April 4, 1884, p. 1; June 11, 1884, p. 3; *Rio News,* June 5, 1880, p. 1; July 15, 1880, p. 1; February 5, 1881, p. 1; *Brasil Agricola,* January 31, 1881, pp. 74–75; Gonçalves, *A instrucção agricola e o trabalho livre,* pp. 24–45.

87. *Rio News,* February 5, 1881, p. 1. The editor of the *Gazeta do Povo* discussed the need to prepare to work with freedmen, emphasizing that after emancipation "the Brazilian slave will not return to the African coast, land of his ancestors" (January 12, 1888, p. 1).

apathy and alienation if not offered unfettered arrangements.[88] Rui Barbosa was especially active in efforts to obviate national legislation that would hamper the *libertos'* bargaining power. He believed that the contracts were strictly matters of negotiation between employers and employees; state interference was unconstitutional and tantamount to socialism.[89]

On the other hand, Alcibiades Peçanha argued that socialism was exactly what the exploited freedmen needed. Blacks usually stepped out of slavery with experience limited to agriculture and possessing very few skills. Tragically, they were entering the labor market at the time when people were moving from the rural, agricultural pursuits to new opportunities in the urban, industrial areas. If somehow freedmen could strengthen their bargaining positions, they too could gain employment in the fledgling industrial sectors and compete favorably with foreign workers. Left to themselves, however, the *libertos* would be powerless, quickly sinking into a form of servitude similar to the situation in Europe in medieval times. Only "socialism" could prevent this, argued Peçanha, by bringing black freedmen and other Brazilian laborers together. Through solidarity, they could organize unions to fight against exploitation by their employers.[90]

Thus many abolitionists believed that the work force of black freedmen could help the planters to solve the manpower problem, and they proposed specific programs to strengthen the blacks' role in that solution. They challenged the popular assumption that the liberated would equate freedom with leisure. Given decent opportunities—education, property ownership, monetary incentives, improved working conditions—they would become dependable laborers. By expressing deep concern for the fate of the black and faith in his ability to accept liberty responsibly, abolitionists denied the existence

88. *Província de São Paulo,* April 8, 1888, p. 1.

89. Rui Barbosa, *Emancipação dos escravos: Parecer formulado pelo deputado Rui Barbosa* (*projecto n. 48*) (Rio de Janeiro, 1884), pp. 146–57.

90. *Gazeta do Povo,* March 23, 1888, p. 1.

of a manpower shortage of vast dimensions.[91] Why look only to slaves or foreigners to man the plantations? If the system could make toil worth the effort, abundant freedmen would be ready to handle the jobs. Emancipation would produce workers aplenty for those willing to compensate for the inequities of slavery and make the free labor system attractive for blacks.

91. For skeptical comments regarding the much discussed "manpower shortage," see Guimaraes, *A agricultura em Minas,* pp. 14–15; Peixoto, *A crise do assucar,* pp. 153–58; F. W. Dafert, *"A falta de trabalhadores agricolas em São Paulo," Relatório annual do Instituto Agronômico do Estado de São Paulo (Brasil) em Campinas, 1892* (São Paulo, 1893), pp. 201–09.

III

The National Crisis and Abolition

7: The Radicalization of Stances: Abolitionism and Antiabolitionism

AFTER PASSAGE of the Saraiva-Cotegipe Law, the positions of many abolitionists and slaveholders hardened significantly. Radical abolitionists loudly repudiated the effectiveness of moderate tactics; intransigent slave proprietors announced their determination to crush further abolitionist challenges. The battle lines were drawn as leaders from both sides of the controversy prepared to match words with action. As radicals from each camp gained the spotlight, the much more numerous groups in the middle positions of the controversy looked on nervously. Most Brazilians were growing tired of the mounting political crises. With their options seeming to narrow down principally to a choice between immediate abolition or extending the life of slavery under Minister Cotegipe's terms, they wondered which policy was more likely to return the country to some measure of political and domestic tranquility. For all practical purposes, the outcome of the rising confrontation between radical abolitionists and radical slavocrats would determine their decision and, consequently, the fate of slavery.

The rapid evolution of the abolitionist position was extraordinary. When abolitionists began their campaign as a small but dedicated minority in 1880, many of them realized the immensity of the task and toned down their demands to levels that indicated a willingness to compromise with the powerful slaveholding interests. As the campaign progressed, the interest in compromise gradually faded until, in the last year of slavery, the cry of almost all of the abolitionists was "Immediate and unconditional emancipation!" Moreover, abolitionists changed their views about the means to achieve their goal. While most began the movement emphasizing peaceful, political approaches to the problem of slavery, they closed their campaign by advocating direct resistance against the institution, even by breaking the law. In short, the movement became increasingly radical.

Although the most salient departures from moderate abolitionism date from the reaction to the Saraiva-Cotegipe Law, some of the changes toward a more radical posture were evident in the early years of the campaign. For example, in the 1883–1885 period many abolitionists began to feel that it was much more worthwhile to put their financial resources into propaganda campaigns than to purchase a few isolated liberations. The whole concept of raising funds through ceremonial meetings and programs conducted by emancipation societies fell under the charge of immorality. Since abolitionist literature repudiated the idea of human bondage, it seemed inconsistent to pay slaveholders to free their bondsmen. The practice might be considered informal recognition of the right to own slaves. Practical concerns also guided the change in policy. With slave prices at high levels in the South, the collection of funds could, at best, unshackle only a small number of Negroes. A different approach to abolition had to be found. As the editor of the *Gazeta da Tarde* explained the need for change, "The small capital used for the printing of *Uncle Tom's Cabin* gave incomparably better results than a thousand times that capital used for emancipations and thus handing it to the enemies of emancipation." [1]

Related to this change in attitudes was a significant reconsideration of the abolitionist position on the larger, political question of indemnification. Earlier, many abolitionists had been willing to include financial remuneration for

1. *Gazeta da Tarde,* June 7, 1886, p. 1.

the slaveholders as an integral part of major emancipation legislation. By 1884, however, most abolitionists dropped the idea, and by 1885 even many emancipators did not see the demand for compensation as plausible.

Abolitionists developed three major arguments to explain their disapproval of monetary indemnification. The first explanation resembled their rationale for rejecting purchase of individual liberations. Because abolitionists emphasized humanitarian sentiments, they reasoned that they could not sanction payment for an institution they described as illegitimate. Immoral slavery had done the Negroes a great injustice, they said, and masters should not be paid for having made them slaves.[2] Second, abolitionists argued that the slaves had already paid for themselves. Estimates ranged from two to five years for the amount of time required for the slave to make up in production profits to his master the cost of his market price and living expenses. Therefore, the abolitionists calculated that the slaves had paid for their own freedom many times over.[3] Finally, the enormous cost of redemption had to be considered. Joaquim Nabuco described the problem in a speech to his constituents in the 1884 election campaign:

> Gentlemen, immediate emancipation with indemnification is foolishness. We do not have the means to fill our annual deficit; where are we going to get 300 or 600 thousand contos to redeem our slaves? . . . Brazil is not sufficiently rich to pay for its crime! [4]

The most serious indications of radicalization within the movement came from frustrated abolitionists who became outspokenly intolerant of the way their appeals for emancipation reform seemed to elicit more reaction than action in

2. Frank Bennett, *Forty Years in Brazil* (London, 1914), p. 112; Abdias do Nascimento, *et. al., O negro brasileiro: 80 Anos de abolição* (Rio de Janeiro, 1968), p. 21.
3. *Gazeta da Tarde,* June 5, 1883, p. 2; January 18, 1884, p. 2.
4. Joaquim Nabuco, *Campanha abolicionista no Recife* (Rio de Janeiro, 1885), pp. 36–37.

government circles. "With abolitionist propaganda you don't win fame," complained Gaspar da Silva of the São Paulo Abolitionist Center. "You get antipathy, you get insults, you get coarse remarks. . . ."[5] Some hinted that more extreme tactics might be necessary if they continued to be denounced and blocked in their propaganda efforts. Angered by the slavocrat attempts to suppress abolitionist activities, an anonymous writer in the *Gazeta da Tarde* warned that history would not show the abolitionists to be the first to take the dangerous road to insurrection in efforts to guarantee their rights:

> If we go out into the street armed, it will be after provocations and violence on the part of our adversaries, by the right of legitimate defense and in favor of a great cause that is, at the same time, a cause of the law and of Liberty![6]

Such pronouncements remained exceptional before 1885. It was the remarkable spread of antislavery sentiment throughout Brazil that did much to inflate the confidence of abolitionists and inspire hope that their growing popularity could influence the decisions of Parliament. Increasingly, they claimed the support of "the people" and concluded that their movement represented the sentiments of the majority of the population. Perceiving that their campaign succeeded in fermenting the social and political situation greatly, abolitionists spoke with more and more assurance of the "inevitability" of the early death of slavery. Their hopes soared especially during the year of haggling over the Dantas proposals. By exerting great effort to appeal to the masses of non-slaveholders and encourage them to break their silence to join the campaign in impressive numbers, abolitionists expected to capitalize on a groundswell of support that would put new forms of pressure on the statesmen of the empire. But as Dantas' work became bogged down in the mud of pro-

5. *Gazeta da Tarde,* May 15, 1883, p. 2.
6. *Ibid.,* December 7, 1883, p. 1.

slaveholder obstruction, abolitionist frustration and impatience mounted.

The failure of Senator Dantas to bring his optimistic goals to fruition illustrated the shortcoming of the antislavery strategy which predominated in 1885. When Dantas assumed office as Prime Minister, he announced a project which he hoped would respect both humanitarian sentiments and the rights of property. His abortive efforts demonstrated the difficulty of trying to compromise the two issues. Following their major failure, abolitionists asked an old question with new urgency: What could be expected from a "Parliament of slaveholders"? As long as influential planters controlled the instruments of power, it seemed the interests of "property" would always be considered paramount to the interests of "humanity." Even as late as 1886, the best that slavocrat Antônio Coelho Rodrigues could offer abolitionists was a suggestion that any solution adopted be reasonable, voluntary, and peaceful while preparing slaves for free labor, preventing vagabondage and avoiding economic harm to the planters. Rigid adherence to all of these qualifications could delay abolition indefinitely.[7]

Abolitionists now reconsidered their approach. Appeals to the benevolence of the slaveholders, so popular in the early years of the campaign, now appeared misguided. In June 1885 Rui Barbosa said he understood why abolitionists spent much time asking the proprietors to view the problem with a spirit of charity and philanthropy, but it would be unrealistic to expect the heroic initiative of abolitionism to come from the slaveholders:

> The planters do not represent abolitionist opinion, and by the irrefutable force of their interests, distrust it, fear it, and oppose it more or less directly, more or less energetically. The situation belongs to the abolitionists;

7. *Annaes da Câmara* (1887), V, 379; Broadside by Joaquim Nabuco, without title, July 7, 1881, Instituto Joaquim Nabuco; Almelia de Rezende Martins, *Um idealista realizador: Barão Geraldo de Rezende* (Campinas, n.d.), p. 362.

> because they are the ones who created it, imposing the slavery issue on the parties.[8]

Passage of the Saraiva-Cotegipe Law marked a turning point in abolitionist strategy. As mentioned in Chapter III, the original project of emancipationist Souza Dantas was so completely changed that the final form proved more satisfactory to the slave proprietors than to the abolitionists. Among the most noxious aspects of the law was a provision establishing a fine of 500 to 1,000 milreis for anyone found guilty of attempting to lure away or shelter slaves. Joaquim Nabuco later conjectured that the defenders of slavery would have better served their interests by accepting the Dantas plan because their rejection of it made abolitionists less tolerant of temporizing solutions and more insistent on immediate, unqualified emancipation.[9]

To many abolitionists, it now seemed that the goal of complete liberation at an early date could not be achieved without extralegal activities. The rhetoric of their antislavery propaganda became more radical as leaders announced their readiness to sponsor direct resistance to the slavery regime. In a new war chant in 1886, José do Patrocínio declared:

> Abolitionist propaganda should not show any more scruples. . . . Slavery should not exist tomorrow, because it is tolerated too much today. The society is not obligated to respect laws that defend institutions contrary to its political, moral and economic development. Now slavery is one of those institutions. Where it has reigned it has polluted the souls and sterilized the soil. . . . No

8. Rui Barbosa, *Conferência abolicionista realisada a 7 de junho de 1885 no Theatro Polytheama da Corte* (Bahia, 1885), pp. 12–13, 51–52.

9. *Gazeta da Tarde,* June 7, 1886, p. 1; September 21, 1886, p. 1; Christiano B. Ottoni, *Autobiographia de C. B. Ottoni* (Rio de Janeiro, 1908, p. 280; Tobias do Rêgo Monteiro, *Pesquisas e depoimentos para a história* (Rio de Janeiro, 1913), Introduction, p. 9; M. Gomez de Mattos (*et. al.*), Commissão Central Emancipadora—Recife to Joaquim Nabuco, June 12, 1886, Instituto Joaquim Nabuco; *Gazeta da Tarde,* June 7, 1886, p. 1; September 21, 1886, p. 1.

> one is obligated to respect slavery; by the contrary, every citizen ought to combat it by every means.
>
> Against slavery all means are legitimate and good.[10]

João Ramos, a leader of the Underground Railroad in Pernambuco, stressed the same theme: All approaches were acceptable in the fight to bring down the institution.[11] Specifically, this meant that abolitionists should direct their propaganda to the slaves as well as the free masses. The *Gazeta da Tarde* warned:

> Remember that our century has sometimes demonstrated that the power is not with the legislature, nor the minister, but with the people, who once in a while impress upon their pseudo masters that slavery only subsists while the slaves tolerate it.[12]

Antislavery spokesman Luís Anselmo Fonseca suggested that the slaves stage a "revolt of inertia." He also urged the bondsmen to flee from the *fazendas* and declared that such behavior was in accord with the principles of the Church and the teachings of Jesus.[13] Some critics of slavery openly countenanced revolt. Raúl Pompea, for example, argued that insurrection was consistent with human nature.[14]

During the 1886–1888 period, abolitionists who combined radical rhetoric with radical action drew considerable attention and rocketed to prominence in the galaxy of abolitionist heroes. Of this group, Antônio Bento achieved highest stature. Bento was a relatively obscure abolitionist in São Paulo until his radical words and deeds of the post-1885 period gave him

10. *Gazeta da Tarde,* June 22, 1886, p. 1.
11. Olegario Mariano, *A abolição da escravatura e os homens do Norte: Conferência pronunciada na sessão inaugural do auditório da Gazeta em São Paulo, aos 3 de novembro de 1939* (São Paulo, 1939), pp. 177–78.
12. *Gazeta da Tarde,* August 13, 1885, p. 1.
13. Luís Anselmo da Fonseca, *A escravidão, o clero, e o abolicionismo* (Bahia, 1887), p. 645.
14. Evaristo de Moraes, *A campanha abolicionista: 1879–1888* (Rio de Janeiro, 1924), pp. 263–64.

notoriety in the slaveholder camp. Through his own newspaper, *A Redempção,* Bento published blunt, hard-hitting blows couched in terms even more severe than those used in most other popular, polemical abolitionist periodicals. Rather than moderating the tone of criticism when speaking specifically of the planter class, Bento's paper featured venomous attacks on the slaveholders. It severely denounced the proprietors as a parasitic class and also condemned those who worked for them. For example, one of its verses included the following lines:

> Further on I saw the overseer, there in the field
> —The ferocious and bloody executioner
> What a bad and rancorous man
> Of unequaled perversity and wicked repute
>
> I was not far from the residence
> of the rich slavocrat fazendeiro
> A bragging, aristocratic noble
> of ugly appearance and soiled face [15]

Most important, Bento directed a well-organized movement to encourage slaves to flee from the plantations and assist them in finding refuge and employment. Bento's notable successes inspired other abolitionists who were engaged in similar activities —figures such as Carlos de Lacerda of Campos and Americo Luz of Ouro Prêto.

The Brazilian Fugitive Slave Law ironically turned out to be a godsend to radical abolitionists just as in the case of the American Fugitive Slave Law of 1850. Framers of the Saraiva-Cotegipe Law designed this provision to protect the slaveholders against the mischievous activities of abolitionists who assisted and protected runaway bondsmen. But implementation of the Fugitive Slave Law only irritated the free population and converted great numbers of them into active abolitionists. As numerous fugitives ran away to seek refuge in abolitionist centers, many Brazilians winced at the sight of slave-catchers pushing their way into homes and public buildings to search

15. *A Redempção,* February 27, 1887, p. 2.

for their prey and directing the chained escapees back to the plantations. This situation turned the slavery issue into more than just a matter of philosophical and political debate; increasingly it touched the personal lives of Brazil's urban citizens who viewed the tragic scenes in their own neighborhoods. In 1887–1888, many townspeople began to assist the radical abolitionists by disobeying the Fugitive Slave Law and interfering with efforts to capture runaways. Even "dignified" abolitionists like Rui Barbosa and Joaquim Nabuco broke from restraint and dropped their insistence that abolitionism be kept within legal channels. Indignant over the Fugitive Slave Law, Barbosa predicted a response similar to the reaction of abolitionists in the United States. "I would like to know if there is, in this auditorium, a coward so vile as to obey such a law," he asked a crowd of followers. Barbosa announced that if slave-hunters invaded his home looking for fugitives, he would throw them out with bloody force.[16] Joaquim Nabuco called for national resistance against slavery and announced, "The moment has arrived in which action ought to be substituted for propaganda. . . ."[17]

During this time the large middle group of "emancipationists" began to move to the left on the slavery question. Senator Christiano Ottoni's views exemplify the opinion of many emancipationists who became more and more amenable to reform as the antislavery movement spread across the empire and took a more radical turn. At the time of the debates over the Rio Branco Law, Ottoni stood with the conservative opposition on many points, criticizing various emancipation proposals as too progressive. But the publication in the early 1880s of the first fairly reliable statistics on the effects of the 1871 legislation led him to reconsider his position and become an important spokesman for a more productive law. Ottoni still saw indemnification as a legal necessity and a gradual

16. Barbosa, *Conferência abolicionista,* pp. 40–41; Rui Barbosa, *Abolicionismo,* in *Obras Completas de Rui Barbosa* (Rio de Janeiro, 1955), Vol. XIV, Tomo I, pp. 18–23.

17. *O Paíz,* October 25, 1887, p. 1.

phase-out of slavery over several years as imperative to avoid economic disaster. Yet he remained flexible on these points and continued to sway as the abolitionist breeze swirled to gale force. During the year of controversy over the Dantas proposal, Ottoni renounced his demand for pecuniary indemnification, substituting a plan requiring freedmen to labor for a specified term. Most important, he gave his support to the drive for new legislation, albeit moderate, because he feared the alternative of inaction:

> I am persuaded that, if the public powers do not demonstrate their intention of accelerating liberation by serious acts, it will be done violently, by means of true anarchy and civil war, characterized by assassinations with the whip, inspired by fear of the masters; partial insurrections, killings, horrors. I pray to God that this fear is imaginary.[18]

Ottoni had hoped that the Saraiva-Cotegipe Law would provide answers to the problems with the proper spirit of compromise, but within a short time he realized that the law was hopelessly inadequate in the eyes of the swelling abolitionist population. Guided more by respect for the realities than a pressing moral impulse, Ottoni moved from the "emancipationist" to the "abolitionist" camp. He sought to expedite liberation to prevent the sparks of abolitionist activity from touching off a powder keg. Despite the temporary tranquility, there was still fire below the ashes, warned Ottoni in February of 1887, and the fire could rage again.[19] Several other important political leaders who had been identified as "emancipationists" also responded to a variety of pressures and switched to an "abolitionist" position in the 1885–1886 period. They repudiated the right to monetary indemnification and began advocating complete abolition within a few years. Indicative of this development were the conversions of Manuel Pinto de Souza Dantas of Bahia, José Bonifácio of São Paulo, and Affonso Celso of Minas Gerais.

18. Ottoni, *Autobiographia de C. B. Ottoni,* p. 270.
19. *Ibid.*, pp. 264, 267, 286, 292; *Annaes da Câmara* (1884), June 9, pp. 33–34; *Annaes do Senado* (1886), September 28, p. 279.

On the other hand, many slaveholders tried to tighten their grip on the situation by implementing restrictive, often repressive policies in the face of increased abolitionist agitation. Their reaction developed in response to the first signs of a growing abolitionist movement, then became more forceful as antislavery sentiment gained strength.

Throughout the 1880s, pro-slaveholder spokesmen pointed to the dangers of abolitionism as the main justification for taking direct action against the movement. They scored the abolitionists for employing illegal, subversive means to upset the order of rural society, charging that these actions could be associated with new outbreaks of slave rebellions and assassinations of masters and overseers. Antislavery leaders were preaching directly to the slaves, telling the captives they had the right to repel force with force and, therefore, should murder their superiors.[20] It was reported that the *fazendeiros* were working in an environment of constant anxiety because of the frequent bloody scenes caused by the agitators of slaves.[21] As one defender of slavery described the situation, "The nation appears tranquil on the surface but it is in revolt in depth. . . ." [22] If the abolitionist challenge could not be repelled, it appeared that the plantation society would be dragged into a serious social and economic crisis. Senator Gasper Silveira Martins had recognized the potential danger as early as 1880 when he charged that the efforts of the antislavery press to excite the slaves weakened the moral force of the masters and gave the captives incentive for insurrection. Such agitation would leave the families of the most important class in the country "to the ferocity of a barbarous race. . . ." Silveira Martins believed that "what is mortally wounded in this dispute is the moral force of the master, the principle of authority, the law! And what is the consequence of this

20. *Gazeta da Tarde,* January 11, 1881; *Annaes do Senado,* 1880, pp. 521–22; *Rio News,* May 3, 1884, p. 2.

21. *Annaes da Câmara* (1884), I, 223.

22. Antônio Coelho Rodrigues, *Manual de um subdito fiel ou cartas de um lavrador a sua magestade o Imperador sôbre a questão do elemento servil* (Rio de Janeiro, 1884), p. 68.

general disrespect but general anarchy?"[23] In the same year one of the powerful Hard-Core *fazendeiros* of northern São Paulo, Moreira de Barros, had warned his fellow slaveholders that the antislavery propaganda which seemed insignificant at the time could some day cause the complete ruin of the agricultural class. Planters in the United States had not realized the danger of the challenge until it was too late. Brazilian *fazendeiros* would not make the same mistake, insisted Moreira de Barros, because they would smash the movement before it gained momentum.[24]

In the early part of the decade, planters' clubs became a popular form of opposition. Two waves of organizational activity occurred, each in response to the intensification of the abolitionist campaign. The first wave appeared in late 1880 and early 1881, at the time of Nabuco's challenges in Parliament and the formation of the Brazilian Anti-Slavery Society. The second came in response to abolitionist activities during the period of Dantas' rise to power in 1884. At that time, slaveholders formed powerful groups such as the Centro do Café, Centro da Lavoura, and the Club da Lavoura to coordinate activities. In Limeira, Lorena, Brotas, Pinhal, and numerous other small communities, planters copied larger organizations on the local level. Many clubs operated under the guise of interest in matters of agriculture as well as politics, but the *raison d'être* of almost all of them centered on the campaign against abolitionists. A few planters joined clubs with the belief that cooperative groups would offer much-needed information about new techniques in agriculture, but they soon resigned in disillusionment.[25]

23. *O Cruzeiro,* November 2, 1880, p. 2.

24. Later, when the abolitionist movement began to draw much popular support, pro-slaveholder spokesmen urged aggressive action. "You don't respond to violence by begging for mercy!", shouted Martinho Campos. Similarly, Martim Francisco warned, "In our province we even resist with firearms," and the newspaper *Diário do Brasil* asked slaveholders to reply in kind to the "robberies" of the abolitionists. See Carolina Nabuco, *The Life of Joaquim Nabuco* (Stanford, 1950), pp. 57, 78; *Gazeta da Tarde,* January 8, 1881, p. 2; August 5, 1884, p. 1; January 5, 1885, p. 1.

25. *Rio News,* March 24, 1881, p. 3.

The planters' clubs called for vigorous counter-propaganda to check the antislavery movement. Their leaders vowed not to patronize doctors, lawyers, or merchants who supported abolitionism and spoke against the "inertia" of public authorities in facing provocation.[26] They also announced their determination to meet abolitionist threats forcefully. This was reflected, for example, in an article in the constitution of one of the clubs, which read:

> The standing committee is authorized to use such measures as it may seem efficacious against those who start an abolition press in the municipality or who shall have any dealings with abolitionists either within it or outside it.[27]

Slaveholders employed a variety of means to try to silence abolitionist voices. When abolitionist meetings drew widespread attention, they responded with deceptive tactics. Frequently they pressured public authorities into having the abolitionists' public conferences transferred to different assembly halls shortly before the conferences were scheduled to start in order to confuse the people attending them.[28] André Rebouças described such an incident in which his group was denied use of one of the principal theaters in Rio de Janeiro. Quickly the abolitionists moved to an alternate meeting place where, with the public waiting outside, Rebouças and José do Patrocínio swept the theater aisles.[29] Sometimes slaveholders hired men to assault street vendors who sold the *Gazeta da Tarde*.[30] They also applied pressure to purge newspaper editors and writers who were favorable to abolition. In 1884, when the Dantas proposals electrified debates, Joaquim Serra was obliged to leave the publication *Folha Nova,* and an attempt was made to dismiss the manager of the *Província de São*

26. *Gazeta de Campinas,* February 12, 1881, p. 2; *Província de São Paulo,* January 16, 1881, p. 2; January 20, 1881, p. 1; *Brazil,* May 20, 1884, p. 2; May 25, 1884, p. 2; June 1, 1884, p. 2; June 3, 1884, p. 1.
27. Quoted by Christiano Ottoni in *Rio News,* July 5, 1884, p. 2.
28. Osório Duque-Estrada, *A abolição: 1831–1888* (Rio de Janeiro, 1918), pp. 208–11.
29. André Rebouças, *Diário e notas autobiográficas.* Edited by Ana Flora and Inácio José Veríssimo (Rio de Janeiro, 1938), p. 293.
30. *Gazeta da Tarde,* January 8, 1881, p. 2.

Paulo.[31] This resistance campaign carried over into the political arena. Slaveholders succeeded in purging José Mariano from the Chamber of Deputies because of his abolitionist activities, and in Rio de Janeiro Alvaro de Lacerda was not allowed to take his seat in the provincial assembly.[32] Political leaders made a similar attempt against Joaquim Nabuco by influencing the Chamber of Deputies to vote, 58–51, to take away his seat, but another abolitionist deputy then relinquished his chair to Nabuco.[33]

After the passage of the 1885 law, the pro-slavery Conservative party government of the Baron of Cotegipe resolved to abandon concessions and stage a battle to the death. The Cotegipe group used all the tricks of electoral manipulation at its disposal to block abolitionists from gaining voices in the government, and they were successful until the abolitionist wave of 1887–1888 overwhelmed them.

To complement Cotegipe's work, from 1885 on, slave proprietors, their hirelings, and local political associates became conspicuously active in direct efforts to crush the antislavery movement. Planters' clubs in Campos paid the rent for the city's police station and subsidized the policemen's salaries, while a group in Campinas set up a fund of 40 contos for use in any way that would contribute toward extermination of the abolitionist campaign. Planters' organizations also subsidized pro-slavery newspapers.[34] Opponents of abolitionism used harassing tactics too. They set off firecrackers at meetings, hecklers intimidated the speakers, and rowdies broke in armed with revolvers, turning the conferences into scenes of chaos.[35] Often they resorted to brazen acts of violence. A group of toughs broke into the offices of the *Gazeta da Tarde,* and in

31. Stanley J. Stein, "The Historiography of Brazil: 1808–1889," *Hispanic American Historical Review* (May 1960), p. 276; Rebouças, *Diário e notas autobiográficas,* p. 303.

32. *O Paíz,* November 23, 1887, p. 1.

33. Rebouças, *Diário,* p. 304.

34. *O Paíz,* October 17, 1887, p. 1; Fonseca, *A escravidão, o clero e o abolicionismo,* pp. 569–70; *Gazeta da Tarde,* January 19, 1887, p. 2.

35. *Gazeta da Tarde,* May 7, 1887, p. 2; August 9, 1887, p. 2.

Campos ruffians attacked the offices of the *Gazeta do Povo* and totally destroyed the press of the *Vinte e Cinco de Março*.[36] Policemen actually joined a throng of enraged citizens in destroying the equipment of one of the abolitionist organs in Recife, *O Rabate*.[37] Adversaries of the abolitionists also beat individuals on the streets, and in some places antislavery leaders could not risk leaving their homes at night.[38] Threats were made on the lives of radical abolitionists, such as Antônio Bento and Carlos de Lacerda, and each of them lost a close associate through murders committed by henchmen of the slavocrats.[39] The terror even affected representatives of the law. Antiabolitionist groups threatened reformist judges with assassination, physically pulled magistrates off the bench when they delivered decisions in favor of slaves, and invaded the homes of some abolitionist lawyers and judges.[40]

The situation became especially explosive in the city of Campos in the province of Rio de Janeiro. In 1887 during a time of extensive slave insurrections in the area, Alvaro de Lacerda, a member of the provincial assembly, planned to give an antislavery speech before a public gathering. When the authorities prohibited the meeting, Lacerda spoke to the group from a window in his home. Suddenly, policemen charged into the crowd. The people hurled stones at the police, but finally the crowd was dispersed with gunshots. A few days later Lacerda called another meeting. As the police began searching those who entered the hall for weapons, a group of angry Negro freedmen attacked the police with stones, bottles, and firearms. Fighting again broke out, and for several days Campos remained in a state of high tension and chaos as bands of policemen and hirelings of the slavocrats patrolled the city

36. *Ibid.*, January 5, 1885, p. 1; *Cidade do Rio,* October 26 and 27, 1887; November 10, 1887, p. 1.

37. *Revista Illustrada,* August 13, 1887, p. 8.

38. *A Redempção,* July 28, 1887, p. 3; *Gazeta da Tarde,* May 10, 1886.

39. *Gazeta da Tarde,* May 14, 1886, p. 1; Moraes, *A campanha abolicionista,* p. 241.

40. *Annaes do Senado* (1884), June 9, pp. 42–43.

with guns. The incidents resulted in the wounding of several citizens and one death. A municipal judge who viewed the bloody hostilities shouted: "Stop! Don't continue! I am horified! Never have I seen such scenes in my land!" [41]

When abolitionist agitation became especially threatening in 1887, Cotegipe's government turned to a policy of outright repression. The ministry officially banned abolitionist meetings in August of that year.[42] The decree was effective for a while in the city of Rio de Janeiro, where the police physically intervened to dissolve several conferences and patrolled the streets in a manner resembling martial law.[43] The newspaper *Novidades* justified the strong action taken by the government because, it declared, while the meetings were working under the pretext of abolitionist goals, they were really planning revolutionary action. The police were correct in impeding a meeting for the sake of public order. A meeting is "tolerated"; it is not a "right." These conferences were dangerous, explained the editors, because they were the work of anarchists and subversives seeking an attack on the country's basic institutions.[44] Although the government's repression of meetings temporarily inconvenienced the abolitionists, within a short time the policy began to backfire. It gave antislavery groups tremendous emotional support from citizens who were outraged by restrictions on the right of assembly. Despite the ban, 2,000 protesters gathered in the city of São Paulo and 1,000 in Ouro Prêto to voice their indignation.[45] It soon became strikingly clear that the policy only served to bring greater embarrassment to the government.

The slaveholders' desperate resistance to the growing abo-

41. *Cidade do Rio,* November 21, 22, 23, 1887; *O Paíz,* November 21, 22, 23, 1887.

42. Fonseca, *A escravidão, o clero e a abolicionismo,* pp. 569–70. Rui Barbosa called the suspension of constitutional guarantees "a provocation to civil war." Barbosa, *Abolicionismo,* p. 23.

43. *Rio News,* August 15, 1887, p. 2.

44. *Novidades,* August 12 and 13, 1887.

45. *Gazeta da Tarde,* August 12, 1887, p. 1; *Revista Illustrada,* September 30, 1887, pp. 4–6.

litionist threat was understandable, but the more they tried to stop it, the more their policies seemed to strengthen the forces of opposition. In earlier years slaveholders had been able to identify themselves as the defenders of public order and tranquility, but now their efforts to apprehend fugitives and repress abolitionist activities made them look more like instigators of disorder. By making a determined stand to resist significant change at a time when the protests increasingly seemed to be getting out of hand, they further inflamed opponents of slavery and pushed many of the non-committed into the abolitionist camp. As Joaquim Nabuco so well expressed the situation in his memoirs: "No one knows who did more for abolition: if it was those who wanted everything, or those who wanted nothing." [46]

Slavery in Brazil now moved into its final crisis, a breakdown which underscored the substance of the slaveholders' oft-stated fears. For decades they had warned about the dangers of raising the captives' aspirations and whetting their appetite for freedom. Proprietors frequently complained that the greatest threat of reform legislation lay in the possibility that it could heighten the slaves' awareness of potential liberty. When resigned to a lifetime in slavery, bondsmen were relatively manageable; but once stirred by the prospect of freedom, their attitude could become rebellious. This much-feared prospect became a reality in 1887–1888.

46. Joaquim Nabuco, *Minha formação* (São Paulo, 1934), p. 200.

8: The Collapse of Slavery

IT IS CHARACTERISTIC of many revolutionary situations that the radical developments which lead to them occur not when the condition of the aggrieved is at its lowest ebb but when moderate improvements in conditions awaken the masses with the hope of change. Indeed, the reforms brought about by the Supreme Court decisions, civil-rights activities, and new federal legislation in the United States between 1954 and 1965 contributed significantly to creating an environment in which the strong demands and militant activities of the "Black Revolution" of the late 1960s could flourish. To a degree, this pattern applies to Brazil's slavery crisis. If the developments of September 1887 to May 1888 may be considered "revolutionary," the sources of this upheaval can be traced, in part, to the changes that occurred in the two preceding years when a campaign to effect legal reforms within the system of slavery made impressive gains. These changes were not directed toward abolition *per se,* for the obstacles erected by the Cotegipe regime temporarily hindered the possibilities of such a comprehensive approach to emancipation. Instead, the developments represented an attempt to make the institution of slavery more humane and to guarantee the bondsmen's legal rights. Ultimately, these changes undermined the moral authority of the *senhores* and created conditions favorable to the radical abolitionists. Antislavery activists who had adopted extremist tactics capitalized on the weakening of slavery's institutional underpinnings. When the contagion of abolitionist agitation reached the slave quarters, many bondsmen were already aware of the growing limitations on the slave proprietors' coercive powers. The slaves' response to the abolitionists' promises of asylum and the deterioration of planter control strained the order and stability of Brazilian society in the last volatile year of slavery, as a wave of violence and upheaval accompanied the abolitionist campaign.

It was in the aftermath of the Saraiva-Cotegipe Law, when the Imperial Government's official stand on abolition had hardened significantly and several abolitionists began planning radical tactics, that some important individuals turned their attention toward modifying and reinterpreting the legal provisions regarding the status of slaves. If slavery was not to be abolished outright in the immediate future, at least they hoped to ameliorate the condition of the bondsmen. This legalistic approach especially provided opportunities for leadership from professional people of high social and political status such as lawyers, senators, and judges—individuals who usually held secure political positions which provided effective sounding boards to press for changes in legislation and judicial procedures. Lawyers scrutinized the smallest details of the laws, requesting that legislative provisions be interpreted liberally to protect the slaves against cruel treatment and to grant them liberty whenever possible. In the meantime, while deputies tried to avoid discussion of issues related to the antislavery campaign, senators approached some major questions head on, especially the matter of prohibiting certain forms of slave castigation. Their courage in raising such issues can be traced, in part, to the independence afforded them by the constitutional system. The composition of the Senate did not fluctuate radically with changes in ministries as did the Chamber of Deputies. Senators served life terms and did not fear addressing sensitive topics as much as members of the lower house, who experienced weighty day-to-day pressures from their constituents, and the chief minister, who helped secure their election.

Ironically, in their campaign to humanize the conditions of slavery, leaders of the legalist movement focused a good deal of attention on the much criticized Saraiva-Cotegipe Law. In spite of their strong reservations about the law, lawyers and senators found means to interpret some of the provisions liberally. They maintained that the 1885 legislation redefined the legal position of the slaves, because many of its clauses placed slaves under the civil codes (including civil criminal codes), thus giving them quasi-civil status. Rather than being true bondsmen, slaves really lived in a transitional state, with the government committed to protecting their rights in the short run and emancipating them in the long run. They pointed out that the law guaranteed the slave's right to deposit funds to purchase his freedom and provided for eventual liberation through tax-supported funds and a table of depreciating values. Such evidence led Affonso Celso, José Bonifácio, and Rui Barbosa to interpret the slave's condition flexibly, viewing it as analogous to the status of privileged bondsmen in Roman times.[1]

Antiabolitionists would not accept flexible construction of the law. Cotegipe rejected it flatly. J. Baptista Pereira, who specialized in interpreting the complex provisions of the Saraiva-Cotegipe Law, berated his fellow lawyers for endorsing the new arguments. Slaves were still slaves, he insisted. As long as they could be bought and sold as objects of commerce and be listed as the legal property of individuals, their condition as chattel laborers could not be denied. Pereira worried that the courts might adopt the "quasi-civil status" argument. In this event, the presumption of liberty in controversial cases would rest with the slave, and the burden of proving otherwise would be the responsibility of the master. Eventually, loose construction of the law could serve to emancipate many slaves. Judges would become abolitionists, thought Pereira, in essence legislators. Actually, under Brazilian practice judges had very modest roles in interpreting the laws, he argued. Any radical resolution of the slavery problem was a job for the legislatures, not the courts.[2]

The legal position of Pereira and others represented a significant about-face from pro-slaveholder policy of earlier years.

1. *Rio News,* September 24, 1886, pp. 2–4; J. Baptista Pereira, *Da condição actual dos escravos—especialmente após a promulgação da lei n.3270 de 28 de Setembro de 1885* (Rio de Janeiro, 1887), pp. 7–12, 22–25, 29–31; Affonso Celso, *Reposta de uma impugnação* (Rio de Janeiro, 1885); Rui Barbosa, *Abolicionismo* in *Obras completas de Rui Barbosa* (Rio de Janeiro, 1955), Vol. XIV, 1887, Tomo I, pp. 35–66.

2. Pereira, *Da condição actual dos escravos,* pp. 7–12, 22–25, 29–31.

At the beginning of the abolitionist campaign slave proprietors could effectively influence judges' decisions, and they sanctioned power for the courts. In one famous instance, when an abolitionist asked the Prime Minister if the 1831 law was still in effect, the government leader replied that such matters were the responsibility of the judicial branch.[3] During the 1886–1888 period, however, the rising tide of urban abolitionism inclined judges to make decisions in favor of slaves. In several important cases, magistrates declared them free or assessed their value at one-tenth or one-twentieth of what masters considered the market rate.[4]

The new inclination of judges helped not only to clear the way for progressive interpretations of the 1885 law but also for the first time to put teeth into the 1831 legislation which had provided for the liberation of Africans illegally transported to Brazil. Abolitionists demanded that the courts make masters responsible for proving the servile status of their bondsmen. Most important, abolitionists asked for a declaration of liberty when masters listed their slaves' country of origin as "unknown" in the registration provided by the Saraiva-Cotegipe Law. Checking the category of "unknown" was presumably an attempt to hide African origins, said the abolitionists; therefore, the benefit of doubt should be given to the slaves. When data from Campos for 1887 showed that about 13,000 slaves had not been properly registered in the area because of their African background, antislavery leaders held protest meetings to publicize the injustices. Even the Minister of Agriculture of the Imperial Government admitted that the information revealed gross irregularities. In the last years of slavery abolitionist lawyers achieved some notable successes in freeing slaves by haunting slaveholders with the law that had been largely ineffective for more than half a century.[5]

3. *Gazeta da Tarde,* January 4, 1881, p. 2; *Rio News,* November 15, 1880, p. 2.

4. Edison Carneiro, *Ladinos e crioulos: Estudos sôbre o negro no Brasil* (Rio de Janeiro, 1964), p. 61.

5. *Província de São Paulo,* July 19, 1887, p. 1; *Rio News,* June 24, 1887, p. 4; Barbosa, *Abolicionismo,* pp. 37–42; *Gazeta do Povo,* November 4, 1887, p. 2.

In the environment of an expanding abolitionist movement, some judges extended their powers to the point of testing the fugitive-slave provision of the Saraiva-Cotegipe Law. The most celebrated case occurred in January 1888, when Antônio Rodrigues Monteiro de Azevedo freed two individuals on a charge of sheltering runaway slaves, declaring that their act was not criminal. Azevedo's decision caused a great sensation, paving the way for abolitionists to break the Fugitive Slave Law with impunity.[6]

Perhaps the most important legal reform of the post-1885 era was the law prohibiting use of the whip to punish slaves. It cut right to the heart of the servile institution: the element of coercion. In 1886 the abolitionist press gave special attention to the horrors of slavery, reporting on cases involving brutal treatment of bondsmen and arranging for public display of slaves deformed by torture. Then the editors discovered a political bombshell—a tragic case in which a severe thrashing had inflicted mortal wounds on two captives in Paraíba do Sul, in the province of Rio de Janeiro. Angry citizens cried out against the barbarity, and abolitionists asked for revocation of a specific provision in the criminal code which allowed masters "moderate" powers of castigation. The law dated back to 1835, a time of slave rebellions, when apprehensive leaders designed the legislation as a deterrent to insurrection.[7] Usually there could be little outside control over the use of flogging as a disciplinary measure, and the limitation of "moderate" castigation set by the 1835 legislation carried little weight. Slave proprietors viewed the whip as an essential instrument in maintaining the psychology of fear, and, understandably, they viewed the attempt to check their punitive powers a dangerous move.[8] They predicted that repeal of the

6. *O Paíz,* February 4, 1888, p. 1; Osório Duque-Estrada, *A abolição: 1831–1888* (Rio de Janeiro, 1918), p. 226.

7. C. B. Ottoni, *Autobiographia de C. B. Ottoni* (Rio de Janeiro, 1908), pp. 57–58; *Annaes da Câmara* (1886), October 1, p. 342.

8. Ottoni, *Autobiographia,* pp. 340–42; C. B. Ottoni, *O advento da república no Brasil* (Rio de Janeiro, 1890), pp. 53–56; *Annaes da Câmara* (1886), October 1, p. 342. Just the threat of flogging served to

1835 law would lead to an outbreak of assassinations and jeopardize the safety of the *senhores* and their families. Only the death penalty would remain to deter the most extreme acts of violence, and that had little effect because the Emperor, who opposed capital punishment, usually intervened to commute sentences.[9]

The power of public opinion became too strong for the slaveholders to reverse. Moreover, the issue trapped them in their own arguments. During their debates in favor of the Saraiva-Cotegipe Law they had claimed the legislation would make Brazilian slavery more humane, eliminating the most notorious injustices. Then why fear the exclusion of cruel forms of punishment? asked the supporters of the antiwhipping law. The time had come to prepare bondsmen for their future role as citizens, a goal that could hardly be achieved while they were subjected to barbarous treatment. In ordinary civil matters no individual had sole authority to mete out punishment; magistrates or the court decided on the verdict and penalty. A modern society could no longer tolerate the arbitrary, extralegal regime of the *fazendeiros*.[10] Moved by the public outcry over the case of Paraíba do Sul and impressed by the logic of the debates, senators voted for the prohibition. Some supported the idea as a step toward abolition; others thought it necessary because inaction would hand extreme abolitionists an explosive issue. Once the measure passed the Senate it had the legal punch necessary to be effective, and deputies in the Chamber could do little but add their support. In October 1886 the whipping of slaves became officially outlawed.

Some masters flouted the law and continued to use the whip. In a horrible incident just a year later, a *fazendeiro* in

---

frighten bondsmen into submission. When a recalcitrant or runaway slave had to face punishment, masters often gathered other captives together to witness the event, believing the mental pain suffered by the onlookers would provide an unforgettable example.

9. *Annaes do Senado* (1886), September 28, p. 284; October 11, p. 288; *Annaes da Câmara,* October 11, pp. 292, 307; October 13, p. 481.

10. *Annaes da Câmara* (1886), September 30, p. 289; October 11, pp. 307–08; October 13, p. 482.

Santa Maria Magalena ordered his overseer to give four slaves sixty lashes each on their hands and feet. All four died. Police authorities tried to take the proprietor into custody, but he escaped with the help of other *fazendeiros.*[11] Other, less dramatic abuses occurred too, but the central fact remained that a principal safeguard of the servile regime no longer had official sanction. Senator Silveira da Motta was close to the truth when he said, "Slavery cannot be maintained without corporal punishment."[12]

The abolition of whipping and gains of abolitionists in the court system in the 1887–1888 period gave slaves new confidence in manifesting their grievances. Once they became unafraid that they would face retribution for calling attention to their problems, numerous bondsmen converged upon the cities to protest. In Campinas a slave campaigned among his fellows, urging them to state their cases before the municipal police. One poor captive turned up at the police station with an iron collar around his neck. Later, a group of more than forty blacks presented themselves to the authorities, complaining of maltreatment by their overseer.[13] A group of twenty-nine slaves told the police in Ouro Preto they would return to their plantation only under the condition that their overseer agreed to retire! Others appealed to the judges; in Minas Gerais several bondsmen complained directly to the provincial president.[14]

Thus, in a general sense, the legal bases of slavery in Brazil became more humane in the last three years before abolition than at any time in the nation's history. Although the *abolitionist* movement suffered a setback in 1885, the *antislavery* movement did not. By passing the Saraiva-Cotegipe Law, Parliament

11. Luiz Luna, *O negro na luta contra a escravidão* (Rio de Janeiro, 1968), p. 75; *Relatório* of the Secretary of Police of Rio de Janeiro province, Salvador A. Moniz Barreto de Aragão, June 30, 1888, p. 8; *Revista Illustrada,* October 22, 1887, p. 6.

12. *Annaes do Senado* (1886), September 29, p. 288.

13. *Rio News,* April 15, 1887, p. 3; April 24, 1887, p. 4; *Jornal do Recife,* January 21, 1888, p. 1.

14. *Cidade do Rio,* April 9, 1888, p. 1; Almelia de Rezende Martins, *Um idealista realizador: Barão Geraldo de Rezende* (Campinas, n.d.), p. 359. *Província de Minas,* January 20, 1888, p. 1.

announced it was not ready for quick dismemberment of the institution, but shortly after the decision, senators, government ministers, and local political and judicial leaders succeeded in liberalizing the condition of slaves. Proprietors were prohibited from flogging their bondsmen, slaves began to bring their grievances to the attention of public authorities, and judges, living in urban centers where abolitionism made significant gains, increasingly delivered decisions in favor of the captives. In a variety of cases involving the legal status of slaves, the burden of proof suddenly fell on the masters. These changes challenged the "moral authority" of the *senhores* —their ability to determine their own rules. Despite the presence of various laws to protect bondsmen and help emancipate them, proprietors had traditionally operated with minimal imposition from outside authorities. Ordinarily the *senhor* was final arbiter on his estate, a condition essential to his dominion over servile workers. The system was based on *evasion* of formal laws, not their execution. Effective control depended on the power of masters to interpret regulations according to their own interests and to exclude themselves from rules they found undesirable. Senator Silveira Martins identified the problem with sharp insight when he said, "The servile regime is an exception. When the exceptional laws disappear, slavery is finished." [15] Developments in the 1880s showed that slavery could not be liberalized effectively and remain viable. The institution rested on coercion; liberalization undermined its foundations.

During this time slaves became vaguely aware that the *fazendeiros'* power was no longer absolute, that somehow their masters were being restrained in dealing with them, and that outside the plantation a movement was fast gaining force which questioned the very nature of their status. With the boundaries of the masters' authority becoming clearer and the slaves' opportunities to redress grievances more abundant, conditions turned propitious for the work of radical abolitionists. The

15. *Annaes do Senado* (1886), September 29, p. 288.

environment of legal ferment prepared the ground for extralegal activities. In 1887 abolitionist agitation suddenly touched off a new crisis which first reached explosive proportions in São Paulo and then threatened to engulf other provinces in the early months of 1888.

Until the last phase of the antislavery campaign, both Progressive Planters and Hard-Core Slaveholders from São Paulo stood opposed to abolitionism along with their counterparts in Minas Gerais and Rio de Janeiro. These *fazendeiros* of the "King Coffee" provinces, who possessed more than two-thirds of the slaves in Brazil, formed a bastion of reaction in the debates over slavery. During the 1880s São Paulo surpassed all other provinces in coffee production, and this dynamic economy placed its leaders in a strategic political position. If their resistance could be broken, abolitionism would win a crucial victory. Angered by the unyielding attitude of São Paulo politicians, abolitionists singled out the province as the key post in the slaveholders' perimeter of defense. As late as 1883, the *Rio News* reported that "in São Paulo, there is not only no enthusiasm, but there seems to be decided opposition to emancipation," and José do Patrocínio called São Paulo "the strong fortress of heinous slavism." [16]

Despite the appearance of slaveholder control in São Paulo, conditions existed in the province which could change the situation dramatically. One of the significant but subtle threats to the Paulista proprietors' regime concerned the diversity of the slave population. The great expansion of the São Paulo coffee culture was a phenomenon of the nineteenth century, so that the large majority of the slaves cultivating the land in that province had been brought there within the last sixty years before abolition. Many slaves were natives of Africa who had been transported to Brazil between the time of the promulgation of the law against the slave traffic (1831) and the period when this law became effectively enforced (after 1850). The number of slaves illegally transported from Africa rose sig-

16. *Gazeta da Tarde,* May 31, 1883, p. 1; *Rio News,* February 24, 1883, p. 2.

nificantly between 1845 and 1849, and this illicit traffic claimed mostly young victims. Many of these slaves were still alive and working as bondsmen during the crisis of the 1880s. As the fastest growing region in Brazil in the second half of the nineteenth century, São Paulo received many of the newly imported slaves. Consequently, in the period of the abolitionist movement a large segment of the province's slave population consisted of first-generation Africans or their children. For example, a resident of Jacareí, São Paulo, noted:

> The present slaveholders in Jacareí knew very well that that city was the depository of Africans who were brought from the coast of Africa, after the law, to be sold illegally as slaves.
>
> The majority of the cultivators of Jacareí originated from the immoral and indecent slave traffic.[17]

A large proportion of captives, moreover, had been recently transferred there from the northern provinces of Brazil through the interprovincial slave traffic. Hence, the slave population of São Paulo contained many uprooted people whose ties to the plantations were more tenuous than those of slaves born and raised on the same *fazenda.* As early as 1880 Joaquim Nabuco warned that São Paulo was "endangering its development by receiving in its bosom those elements of disorder and turmoil." [18]

It took an active antislavery movement to stir these restive bondsmen into mass action. The rapid economic progress of São Paulo in the 1880s provided a favorable environment for abolitionist thought. Urban centers rose, attracting a growing

17. Antônio Gomes de Azevedo Sampaio, *Abolicionismo: Considerações geraes do movimento anti-escravista e sua história limitada a Jacarehy* (São Paulo, 1890), p. 55.

18. Gilberto Freyre, *The Mansions and the Shanties: The Making of Modern Brazil* (New York, 1963), pp. 331–32; *Annaes da Câmara* (1880), V, 35. The history of slave escapes, *quilombos* (fugitive communities), and slave rebellions in Brazil involves many examples of upheavals that resulted from the transference of groups from one culture or region to another. The quilombo of Palmares in the seventeenth century and the slave uprisings in Bahia in the nineteenth century are among the most outstanding examples.

population of immigrants, freedmen, and emigrants from other sections of the province and the empire in search of new employment opportunities.[19] Antislavery opinion became especially strong in the cities where liberal ideas found acceptance. Most of the abolitionists conducted their campaigns from the urban centers, and many fugitives found asylum there through the aid of sympathetic public authorities and citizens.

The upheaval that rocked São Paulo's plantation society in the last years of slavery was provoked to a large extent by the radicalization of abolitionist tactics. Frustrated by political setbacks and the ineffectiveness of emancipation funds, many antislavery leaders called for a more daring approach through direct appeals to the slaves on the plantations. They now prepared to take emancipation into their own hands by whisking the bondsmen away from their masters. The underground movement became most effective in São Paulo, where Antônio Bento was its principal leader. By coordinating the efforts of assistants called *caifazes,* Bento systematized the operations. For his bold exploits, contemporaries referred to him as "Liberator of the Province," "The Cid of Abolition in Southern Brazil," and Brazil's John Brown.[20] With some exaggeration, one writer later stated that "abolition in Brazil was São Paulo;

19. Sometimes immigrants incited the spirit of liberty. The presence of these free laborers in São Paulo working close to the bondsmen did much to undermine slavery. See Emília Viotti da Costa, *Da senzala à colônia* (São Paulo, 1966), p. 304. Also, see the comments regarding immigrants in Sáo Paulo in the *Falla* of the president of Bahia, João Capistrano Bandeira de Mello, October 4, 1887, p. 146. Also important were the free Negroes who empathized with their brothers in bondage; sometimes they escorted their own relatives to freedom. These freedmen, who had grown in number significantly in São Paulo, constituted a troublesome threat to the *fazendeiros.* See Florestan Fernandes and Roger Bastide, *Relações sociais entre negros e brancos em São Paulo* (São Paulo, 1955), pp. 38–54; *Cidade do Rio,* November 24, 1887, p. 1.

20. *O Paíz,* March 19, 1888, p. 1; *Cidade do Rio,* February 18, 1888, p. 1; Evaristo de Moraes, *A campanha abolicionista: 1879–1888* (Rio de Janeiro, 1924), p. 261; *A Redempção,* May 13, 1899, pp. 3–4; *Província de São Paulo,* May 17, 1888, p. 1. After abolition, groups of Negroes gathered in front of Bento's home each year on the anniversary of emancipation to celebrate and dance the samba. Edison Carneiro, *Antologia do negro brasileiro* (Rio de Janeiro, n.d.), p. 65.

abolition in São Paulo was Antônio Bento."[21]

Bento made extensive arrangements to coordinate his escape plots and was ably assisted by people from many different social classes. While farmers and Negro freedmen appealed to slaves on the *fazendas,* railroad coachmen guided the fugitives on trains, and lawyers and businessmen sheltered them in their homes. If a *caifaz* had relatives who were slaveowners, he was expected to assist in the escape of at least one slave from his kinsfolk. Bento dramatized this policy himself by arranging to have the *fazenda* of his brother-in-law abandoned by all the slaves. His sister never forgave him for the joke. In another daring scheme, he suddenly appeared at a dance on a large *fazenda* with a band from his religious brotherhood and ten *caifazes.* The wealthy *senhora* of the estate tried to maintain her composure when confronted with the intruder. But when Bento and his entourage left after an hour, a plantation worker confirmed that almost all the slaves had left the *fazenda.*[22]

Slave proprietors tried in vain to counteract Bento's exploits. They denounced him as a highwayman and a bandit, searched his home for fugitives, assaulted his associates, and killed one of his agents. A hired tough even made an attempt on Bento's life, but two *caifazes* were prepared for the plot. They sent the would-be assassin back to his employer with his head shaved as a reminder that he had met Antônio Bento.[23]

Other abolitionists imitated Bento's tactics. Usually working at night, they carried their appeals directly to the *fazendas;* sometimes they gave antislavery literature to slaves who could read. Once, when a São Paulo planter visited his slaves who should have been at work, he found them surrounding one of their comrades, who was reading aloud a speech of Senator

21. Afonso Schmidt, *A marcha, romance da abolição* (1941), p. 290.

22. Evaristo de Moraes, *A campanha abolicionista: 1879–1888* (Rio de Janeiro, 1924), pp. 261–63; *São Paulo e a sua evolução: Conferências realizadas no Centro Paulista em 1926* (Rio de Janeiro, 1927), p. 36.

23. *Gazeta da Tarde,* October 19, 1885; *Rio News,* April 5, 1888; Reneé Thiollier, *Um grande chefe abolicionista: Antônio Bento* (1932), pp. 29–30; João Dornas Filho, *A escravidão no Brasil* (Rio de Janeiro, 1939), p. 185.

Dantas.[24] Often the nocturnal agents counseled flight from the *fazendas,* and sometimes they supplied arms to the slaves.[25]

Slaves began to flee from the plantations in increasing numbers. São Paulo had experienced slave escapes throughout the nineteenth century, but most of these incidents had only involved the efforts of individual bondsmen. Occasionally, a group of slaves would attempt to flee together, but if caught they would be paraded through the streets, whipped, or locked in irons, and the leaders of the conspiracy would face severe punishment as an example to others.[26] For a long time the probability of capture and the penalty for escape remained effective deterrents against collective efforts. In 1887 and 1888, however, the problem of mass exodus from the plantations reached crisis proportions in São Paulo. As abolitionism spread across the province and the cities became hot beds of antislavery agitation and sanctuaries for runaway slaves, the slave proprietors began to lose control of the situation. They could no longer keep the abolitionist "troublemakers" off the plantations or silence the propaganda campaign. Large groups began to leave the *fazendas* in search of freedom. As the newspaper *O Paíz* put it, conditions were getting to the point that the slave who did not flee was the one who loved his master more than himself.[27]

Once abolitionists gained control of important cities, the position of slave proprietors in neighboring regions became untenable. Pockets of abolitionist agitation appeared proximate to the principal plantation areas. Cities such as Fortaleza, Recife, Ouro Prêto, Campos, Rio de Janeiro, São Paulo, and Santos became asylums for runaway slaves. In this regard, the Brazilian experience differed significantly from the situation in the United States. Slavocrats in the American South had been able to contain abolitionist activities geographically. By the

24. *Rio News,* October 15, 1887, p. 3.
25. *Cidade do Rio,* November 24, 1887, p. 1.
26. *Ibid.,* October 11, 1887, p. 1; *Gazeta da Tarde,* October 5, 1882, p. 1.
27. *O Paíz,* October 24, 1887, p. 1.

1830s, Southerners succeeded in silencing abolitionists or frightening them off to the North. Despite the Brazilian slavocrats' serious repressive efforts, however, they were not able to crush discontented elements or localize them effectively. The hour was too late; neither cajoling nor coercion could turn the tide of the urban antislavery movement spirited by both intellectual and economic concerns. Slaveholders found troublemakers in their own back yards. Abolitionists, including many Negro freedmen, worked their way into the slave quarters at night, urged captives to flee, then slipped back into their places of refuge before daybreak. Bondsmen lost their fear of punishment as they became aware of limitations on their masters' power and the new opportunities for effective escape. How could slavery be maintained under such conditions? asked Antônio Coelho Rodrigues. By the ignorance or resignation of slaves? Hardly. In 1887–1888 thousands of bondsmen made rapid exit. Masters were surprised to find that even their most loyal servants had disappeared.

Many of the escapees found employment on other plantations. In previous years planters had preferred to work with slaves, but now they were suffering from manpower deficiency at a time when the coffee economy was rapidly expanding. When abolitionist organizations offered them fugitives, they were happy to accept. It was estimated that by the time of abolition one-third of the São Paulo *fazendas* included fugitives among their workers.[28]

Many others fled to the cities. The runaway bondsmen especially viewed the coastal city of Santos as a promised land, because it seemed beyond the reach of the slave-chasers, and its thriving coffee export business presented numerous employment opportunities. As late as 1886 slave proprietors still had sufficient influence in the city to arrange for the return of fugitives to the *fazendas*. But Santos soon broke under the strain of violence. In one case, a screaming group of railroad

28. Antonio Manuel Bueno de Andrada, "*Depoimento de uma testemunha,*" *Revista do Instituto Histórico e Geográfico de São Paulo,* XXXVI (1939), p. 221.

porters attacked police and guards with sticks and stones at a station, enabling a fugitive slave to escape from the officers. The acts of disobedience became increasingly audacious as large groups of armed citizens and fugitive slaves broke into the city jailhouse to free captured runaways, attacked police in the streets during the night, and destroyed equipment in the office of the city's pro-slaveholder newspaper. Under great pressure, resistance collapsed in Santos in November of 1886, and the fugitives poured in. A new shanty town rose on the hills around the city—the *quilombo* (community of runaway slaves) of Jabaquara, and by the end of 1887 more than 10,000 people settled there under the leadership of the Negro leader Quintino Lacerda. An ex-slave, Lacerda led servile insurrections and organized resistance forces to rout troops sent to apprehend the escapees. He watched over the construction out of mud and straw of an African-style fortress-city, established an administration to plan a governmental system, stimulated commercial activity, and obtained a subscription to finance some of the building. In his deft hands, the fame of Jabaquara spread quickly.[29]

Many fugitives used the São Paulo railroad to get to Santos. Aided by abolitionist leaders and sympathetic railroad conductors, they were able to arrive at their destination with little difficulty. Abolitionists met the fugitives at the terminal and directed them to safety. As abolitionists often accosted all people of color who departed from the trains, assuming they were runaway slaves, occasionally they made embarrassing mistakes. Sometimes the slaves had to leave the *fazendas* hastily without adequate preparation. Many were dressed only in

29. Tobias do Rêgo Monteiro, *Pesquisas e depoimentos para a história* (Rio de Janeiro, 1913), p. 169; *"Quilombolas e Jabaraquara,"* in *O Estado de São Paulo,* June 24, 1956; *Annaes da Câmara* (1888), I, 51–52; *Diário de Santos,* May 16, 1888, p. 1; Luna, *O negro na luta contra a escravidão,* p. 116; *Relatório* of the president of São Paulo, Barão do Parnahyba, January 17, 1887, p. 33; *Relatório* of the Chief of Police of São Paulo province, Luiz Lopes Baptista do Anjos Junior, 1887, pp. 3–5. The Baron of Cotegipe worried that the creation of an asylum in Santos could lead to disruptions throughout the province. See Baron of Cotegipe to Dm Pedro II, November 22, 1886, CXCVI–8888, Arquivo do Museu Imperial.

light clothing or old rags; some were almost nude. Their scanty food supplies dwindling, they spent many days walking along the road with their women and children. According to a story in *O Paíz,* a pursued band of desperately hungry and tired fugitives hurled two children into a river because they had to be carried and were slowing down the caravan.[30]

Violence resulted as local authorities sent out special police forces to capture the fugitives. When such a group surprised a camp of twenty-two runaway slaves in São Paulo, five of the escapees were shot to death.[31] But many fugitives possessed firearms and were prepared for encounters with their pursuers. When a planter found two of his runaways hiding in a wagon at a São Paulo railroad station, he drew his revolver and ordered them to return to their quarters. But the slaves also produced revolvers and refused to go.[32] The sight of so many aroused fugitives in possession of weapons alarmed even some of the abolitionists, who sent emissaries to pacify the armed escapees and direct them on their way without bloodshed.[33] Nevertheless, several confrontations occurred along the highways and in the *quilombos,* incidents involving assault and robbery by wandering bands of fugitives and battles resulting in the death of both slaves and slave-hunters. With escapes increasing at a rapid pace, the prospects for more violence were ominous.[34]

A major clash between armed fugitives and slave-hunters occurred in October 1887. One of Antônio Bento's *caifazes,* a freedman named Pio, was leading a group of 150 runaway slaves toward Santos when he encountered a small police force near Itú.[35] As the police were greatly outnumbered, and they saw that the slaves had about forty firearms, they decided not

30. *Cidade do Rio,* January 11, 1888, p. 2; *O Paíz,* November 23, 1887, p. 1.

31. *Rio News,* August 24, 1887, p. 4.

32. *Ibid.,* November 5, 1887, p. 3.

33. *Cidade do Rio,* October 27, 1887.

34. *Relatório,* Chief of Police of São Paulo province, Salvador Antônio Muniz Barreto de Aragão, 1887, p. 19.

35. Among the runaways were the wife and children of the freedman Pio.

to attempt capture. But after some confusion and shouts of "Liberty or death!" an exchange of gunfire occurred which left one policeman dead and several from both sides wounded. Another confrontation the next day caused more bloodshed, as the fugitives badly mauled a contingent of twenty policemen. The people of Itú were so much alarmed by these clashes that the provincial government had to send a special guarded train to re-establish confidence. Before the forces could arrive, however, the slaves defiantly walked through the center of the city, passing directly in front of the jailhouse. Finally, a force of forty police cavalrymen found the slave band and asked them not to go any farther, indicating that a large group of thugs hired by the slaveholders was hiding in the hills ahead. A police officer sympathetic to the slaves urged Pio to turn back, but, fearing deception, the freedman viciously struck down the officer and ordered his followers to continue the march. Other policemen then killed the Negro leader, but the determined slaves moved on toward Santos, only to be cut to pieces by an ambush.[36] About forty of the original group escaped completely, and only half of these finally walked into Santos, where the nervous population received them cautiously. As one telegram from the city reported: "The attitude of the fugitive slaves has caused great sensation here by the presumption of an imminent massacre." [37]

Indeed, some of the slaves' activities turned into full-fledged insurrections. Actually, these violent revolts had shown a dangerous increase as early as 1882 when the effects of rising abolitionist agitation were first felt on the *fazendas*. At that

36. Doctors who performed an autopsy on Pio claimed that he had not had anything to eat for three days before his fatal encounter with the police. Many others in the fugitive group were also desperately hungry, having nothing but a few pieces of *palmito* (palm heart) during the trip.

37. *O Paíz,* October 20, 21, and 22, 1887; *Diário de Santos,* October 21, 1887, p. 1; October 25, 1887, p. 1; *Correio Paulistano,* October 21, 1887, p. 1; Andrada, *"Depoimento de uma testamunha,"* p. 224; *Relatório,* Chief of Police of São Paulo province, Salvador Antônio Muniz Barreto de Aragão, 1887, p. 6; *A Redempção,* October 27, 1887, p. 2; *Gazeta do Povo,* October 21, 1887, p. 1.

time the government of São Paulo took special measures to improve the effectiveness of its provincial police.[38] At first the insurrections were isolated, but some feared that the conflict might expand and become a racial slaughter similar to the cataclysm of Santo Domingo. The *Rio News* warned: "The great danger lies more in the possibility that some slave or freedman of exceptional ability and strength of character may take the cause in hand and stir his race into general revolt." [39]

The pace of revolts accelerated in São Paulo in 1887, and in some regions uprisings involved large numbers of slaves from neighboring *fazendas*. From Capivari, Campinas, Amparo, Itú, Indaiatuba, Piracicaba, and other sections, reports poured in of armed insurrections.[40] The most rebellious slaves attempted to assassinate authorities on the *fazendas*. They usually made overseers their first victims, as these were the persons most immediately responsible for directing and disciplining them. Reports of assassinated overseers multiplied in 1887 and 1888.[41] In some cases the rebels tried to murder their masters. For example, slaves on the *fazenda* of the Baron of Serra Negra detailed a plan to revolt, kill their master, and flee en masse, but when they carried out the conspiracy, some loyal slaves defended the Baron and saved his life. Some other masters were not so fortunate.[42]

Christiano Ottoni had recognized the serious implications of such violent developments as early as 1884:

38. *Gazeta da Tarde,* November 10, 1882, p. 1; December 29, 1882, p. 1; *Rio News,* January 5, 1883, p. 2.

39. *Rio News,* January 5, 1883, p. 2.

40. *Diário de Santos,* October 28, 1887, p. 2; *Correio Paulistano,* October 19, 1887, p. 1; *Relatório,* Salvador António Muniz Barreto de Aragão, p. 9.

41. *A Redempção,* January 27, 1887, p. 3; *Relatório,* Salvador António Muniz Barreto de Aragão, pp. 11–12; *Gazeta da Tarde,* July 29, 1886, p. 1; Adelino R. Riccardi, *"Parnaiba, o pioneiro da imigração," Revista do Arquivo Municipal de São Paulo,* IV, No. 44 (1938), 138.

42. Costa, *Da senzala à colônia,* p. 310; *Relatório* of the president of São Paulo province, Francisco de Paulo Rodrigues Alves, January 10, 1888, p. 8; Francisco José de Oliveira Vianna, *O ocaso do império* (São Paulo, 1925), p. 72. The Baron of Serra Negra had recently purchased slaves from another planter, Manuel de Moraes Barros.

> What we are witnessing now has never been seen before. The few crimes of this kind, committed at long intervals, did not represent the serious characteristics which distinguish these crimes now. But besides being less frequent formerly than now, they did not offer the symptoms which we now observe. The criminal fled, or he denied the fact, or he tried to escape the penalty of the law; now, however, he murders, and he goes immediately to the authorities and delivers himself up, saying: we have committed a murder; we want to be punished. It is this which increases the gravity of the situation.

See the *Rio News,* June 24, 1884, p. 3.

Frustrated by their difficulty in preventing the spread of anarchy on the *fazendas,* some slave proprietors decided upon radical action. In October 1887, two hundred armed residents of Frade invaded a *fazenda* that had been the scene of a recent insurrection. The enraged citizens were determined to kill the insurrectionist leaders, but when they arrived, they found the *fazenda* completely abandoned.[43] *Fazendeiros* also gathered their employees together for raids on small towns known for abolitionist activity, surrounding and entering homes in search of fugitives.[44]

One of the most tragic cases of violent slaveholder reaction occurred in Rio do Peixe. A police delegate of the municipality who sympathized with the antislavery movement was sheltering fugitives in his home. In February 1888, when many *fazendas* in the region were being abandoned, the angry slave proprietors decided to take action. They were led by two naturalized Brazilians, James Ox Warne and John Jackson Clink, immigrants from the United States, who had fought for the Confederacy during the Civil War. The two incited the planters by telling them that they had "cockroach blood" and that under such circumstances a revolution would have occurred

43. *O Paíz,* October 25, 1887, p. 1.

44. *Anais da Assembléa Legislativa da Província de São Paulo* (1888), pp. 83–85.

in any other country. After the harangue a party of 140 planters broke into the delegate's house. A planter who had just lost all of his slaves struck the first blow. Then the others quickly joined in to bludgeon the young man to death. Within a few days the name of the slain delegate became famous across the empire as newspaper editors bitterly condemned the murder. Suddenly, the abolitionist movement found a new martyr. Under great public pressure, the government of São Paulo pressed charges against those responsible for the crime, but the authorities became embarrassed when they learned that many prominent persons were among the accused. Of the twenty individuals indicted for murder, all were eventually acquitted.[45]

In desperate efforts to impede the increasing escapes, planters tried a variety of methods, some of them resulting in comic situations. One *fazendeiro* in Campinas brought a lawyer to his plantation to speak to the slaves and convince them not to flee. Within a short time his *fazenda* was almost completely abandoned.[46] Another planter tried to discourage escape by forcing his male slaves to dress like women and the female slaves like men.[47]

As the slave proprietors learned that they could not resist alone, they became more dependent on the public forces. Through the nineteenth century, they had relied upon the *capitães-do-mato,* the hired slave-catchers. Since the *capitães-do-mato* had frequently been successful in their hunts, they were paid well, but in the 1880s their work became more difficult.[48] The free masses no longer condoned their activities, and, especially in the cities, the public became determined to hinder their work. Also, by now the problem was too big for them to handle alone; the mass migrations from the *fazendas*

45. *Relatório,* Salvador Muniz Barreto de Aragão, p. 8; *O Paíz,* February 15, 1888, p. 1; March 3, 1888, p. 1; *Rio News,* February 24, 1888, pp. 3–4; July 15, 1888; *Revista Illustrada,* March 17, 1888, p. 6; *Jornal do Recife,* February 21, 1888, p. 1.

46. *A Redempção,* April 28, 1887, p. 3.

47. *Ibid.,* July 28, 1887, p. 3.

48. Costa, *Da senzala à colônia,* p. 312; Luna, *O negro na luta contra a escravidão,* p. 111.

required the assistance of larger police forces. Realizing the potential danger as early as 1881, members of the Agriculture Club of Campinas appealed for more public forces.[49] Both local and provincial police were increased in the next few years, but this was not sufficient to meet the crisis. When the flights reached flood stage in 1887, the provincial forces of São Paulo included only 530 permanent police corpsmen and 240 urban police—a force which the president of the province considered grossly inadequate for the needs.[50]

As the majority of the population of São Paulo now abhorred the idea of slave-capturing, police forces sent to hunt fugitives became the object of public wrath.[51] Large groups of people gathered in public places in the cities to prevent the return of fugitive slaves. When a police chief arrived in Santos in 1887 to escort four fugitives back to their masters, he was rudely surprised by a crowd of angry citizens, who assaulted his force of forty policemen with clubs and stones. Finally the police chief and his contingent scurried off without the slaves.[52] Many other encounters occurred between the public and the slave-chasers, clashes in which crowds jeered and stoned the police.[53] A day of violence in Campinas involving exchange of gunfire between citizens and police resulted in the wounding of several people, including the president of the municipal legislature. The tumult also left the jailhouse and city lights badly damaged.[54] When slaves abandoned a *fazenda* near Piracicaba, police captured them, but as they returned to the city by train, a huge throng met them at the station and freed the slaves again. The event produced great excitation among the city's fugitive slave population, and the next day

49. Nícia Vilela Luz, "*A administração provincial de São Paulo em face do movimento abolicionista,*" *Revista de Administração,* VIII (December 1948), p. 95.

50. *Relatório,* Francisco de Paulo Rodrigues Alves, pp. 22–23.

51. *O Paíz,* October 21, 1887, p. 1.

52. João Dornas Filho, *A escravidão no Brasil* (Rio de Janeiro, 1939), p. 186.

53. *O Paíz,* January 23, 1888, p. 1; *Relatório,* Salvador Muniz Barreto de Aragão, p. 7.

54. *O Paíz,* January 24, 1888, p. 1.

more than 1,000 blacks ran through the streets engaging in numerous disorders and exchanging gunfire with whites. Some families in Campinas, Piracicaba, and other cities that experienced the upheaval remained locked in their homes for days or took the train to the capital city in search of safety.[55]

Violence also shook the city of São Paulo. In October 1887 a very serious incident began when a large group of Negro freedmen interrupted a traditional festival at the church of São Francisco. Many of the area's finest families were in attendance. When one of the freedmen was arrested, a brawl broke out between the Negroes and the police, and quickly the festival scene became a battlefield. The blacks, many of whom possessed firearms, were finally dispersed when a special infantry force arrived. The next day the blacks returned while a police corps music festival was being held in the garden of the government palace. Amid shouts of "Liberty or death!" and "Death to the slavocrats!" the blacks surged upon the police. Panic reigned among the families in the palace garden until another special force of infantrymen arrived to repel the attackers. The tumult in the capital city deeply impressed citizens of São Paulo with the explosiveness of the slavery question.[56]

The crisis was now beyond the control of planters' hirelings or the provincial police. By the early months of 1888 the task of slave-catchers became almost impossible; in Mogymirim, for example, crowds forced three of them to parade through the streets with horns and kerosene cans on their heads.[57] As the inadequacy of the police efforts became more glaring each day, slave proprietors began to appeal to the army for assistance. Newspapers sympathetic to the planters cried out against the lack of military involvement in the crisis. Articles and letters appearing in the *Liberal Paulistano* and *Novidades* criticized the government for folding its arms in the face of

55. *Jornal do Recife,* January 21, 1888, p. 1.

56. *Relatório,* Salvador Muniz Barreto de Aragão, p. 6; Ricciardi, "*Parnaiba, o pioneiro da immigração,*" pp. 180–81.

57. *Rio News,* March 5, 1888, p. 3.

difficulty.[58] Slavocrat politicians voiced their discontent too. The Baron of Cotegipe grumbled about the government's difficulty in finding authorities who would face the danger, and Andrade Figueira demanded that the army be given the duties of the *capitão-do-mato*.[59]

Joaquim Nabuco strongly opposed Figueira's proposal, charging that the use of soldiers to chase slaves would dishonor their occupation. "Is there a lower and more degraded profession than that of *capitão-do-mato?*" [60] Nabuco had long been the principal spokesman for the legal, political approach to abolitionism, but now he accepted the radical consequences of the mass flights from the *fazendas*. Nabuco justified the escapes by reasoning that "in the absence of law and justice [flight] has been the only Providence of the slave in our country." In 1887 he appealed to the government not to send the army as "bloodhounds" against runaway slaves.[61]

Many members of the military corps expressed sympathy for the abolitionist movement. Some of the interest originated from Brazil's participation in the war against Paraguay (1866–1870). About 20,000 Negro slaves were given their freedom for fighting in the war, and the experience of working with bondsmen left many military leaders impressed with their cause. By the 1880s there were large numbers of Negroes and mulattoes in the lower ranks of the army who opposed slavery.[62] The higher echelons included many officers from the urban, antislavery groups who wanted to modernize the military, and they easily associated themselves with abolitionist

58. Reported in *Correio Paulistano,* November 11, 1887, p. 1; *Novidades,* April 26, 1888, pp. 2–3. Also see the statement of the Baron of Rezende, quoted in *A Redempção,* April 22, 1888, p. 2.

59. *Fuga de escravos em Campinas: Discursos pronunciados no Senado pelo Exm. Sr. Barão de Cotegipe* (Rio de Janeiro, 1887), p. 16; *Cidade do Rio,* October 9, 1887, p. 2.

60. *Annaes da Câmara* (1887), V, 350.

61. *O Paíz.* See the issues of October 18, 19, 21, and 23 of 1887. Also, see the broadsides in the Instituto Joaquim Nabuco: *"Um voto de censura contra o procedimento do governo"; "A' S.A.I. O Snr. Conde D Eu"; "Ao Exercito Brasileiro."*

62. Percy Alvin Martin, "Slavery and Abolition in Brasil," *Hispanic American Historical Review,* XIII (May 1933), p. 174.

goals. Some army leaders even belonged to abolitionist clubs and spoke at antislavery meetings. Especially important at the officer level were the members of the Club Militar. Presided over by Marshal Manuel Deodoro da Fonseca and influenced by the intellectual leadership of the Positivist Benjamin Constant, this organization took a strong antislavery stand.[63] In October 1887 the Military Club directed a petition to the Princess Regent requesting in the name of humanity, Christian charity, and civilization that the military not be obligated to chase fugitive slaves.[64]

Humanitarian sentiments were not the only motives for the declaration. It was presented at a time of disorders on the plantations, when the question of military involvement was crucial. During the tense days in late October, abolitionist groups implored army leaders not to dishonor their organization by fighting in defense of slavery. By speaking out early and clearly on this sensitive issue, the members of the Military Club protected their own interests. Since the military was being requested to intervene and stop the escapes, the Military Club sought to clarify its position before being summoned to a task it deemed not only repugnant but also unpopular and dangerous. Thus the document reflected both humanitarian and practical concerns.

The petition represented the attitude of the Military Club and not necessarily that of the entire officer corps. Some officers who had been drawn from the rural aristocracy skirted the issue of slavery and did nothing for the abolitionist movement. Both before and after presentation of the petition, some military personnel carried out assignments to pursue fugitive slaves. In fact, after Deodoro signed and delivered the petition to the Adjutant General, military officials returned it to him. The general headquarters justified its implicit rejection on the

63. On Benjamin Constant's antislavery stand, see Ivan Monteiro de Baros Lins, *Três abolicionistas esquecidos* (Rio de Janeiro, 1938), pp. 13–17; Luna, *O negro na luta contra a escravidão,* p. 215; Barbosa, *Abolicionismo,* p. 72. Raimundo Girão, *A abolição no Ceará* (Fortaleza, 1956), pp. 160–61.

64. *Cidade do Rio,* October 27, 1887, p. 2.

grounds that the Military Club had no legal existence and that military laws prohibited collective representations.[65]

Within a short time, however, the general headquarters adopted the position of the more progressive officers and the Military Club. Two factors explain the non-abolitionist military group's decision not to pursue fugitive slaves. In the first place, these officers too came to realize that the job of slave-hunting was difficult and dangerous and that pursuing fugitive slaves did not offer the military any clear rewards; defending a dying institution would only arouse public wrath against the army and precipitate more violence at a time when upheaval was the most threatening problem of Brazilian society. In the second place, many provincial and Imperial authorities were reluctant to request the aid of the army because they feared the issue might raise a new military question. Already relations were strained between army officers and the Cotegipe ministry because of differences concerning modernization of the army and navy, the role of the military in national affairs, and several complicated personal disputes. Moreover, embarrassing cases of insubordination developed in the army, as some officers and soldiers refused to obey orders from their superiors to apprehend fugitives. With such quarrels already plaguing government-military relations, the political leaders of the country could ill afford to antagonize further the abolitionist group within the military. Consequently, the group of army officers who were ambivalent about the slavery question were not strongly pressed to pursue fugitives, and the abolitionist military leaders had their way. As upheaval spread, the army refused to assume the role of *capitão-do-mato,* a determination that proved a severe blow to the slaveholders' regime.[66]

65. *Correio Paulistano,* November 6, 1887, p. 1; Emília Viotti da Costa, *"Sôbre as origens da república," Anais do Museu Paulista* XVIII (São Paulo, 1964), pp. 112–13; Luis Anselmo da Fonseca, *A escravidão, o clero e o abolicionismo* (Bahia, 1887), pp. 569–70; *Rio News,* June 15, 1887, p. 2; December 24, 1887, p. 3.

66. Osório Duque-Estrada, *A abolição 1831–1888* (Rio de Janeiro, 1918), pp. 205–09, 225–26; Nelson Werneck Sodré, *História militar do Brasil* (Rio de Janeiro, 1965), p. 158; Charles Willis Simmons, *Marshal*

Anxieties increased in proportion to the number of escapes, insurrections, and assassinations. "Brazilian society is passing through a crisis, the consequences of which no one is able to foresee," reported the *Correio Paulistano* in October 1887, warning that "these disturbances of public order cannot help but seriously prejudice commerce and industry and necessarily set back the immigration that flows to the capital city [São Paulo]." [67] An air of discouragement permeated the *fazendeiro* society.[68] Andrade Figueira, one of the chief spokesmen for the slaveholding interests, received many letters from frustrated planters bemoaning the breakdown of order, and the Baron of Cotegipe charged that the "propaganda of anarchy" and subterranean activities of abolitionists were bringing about the disorganization of labor.[69] In the first quarter of 1888 the number of coffee sacks exported from Santos dropped significantly from that for the same period the year preceding.[70] The troubles had reached crisis proportions; as one Paulista politician declared, "There is no confidence in today, or even in tomorrow." [71]

During 1887 planters in other important slaveholding provinces of the Central-South were not plagued by the escapes as much as those of São Paulo. The stagnation of the coffee economy in the Paraíba Valley made it difficult for fugitives to find employment, and the few major urban centers did not

---

Deodoro and the Fall of Dom Pedro II (Durham, 1966), pp. 77–94; Santos, *Os republicanos,* pp. 264–68; Ottoni, *Autobiographia,* p. 346; *Rio News,* August 15, 1887, p. 2; *Annaes da Câmara* (1888), June 4, p. 18; June 7, p. 81.

67. *Correio Paulistano,* October 28, 1887, p. 1.

68. Joaquim Floriano de Godoy, *O elemento servil e as camaras municipaes da província de São Paulo* (Rio de Janeiro, 1887), p. 31.

69. *Annaes da Câmara* (1888), I, 52; *Fuga de escravos em Campinas,* pp. 4–5.

70. *Jornal do Recife,* March 4, 1888.

71. The words of Senator Floriano de Godoy are quoted in Antônio Gomes de Azevedo Sampaio, *Abolicionismo; Considerações geraes do movimento anti-esclavista e sua história limitada a Jacarehy* (São Paulo, 1890), p. 50. The editor of the *Gazeta de Povo* (Campos, Rio de Janeiro) claimed that many feared São Paulo was becoming embroiled in "civil war." Also see João Ferreira de Moura to Visconde de Paranaguá, November 21, 1887, 21.11887, Arquivo do Museu Imperial.

contain as many modernization-conscious antislavery elements as the rapidly growing São Paulo cities. In most areas of Minas Gerais and Rio de Janeiro the rural proprietors, with their great political and social influence, were able to maintain control of the situation until the last months before abolition. As Andrade Figueria noted, planters in Rio de Janeiro succeeded in "suffocating" the movement. Because this condition made flight from the plantations difficult, some slaves in Rio province tried other tactics; for example, many refused to work.[72]

Late in 1887, however, the tremors of São Paulo reached communities in Rio de Janeiro. Carlos de Lacerda, the boldest of the abolitionists in Rio de Janeiro, contributed much to this breakdown. As editor of the radical abolitionist organ in Campos, the *Vinte e Cinco de Março,* and chief organizer of the area's underground railroad, Lacerda worked as an effective counterpart to Antônio Bento of São Paulo. Lacerda had risen to prominence as an abolitionist leader during the period of the Dantas administration and continued his activities under great danger until the day of abolition. His name excited extreme emotions in the sugar plantation area of Campos; slaveholders viewed him as a violent and dangerous activist, while slaves hailed him as their most important and trusted abolitionist friend. From their own perspectives, both parties assessed Lacerda's role accurately.[73] Lacerda's agitation stirred the bondsmen into action. New incidents of upheaval continued unabated until April 1888 when the slaveholders' control suddenly broke completely in some regions and thousands of slaves abandoned the *fazendas.* In one case fifty armed slaves from a *fazenda* near Campos revolted and established their own *quilombo.* Later, a force of sixteen policemen and 200 armed citizens tracked down the insurrectionaries. In several

72. Fonseca, *A escravidão, o clero, e o abolicionismo,* p. 603; *O Paíz,* October 15, 1887, p. 1.

73. Carlos de Lacerda to Colonel F. Solon de Sampaio Ribeiro, November 27, 1890, Lata 419–Doc 42, Arquivo do Instituto Histórico e Geográfico Brasileiro.

incidents on other plantations, slaves killed their overseers, fled from their masters, and burned the sugar-cane fields. Large groups of fugitives worked their way toward the city of Campos during the night, hoping to obtain letters of liberty which Lacerda was rumored to have ready for them.[74]

Violence begot violence as planters in Campos and other areas of Rio de Janeiro replied in kind to the new threats. Some resorted to "lynch law." After the police of Monte Verde apprehended a slave who had disposed of his mistress while the master was away, a crowd of enraged citizens yanked the murderer out of jail, killed him, and tossed the body into a fire. In another incident, 100 men rushed onto a plantation and brutally beat three slaves who had killed their overseer. The situation became especially tense in the town of São Fidelis, which harbored more than 2,000 fugitives in the early months of 1888. Incensed planters thrashed blacks in the streets and planned to attack the town with a large force of armed *fazendeiros* and their hirelings. The newspaper *Gazeta do Povo* reported that the lives of several officials in São Fidelis were in danger.[75]

Slaveholders desperately tried to silence Lacerda. On one occasion during the earlier period of his activities, in May 1884, he had attracted a shouting, gun-wielding crowd of 500 Campos citizens to hear his emotional antislavery oratory. When thirty Campos policemen arrived to disperse the crowd, it appeared that a bloodbath would ensue. But an articulate police deputy addressed the throng, calmed them, and succeeded in avoiding a physical confrontation.[76] In the following years, hostilities became more explosive. Slaveholders ordered thugs to as-

74. Luna, *O negro na luta contra a escravidão,* pp. 75, 112–13; *Brazil,* June 3, 1884, p. 1; Carneiro, *Antologia do negro brasileiro,* p. 258; *Relatório* of the Chief of Police of Rio de Janeiro, Salvador A. Muniz Barreto de Aragão, June 30, 1888, pp. 6–12.

75. *Relatório* Salvador A. Muniz Barreto de Aragão, June 30, 1888, p. 6; Barbosa, *Abolicionismo,* pp. xi, 17–18; *Gazeta do Povo,* October 25, 1887; October 28, 1887, p. 1; April 11, 1888, p. 1; Carneiro, *Antologia do negro brasileiro,* p. 258; *Revista Illustrada,* 1884, n.379, p. 2.

76. *Brazil,* May 18 and 20, 1884.

sassinate Lacerda but failed because he was well protected by armed associates. When Lacerda traveled to Macaé in July 1887, apparently to lure slaves away from their masters, many planters converged upon the town to impede his entrance. The clash left two citizens wounded.[77] More serious were the events in Campos in October of the same year. Police engaged in a shooting match with individuals inside the offices of Lacerda's newspaper. With guns and dynamite, the newspaper employees inflicted wounds on six deputies while suffering three injuries on their own side. Finally, officers surrounded the building, broke through the front door, and captured the abolitionists. After taking them to prison, the police faced several attacks from angry mobs that tried to push their way into the jailhouse to free Lacerda's friends.[78]

The embattled slaveholders were not successful in quelling the disorders, for their control collapsed within a short time. By March and April of 1888 the situation in São Fidelis, Campos, Padua, and other sections of the province deteriorated into what observers described as almost complete "anarchy." Thousands of runaway slaves rushed into the cities. Many made their way to the capital of the empire, establishing a new *quilombo* in the section of Leblon. In the countryside work came almost to a standstill. Communities became unsafe as armed fugitives assaulted travelers and robbed homes at night.[79]

Similar conditions developed in Minas Gerais. At the forefront of the movement in the city of Ouro Prêto was the young and dynamic abolitionist leader Dr. Americo Luz. He too encouraged flights from the *fazendas* and faced great danger for carrying out his strategy. When Luz and other abolitionists traveled to campaign in the town of Muzambinho, four *fazendeiros* organized a force of thugs to ambush Luz and his

77. *Relatório,* Salvador A. Muniz Barreto de Aragão, June 30, 1888, p. 6.

78. *Revista Illustrada,* October 29, 1887, p. 6.

79. *Relatório,* Salvador a Muniz Barreto de Aragão, June 30, 1888, pp. 6–12; *Gazeta de Povo,* March 13, 1888, p. 1; April 11 and 12, 1888.

friends. The plan almost succeeded, but other planters learned of the conspiracy, gathered a counter-force, and repelled the attackers. For a few days false rumors circulated about the outcome of the events in Muzambinho, and many believed that Luz had been killed.[80] Despite the slaveholders' desperate efforts to control the abolitionists and slaves, sections of Minas Gerais too became scenes of mass escapes. In the early months of 1888 the city of Ouro Prêto became a recognized asylum for slaves, and the provincial police chief and other authorities began to worry about the danger of disorders and the lack of jobs for the city's increasing population overflow. In the following months many runaways relocated to seek opportunities in São Paulo.[81]

Where many planters had already emancipated their slaves, as in sections of the Northeast, the fugitive slave problem did not become as great as in the Central-South. In some of the coastal sugar-cane regions where many slaves resided, however, a wave of collective escapes began to appear. During January and February of 1888 large groups of slaves in the Northeast fled from the plantations, particularly in the province of Pernambuco. Some hoped to find safety in the free province of Ceará; others gambled and settled in the city of Recife. In one incident hired thugs attacked a party of seven slaves trying to find their way to Ceará but succeeded in apprehending only one. After the captured fugitive made a second desperate attempt to escape, the group pounced on him and clubbed him to death. *Senhores de engenho* felt great apprehension over the new signs of unrest, and reports of disruption in other parts of the empire only heightened their sense of tension.[82]

By April 1888 the foundations of Brazilian slaveholding

80. *Cidade do Rio,* April 2, 1888, p. 3.

81. *Província de Minas,* January 20, 1888, p. 1; Oliam José, *Abolição em Minas* (Belo Horizonte, 1962), pp. 94–99.

82. *Diário da Bahia,* April 5, 1888, p. 2; *Jornal do Recife,* January 10, 12, 13, 15, 31, February 14, 1888; *Gazeta do Povo,* May 2, 1888, p. 1; *Relatório* of the vice-president of Pernambuco, Ignácio Joaquim de Souza Leão, April 16, 1888, p. 19; *Província de São Paulo,* April 7, 1888, p. 1.

society were collapsing. Especially in the most important coffee-producing provinces of the Central-South, *fazendeiros* saw the rebellion of abolitionists and slaves breaking out of control. The difficulties became most severe in São Paulo, peaking in February 1888, and leaders in Rio de Janeiro and Minas Gerais could not see much hope in reversing the spread of disorders into their own provinces.[83] They also feared that the violent collapse of slavery might polarize relations between the races and eventually explode into outright war. Already in the cases of slave revolts and assassinations, dangerous confrontations between blacks and whites had materialized. It would be ominous if the Negro should begin to conceive of the situation as a battle between races. The newspaper *O Paíz* discussed this delicate problem when it reported that "the army, which does not desire the smashing of the black by the white, would also not allow the black, brutalized by the horrors of slavery, to guarantee his liberty by smashing the white." [84] Leaders from other sections of Brazil watched the deterioration with great anxiety. The editor of the *Diário da Bahia* warned of the dangers of war generated by the oppressed race's passions, and Antônio Coelho Rodrigues of Piauí worried about increased race hatred developing out of the conflicts.[85]

Abolitionists had long warned that the slave quarters contained the germs of revolution.[86] These prophets of doom now seemed correct. Leaders from all political camps began to demand that the government not sit by helplessly while slavery ended by violence. Abolition should be achieved by a pacific solution, they insisted; the matter should not be allowed to pass into the hands of the people in revolt.[87]

83. *Província de São Paulo,* April 8, 1888, p. 1.
84. Quoted in Moraes, *A campanha abolicionista,* p. 314.
85. *Diário da Bahia,* April 3, 1888, p. 1; *Annaes da Câmara* (1888), June 7, pp. 92–93.
86. *Gazeta da Tarde,* January 15, 1881, p. 1.
87. *Annaes da Câmara* (1888), I, 56.

9: Abolition or Anarchy?

THE SWIFT PROGRESS of the antislavery movement in 1887–1888 astounded even the abolitionists. *Fazendeiros* who had been slow to react to appeals for emancipation suddenly began to liberate their slaves en masse, and political leaders who had long defended the interests of slaveholders in Parliament abruptly began to advocate abolition. Some observers interpreted these developments as admirable examples of the spirit of humanitarianism and political compromise. But behind these conversions to abolitionism was the deep anxiety that resulted from a serious weakening of the foundations of slavery and the upheaval that threatened Brazilian society in 1887 and 1888. Temporizing solutions were no longer satisfactory. In the face of the violent collapse of slavery, slave proprietors reconsidered their positions, weighing the pain of abolition against the danger of anarchy and threat of social revolution.

The wave of escapes, insurrections, and upheaval coupled with the uncooperative behavior of urban officials led many planters to change their attitudes about emancipation. Fearing impending disaster unless they took a more flexible stance, they realized that concessions were necessary to keep the bondsmen working.[1] *Fazendeiros* began granting liberty to the slaves if they would make various promises such as not to flee, to remain until the coffee crop was harvested, or to continue to reside on their *fazendas* after liberation.[2] A typical announcement in São Paulo, for example, stated:

> The planters of the municipality of Indaiatuba met and conceded liberty to all the slaves that they possessed, in

1. *Correio Paulistano,* November 4, 9, and 16, 1887.
2. *Ibid.,* November 16, 1887, p. 2; November 22, 1887, p. 2; *A Redempção,* January 5, 1888, p. 2.

> number greater than 700, under the exclusive condition that they continue to work for salary, on the same *fazendas* on which they are located.[3]

When São Paulo first began to experience the mass wave of escapes in 1887, slave proprietors reacted to the problem with proposals for conditional emancipation. Under these arrangements, slaves were to remain at work for a specified period of time, usually between one and three years, after which they would be declared totally free. Sometimes *fazendeiros* promised they would offer the bondsmen a small remuneration at the end of the term. In November of 1887 planters began to plan joint efforts to liberate entire municipalities on the basis of a term of services, and in December the Associação Libertadora (Liberator Association) and the Sociedade Libertadora (Liberator Society) were formed to abolish slavery in São Paulo by December 30, 1890.[4] These planters emphasized a short-term rather than an immediate abolition because they wanted time to prepare for the free labor system without disruption of work. They realized they could obligate slaves to remain on the *fazendas* but that they would have no such authority with freedmen. Hence, they devised the title of "conditional freedmen," designed to provide some psychological satisfaction to the slave while, in fact, maintaining his position of obligatory labor for a time.[5]

As the flights and turmoil continued, planters realized that delay was no longer possible. The situation called for immediate liberation, or the slaves would continue to leave the *fazendas* in great numbers, probably never to return. Indeed many of the fugitives were really "conditional freedmen" who left the plantations dissatisfied with what they considered deceptive promises of liberty.[6] Statistics from São Paulo re-

3. *Cidade do Rio,* December 28, 1887, p. 2.
4. *Correio Paulistano,* November 13 and 17, 1887.
5. Nazareth Prado (ed.), *Antônio Prado no império e na república: Seus discursos e actos collegidos e apresentados por sua filha* (Rio de Janeiro, 1929), p. 75.
6. *Gazeta do Povo,* October 27, 1888, p. 1.

flected the planters' growing awareness of the need for drastic change. Between 1887 and 1888 the number of unconditional emancipations recorded in the newspapers increased significantly. For example, of seventy-nine liberations listed in Campinas in July of 1887, six were unconditional, four were on the basis of indemnity, and sixty-nine were conditional.[7] Five months later, however, a general list of 1,453 emancipations reported 743 unconditional, 395 for the end of the year, 303 for one year of service, and thirty-six for the end of 1889.[8] By March of 1888, immediate and unconditional emancipations in São Paulo clearly prevailed over conditional ones.[9] Some of the cases involved letters of liberty given collectively to more than 1,000 individuals from the same *fazenda*.[10] Slavery was now almost totally demoralized in São Paulo, and in April Campinas fell, the last powerful holdout of the Paulista slavocracy. Meanwhile, emancipations increased in other south-central provinces at a rapid clip. In Rio de Janeiro the most celebrated action involved the joint decision of the Viscount of São Clemente and the Baron of Nova Friburgo, which liberated a total of 1,909 slaves.[11] Campos became a free city in March, and the number of liberations on plantations near the city rose to almost 3,000 in one day in late April.[12] In southern Minas Gerais major cities such as São João d'el-Rei and Diamantina became almost totally free; in the latter area, planters an-

7. *Rio News,* August 15, 1887, p. 4.

8. *Ibid.,* February 15, 1888.

9. *Relatório* of the president of São Paulo province, Francisco de Paula Rodrigues Alves, January 10, 1888, pp. 2–3.

10. *Rio News,* February 24, 1888, p. 4.

11. *Cidade do Rio,* April 4, 1888, p. 1; April 25, 1888, p. 1; *Província de Minas,* April 6, 1888, p. 1; *A Redempção,* April 29, 1888, p. 2; *Revista Illustrada,* April 28, 1888, p. 6. Especially shocking for the defenders of slavery were the actions of the Viscount of Ararama and his relatives, who had been close political associates of slavocrat Paulino de Souza. They liberated more than 1,000 slaves. *Jornal do Recife,* March 28, 1888.

12. *Província de São Paulo,* May 2, 1888, p. 1; *Gazeta do Povo,* March 10, 1888, p. 1. As thousands of slaves fled in the Campos area, a *fazendeiro* and his wife prayed to Saint Anthony, asking that all should remain well. Shortly after, all their slaves escaped. *Gazeta do Povo,* March 23, 1888, p. 2.

nounced liberty for about 800 slaves in one meeting.[13] Similarly, *fazendeiros* in Espírito Santo proclaimed many manumissions, and the newspaper *Província de Espírito Santo* counseled hasty emancipation before the government would free the slaves by decree.[14]

In the early months of 1888 leaders in the Northeast were surprised to find that they no longer ranked in the vanguard of the emancipationist planter class. The rapid transformation of attitudes in the Central-South made coffee *fazendeiros* more progressive on the slavery question than the northeastern planters. Reading the danger signs, slave proprietors in the Northeast followed suit, and within a short time the manumission fever spread through the coastal strip. Some *senhores* acted because they feared an outbreak of disorders in their own regions. For example, when escapes became uncontrollable in sections of Pernambuco, some masters announced complete freedom for their slaves—except those who had run away! Others felt the collapse of the southern slavocracy made abolition a *fait accompli*. To wait for a government decree would only earn them the enmity of their Negro workers. By showing their own initiative to free the slaves, they hoped to receive credit for a benevolent act and cement good relations for the post-emancipation era. In April the municipal assembly of Recife sent a formal appeal to the Imperial Government asking for immediate abolition without indemnification, and by early May a movement was well under way to free the capital of the province.[15] By the time Parliament prepared to meet in Rio de Janeiro to decide on the fate of slavery, news poured in of tremendous activity in the North and Northeast. Bahia reported massive liberations of 130, 150, and 220 slaves on individual

13. *Gazeta do Povo,* April 5, 1888, p. 1; *Gazeta Mineira,* April 5, 1888, p. 2; April 12, 1888, p. 1.

14. *Gazeta do Povo,* April 12, 1888, p. 1.

15. *Diário da Bahia,* April 5, 1888, p. 2; *Jornal do Recife,* January 10, 12, 13, 15, 31, February 14, 1888; *Gazeta do Povo,* May 2, 1888, p. 1; *Relatório* of the vice-president of Pernambuco, Ignácio Joaquim de Souza Leão, April 16, 1888, p. 19; *Província de São Paulo,* April 7, 1888, p. 1.

plantations.[16] Many municipalities and *vilas* in Rio Grande do Norte, Alagoas, Piauí, and Sergipe were almost entirely free, and Pará reported large gains for the antislavery movement centering in Belém, where abolitionists cleared the city of bondsmen on a block-by-block basis.[17] Repercussions of the campaign reached other sections of the empire too. By May the capital city of the interior province of Goiás was almost free, and in Paraná the recently formed Paraná Abolitionist Confederation, under the leadership of an influential army colonel, F. Solon de Sampaio Ribeiro, coordinated the work of diverse antislavery groups.[18]

The emancipatory spirit exemplified by Brazilian planters on the eve of abolition did not represent devotion to principles of liberty or allegiance to the antislavery movement. As the newspaper *Novidades* explained, "No one freed his slaves out of the conviction that ownership was illegal; rather out of the desire for recompense or out of the speculative, ingenuous hope of gratitude." [19] A depressed spokesman for the slave proprietors well summarized the situation when he explained that the events in São Paulo proved "the *fazendeiros* liberate their slaves by the law of necessity, and not by the law of humanity." [20] Humanitarian sentiments were, at best, a minor factor in influencing the emancipatory efforts of *fazendeiros* in the late 1880s.

Representative of the realignment of Progressive Planters in the period of crisis was the political transformation of

16. *Diário da Bahia,* April 19, 1888, p. 1.

17. *Relatório* of the president of Sergipe, Olympio M. dos Santos Vidal, April 3, 1888, pp. 29–30; *Diário de Bahia,* April 3, 4, 5, 24, 27, May 4, 1888; *Cidade do Rio,* April 6, 1888, p. 1; *Província de São Paulo,* April 20, 1888; May 2, 1888, p. 1.

18. *Diário da Bahia,* May 4, 1888, p. 1; Lata 420–Docs 36, 55, 56, 60, 80 in the Arquivo do Instituto Histórico e Geográfico Brasileiro.

19. Quoted in Stanley J. Stein, *Vassouras: A Brazilian Coffee County, 1850–1900* (Cambridge, 1957), p. 225.

20. *O abolicionismo perante a história ou o dialogo das três províncias* (Rio de Janeiro, 1888), p. 118. Emelio Castelar supported immediate liberation of the slaves, declaring, "An epoch of gradual emancipation is an epoch of killing, of revolution, of civil war." See Luís Anselmo Fonseca, *A escravidão, o clero e o abolicionismo* (Bahia, 1887), p. 600.

Antônio Prado. Because of the great weight Antônio Prado carried as a spokesman for many *fazendeiros* in São Paulo, he was cheered as the most significant new addition to the abolitionist camp. Prado, the son of a wealthy planter, became an influential political leader in the decade of the Eighties. His family name commanded great respect; other Prados in the province also achieved fame as planters and politicians. Antônio Prado accumulated vast holdings in coffee plantations, banks, ships, and railroads. He also participated extensively in the civic affairs of the capital of São Paulo. Under the Baron of Cotegipe he served as Minister of Agriculture until he left the Cabinet to take a seat in the Senate in 1887.[21]

Prado incurred severe criticism from abolitionists during his years of political ascendency. When the Dantas debates began, he stood with the hard-liners of his province who believed the "rights of property" and "conditions of agriculture" were the paramount concerns. Prado even considered as too short Saraiva's original schedule to abolish slavery in seventeen years. Later, he exercised considerable influence to pass the Saraiva-Cotegipe Law and then, as Minister of Agriculture, engineered the deceptive measures which made the legislation less progressive than it appeared to be and extended the term of slavery an additional year and a half. (See Chapter III.) As a possessor of many slaves and a powerful political leader who opposed the more advanced reform proposals, Prado was considered a *bête noir* in abolitionist circles. As late as January 1887 the editors of the *Gazeta da Tarde* characterized him as a "slavocrat." [22]

Prado did show a predilection for immigration and free labor, but he was opposed to adopting radical proposals for emanci-

21. Richard M. Morse, *From Community to Metropolis: A Biography of São Paulo, Brazil* (Gainesville, 1958), p. 170; Pierre Monbeig, *Pionniers et planteurs de l'etat de São Paulo* (Paris, 1952), pp. 122–23; Prado, *Antônio Prado no império e na república,* pp. 13–14; *A Redempção,* March 3, 1887, p. 1.

22. Evaristo de Moraes, *A campanha abolicionista: 1879–1888* (Rio de Janeiro, 1924), pp. 97–98, 116, 146; *Gazeta da Tarde,* July 7, 1886, p. 1; January 22, 1887. Also see the issues of September 28 and 29, 1886.

pating the slaves. He cautioned against hasty solutions and claimed that *fazendeiros* needed time to prepare for the transformation to a free labor system.[23] To accommodate the needs of the *fazendeiros,* Prado recommended marking a term of a specified number of years for the abolition of slavery.[24] He believed this was the only means of keeping the Negroes at work because, without the coercive influence of slavery, Prado thought that most of them would run away from the plantations. He had little faith in the freedmen's reliability as workers; rather, he emphasized European immigration as the solution to the manpower problem.[25]

With the upsurge in abolitionist activity, Prado began to change his posture on the slavery question. He spoke in the Senate in favor of the prohibition on whipping, and, in the following year, supported the idea of giving freedom to slaves who had been improperly registered by their masters.[26] Most important, Prado reacted quickly and flexibly in response to the breakdown of order on the plantations. When tumult threatened the stability of Paulista society in 1887, Prado urged the slave proprietors to establish a three-year term for the end of slavery. "The contrary is to attempt the impossible," he warned. "It would be as if one wished to contain a swelling river by means of a dam!" [27] When controversy erupted over the slaveholders' request for government assistance in pursuing fugitive slaves, Prado broke away from the politically reactionary groups and terminated his alliance with the Baron of Cotegipe.[28] He was a conservative on the emancipation question, not a reactionary. When he realized that rigid resistance to abolitionism was no longer acceptable and could lead to

23. Prado, *Antônio Prado no império e na república,* pp. 30, 67–69, 84, 86–87.

24. *Ibid.,* pp. 25, 63, 75, 87.

25. See the article by Afonso de Escragnolle Taunay in *1° Centenário do Conselheiro Antônio da Silva Prado* (São Paulo, 1946), p. 169.

26. *Revista Illustrada,* June 30, 1887; *A Redempção,* April 22, 1888, p. 2.

27. Prado, *Antônio Prado no império e na república,* pp. 228–29.

28. *Cidade do Rio,* November 3 and 19, 1887.

greater troubles, he changed his posture. Sensing the great difficulty of apprehending large groups of fugitive slaves, Prado asked, "Can the public power guarantee to the proprietors the permanency of the slaves on the *fazendas* if the dangerous conditions in São Paulo—that is, the flights en masse—should become generalized?" [29] By insisting that it was the master's job to capture runaway slaves, Prado significantly influenced the government's decision not to pressure the army into taking action in the crisis.[30]

In December of 1887 Prado organized the Society for Liberation and the Organization of Work and called a large group of Paulista planters to its first meeting. In a speech before the assembled *fazendeiros,* Prado explained that the organization would aim to check the flights of slaves and prevent the disruption of agricultural production. "The disorganization of labor, as a consequence of the slaves abandoning the *fazendas,* and the general disturbance of public order are the things that most worry the Paulista *fazendeiro,*" said Prado. "It is that side of the labor question that is of most interest to the association." As the meeting closed, the supporters of Antônio Prado pledged to liberate all of their slaves within three years.[31] Although Prado thought a three-year term of service was the definitive solution to the slavery problem in December 1887, by early 1888 he switched to advocating immediate abolition with the condition of two years of forced residence for the freedmen. Finally, in May 1888, he accepted the idea of unconditional abolition. His concern about the continuing upheaval brought about the rapid change in attitude. The government had to give the *coup de grâce* to slavery, he believed, or else the outcome of the conflict might be injurious to the whole society. Prado believed that it was necessary for the two major parties to come to terms on a policy of immediate emancipation, otherwise "abolition

29. Prado, *Antônio Prado no império e na república,* p. 243.
30. *Correio Paulistano,* January 31, 1888, p. 1; *O Paíz,* February 11, 1888, p. 1.
31. *1° Centenario do Conselheiro Antônio da Silva Prado,* p. 22.

would [be] realized exclusively by popular revolution." As he later explained, "If the slavery question had not been advocated by the government, the tranquility that one notes still would not reign." [32]

Prado's progressive position was of critical importance, and it gave great momentum to the antislavery movement in its final stages. Abolitionists hailed the Paulista's conversion and adopted him as a hero of the movement. In the excitement of national emancipation, abolitionists were willing to forgive Prado for the eleventh-hour nature of his allegiance to the campaign.[33]

Other erstwhile adversaries of the abolitionists also became political chameleons in the period of crisis. One by one the political leaders who previously had been cautious and defensive about emancipation moved into the immediatist camp. Fearing the intensification of disturbances, figures such as Moreira de Barros, Campos Salles, and José Antônio Saraiva resolved to destroy the source of the problem.

Moreira de Barros had long been the chief political spokesmen for Hard-Core Slaveholders in the Paraíba Valley section of São Paulo, and he had been one of the most effective managers of the resistance against the abolitionist movement in Parliament. But in January 1888, after witnessing an avalanche of escapes from the *fazendas,* Barros suddenly announced the unconditional liberation of all his slaves, and he began boasting that he was an "abolitionist." [34] Republican deputy Campos Salles altered his position on abolition so

32. Prado, *Antônio Prado no império e na república,* p. 23; *Província de São Paulo,* April 5, 1888, pp. 1, 25.

33. *Cidade do Rio,* November 23, 1887. In the historical literature Antônio Prado has been treated as a "statesman" who confronted the crisis of slavery with "practical good sense." See, for example, Luís Amaral, *História geral da agricultura brasileira* (São Paulo, 1940), I, 343; Joaquim Nabuco, *Minha formação* (São Paulo, 1934), p. 196.

34. *O Paíz,* January 5, 1888, p. 1; *Cidade do Rio,* January 5, 1888, p. 1; *Correio Paulistano,* January 6, 1881, p. 1. In this regard, the editor of the *Rio News* assessed the situation accurately when he predicted: "When the country can wholly abolish it, slavery will find deserters among its best allies" (October 15, 1880, p. 3).

quickly that he began demanding immediate emancipation while he still possessed slaves. The Paulista *fazendeiro*-politician who later became President of the Republic maintained a cautious interest in gradual emancipation, but in November of 1887 he turned to immediatism. He and his associates withdrew from the Society for Liberation and the Organization of Work because they considered Prado's plan of a three-year term for slavery too conservative. A week later Salles liberated all of his slaves.[35] Another eleventh-hour advocate of immediate abolition was José Antônio Saraiva, the leader of the ministry that designed the 1885 law to delay complete abolition for thirteen years. In February of 1888, however, he gave his full support to the movement and urged the government to adopt promptly a policy of unconditional liberation. "The slavery question can no longer be treated with a project that prolongs the institution, since all resistance is uselessly ineffective," said Saraiva.[36]

With sudden haste similar to the actions of these political leaders, the Church, too, became a late convert to abolitionism. Beginning in July 1887 prelates from diverse sections of the empire issued a series of pastoral letters condemning slavery and calling for abolition, and by October religious orders were rushing to announce emancipation of their slaves.[37] In one of the pastoral letters the Bishop of Diamantina (in Minas Gerais) admitted that clergymen had not been active in the abolition movement, but he ascribed this passivity to the fear of the "grave consequences of a precipitation" and harmful repercussions of abolition.[38] Luís Anselmo Fonseca, author of *A escravidão, o clero e o abolicionismo* (*Slavery, the Clergy and*

35. *Rio News,* January 5, 1888, p. 3; *1° Centenário do Conselheiro Antônio da Silva Prado,* p. 24. Campos Salles' earlier attitude toward emancipation, as expressed in a series of articles in the December 1880 issues of *Província de São Paulo,* is filled with equivocation.

36. *O País,* February 10, 1888, p. 1.

37. *Ibid.,* October 7, 1887, p. 1; October 13, 1887, p. 1; João Dornas Filho, *A escravidão no brasil* (Rio de Janeiro, 1939), pp. 233, 249–51.

38. *O País,* October 24, 1887, p. 1; *Revista Illustrada,* September 11, 1887, p. 2.

Abolitionism), was not impressed by the tardy action of the bishops and declared that they were only speaking out "shortly after slavery became demoralized and abolition captured the land." [39]

As the abolitionist movement gained momentum in 1887 and 1888, antislavery candidates swept the elections in many parts of the empire. In the province of Rio de Janeiro abolitionist Rodrigues Peixoto won an important victory despite all the obstacles put in his way by the friends of Paulino de Souza.[40] In Pernambuco, the Cotegipe ministry mustered all of its political power to try to defeat Joaquim Nabuco, but the abolitionist leader won impressively; and in São Paulo, Alagoas, Bahia, and other provinces, the Cotegipe ministry suffered more humiliating defeats.[41]

In ordinary circumstances the political developments would have been sufficiently portentous to force the resignation of the ministry. But Cotegipe held tightly to the reins of government because he realized that his ministry represented the last hope of the slave proprietors. From the time he had taken control as President of the Council in August of 1885, Cotegipe, who supported the 1885 law as the final solution to the problem of slavery, tried to maintain a program of solid resistance against the abolitionists, sometimes even employing the police forces under government authority to disrupt abolitionist meetings. Until the final crisis, the Baron of Cotegipe succeeded in keeping his planter following in line by describing himself as the necessary protector of public order. As long as he remained leader, Cotegipe assured the slaveholders, emancipation would have to come under conditions of economic stability and domestic tranquility. His theme paid off until 1887 when some leading planters saw that Cotegipe's policy of intransi-

39. Fonseca, *A escravidão, o clero e o abolicionismo,* p. 498.

40. *O Paíz,* November 22, 1887, p. 3.

41. Joaquim Nabuco, *Minha Formação* (São Paulo, 1934), pp. 224–25; Osório Duque-Estrada, *A abolição: 1831–1888* (Rio de Janeiro, 1918), p. 224; *Cidade do Rio,* December 13, 1887, p. 1; January 19, 1888, p. 1; *Revista Illustrada,* January 14, 1888, pp. 4–5; March 3 and 10, 1888.

gence was proving detrimental to order and prosperity. This approach to the problem, which one observer described as "fanatic resistance," seemed only to exacerbate tensions, lower public morale, and increase apprehension about the fate of the nation. Princess Isabel spoke to Cotegipe about the dangerous developments and defeats his friends suffered in the elections. She expressed doubt that his ministry could continue unless it showed new initiative in favor of emancipation, but Cotegipe did not indicate readiness to alter his stance radically.[42]

The controversy that brought Cotegipe's downfall involved the chief of police of Rio de Janeiro, João Coelho Bastos, who had become a principal target of the abolitionists. Cotegipe had worked closely with Bastos to coordinate the government's efforts to repress antislavery activities and return fugitive slaves to their masters. Abolitionists demanded Bastos' dismissal, but they got little response until new disorders in the capital city highlighted the police chief's inability to control the citizenry.[43] In March of 1888 a conflict broke out in Rio de Janeiro between sailors and policemen after the police beat a naval officer. The turbulence spread as citizens of the city joined the sailors in parading through the streets and defying the police. Shooting occurred in several clashes. As the alarmed public blamed the upheaval on the government and the police, the Princess Regent, under heavy pressure, asked Cotegipe to dismiss Police Chief Bastos. Cotegipe, aware of the significance of these developments, then submitted his own resignation. With him went the last hopes of the inflexible slaveholders.[44]

42. Notes and letters of Princess Isabel, March 1888; December, 1888 (?), CXCIX–9030; João Ferreira de Moura to Visconde de Paranaguá, November 21, 1887; 21.11887, Arquivo do Museu Imperial; Baron of Cotegipe to J. Arthur de Sousa Corrêa, March 9, 1888, Instituto Joaquim Nabuco.

43. Duque-Estrada, *A abolição,* pp. 197, 214–15; *Gazeta da Tarde,* October 26, 1885, p. 1; Moraes, *A campanha abolicionista,* p. 155. For a defense of Coelho Bastos' actions, see *Novidades,* January 12, 1888, p. 1.

44. *Diário de Santos,* March 4, 1888, p. 1; *Cidade do Rio,* March 3, 4, and 5, 1888; Carolina Nabuco, *The Life of Joaquim Nabuco* (Stanford, 1950), pp. 163–64. Letters of Princess Isabel, March 1888, CXCIX–9030, Arquivo do Museu Imperial; *Revista Illustrada,* March 3 and 10, 1888.

The Princess Regent chose João Alfredo, another Conservative, to replace Cotegipe. An influential politician from Pernambuco, former president of São Paulo and senator in the Imperial Government, Alfredo had defended the interests of slavery during the debates over the Saraiva-Cotegipe Law, and in 1887 he opposed a proposal that would have marked January 1, 1890, for abolition. After realizing the seriousness of the breakdown of discipline on the plantations, however, he emancipated his own slaves, broke from Cotegipe's group, and joined Antônio Prado in leading the flexible planters to a progressive position on slavery.[45]

When Alfredo took control of the government in March 1888, many believed he would seek to delay abolition. His Cabinet included political leaders who had long fought to extend the life of slavery, men who could be expected to amend an emancipation law with deceptive qualifications. Diverse rumors circulated at the time of Alfredo's appointment. Some suggested that the new chief minister would obligate slaves to remain with their masters until the end of the coffee harvest. The more conservative estimates indicated that Alfredo was considering additional laws to prevent vagrancy and require the Negroes to remain on the plantations for a five-year term of service.[46]

But slavery was a collapsing institution in 1888, and temporizing solutions could not hold back the tide. In the first few months of Alfredo's ministry abolitionism made great gains across the empire. The over-all progress of the movement was so rapid that the degree of its success at the time when Parliament opened in May of 1888 surprised even the most ardent abolitionists. Earlier, between 1885 and 1887, abolitionists and many emancipationists supported several emancipa-

45. *Novidades,* July 11, 1887, p. 1.

46. Moraes, *A campanha abolicionista,* p. 325; *Duque-Estrada, A abolição,* pp. 220–30; *Cincocentenário da abolição em Pernambuco Catalogo da exposição realisada no Teatro Santa Isabel de 13 a 31 de maio de 1938* (Pernambuco, 1938), p. 7; *Revista Illustrada,* 1884, n.378, p. 2; *Província de São Paulo,* May 5, 1888, p. 1; *Annaes da Câmara* (1888), June 7, p. 83; *"Projecto de lei de abolição e projecto de lei de serviços rurales,"* March 30, 1888, Instituto Joaquim Nabuco.

tion projects designed to set various terminal dates for slavery. Although the authors of the plans reacted to abolitionist gains by moving up the suggested dates for the complete extinction of slavery, they did not anticipate abolition without qualifications as early as May 1888. Among the major proposals, all of which were defeated, were José Bonifácio's plan in 1885 to end slavery by 1893, Senator Manoel Pinto de Souza Dantas' plan in 1886 to end slavery in five years, Senator Joaquim Floriano de Godoy's plan in 1887 to end slavery immediately and obligate freedmen to two years of service, Senator Manoel Pinto de Souza Dantas' plan in 1887 to end slavery by December 31, 1889, and Senator Affonso d'Escragnolle Taunay's plan in 1887 to end slavery by December 25, 1889. Even as late as December of 1887 the radical abolitionist José do Patrocínio placed his hopes for abolition on the year 1889, the centenary of the Rights of Man.[47] Now, in May 1888, abolitionists fully realized how much the spreading turbulence in Brazil could help them to effectuate an early solution. When the government presented its proposal, many antislavery leaders discarded their contingency plans for delayed liberation and terms of service. "I didn't believe my eyes, I didn't believe my ears," exclaimed Joaquim Nabuco, "when I heard the noble President pronounce those words—immediate and unconditional abolition." [48]

Actually, the government did not decide to support complete, unqualified abolition until just before Parliament opened. The readiness of deputies and senators for a radical solution could not be ascertained until they began to assemble in Rio de Janeiro and reported on recent developments in their respective areas.[49] It quickly became clear that slavery was collapsing on a much broader scale than many had imagined, and there did not seem to be any prospect that an effective method

47. *Cidade do Rio,* December 16, 1887, p. 1.

48. Joaquim Nabuco, *Discursos parlamentares: 1879–1889* (São Paulo, 1949), p. 442.

49. *Província de São Paulo,* May 5, 1888, p. 1; *Annaes da Câmara* (1888), June 7, p. 83; Duque-Estrada, *A abolição,* p. 237; *Gazeta do Povo,* April 29, 1888, p. 1.

could be found to impede flights from the plantations. No accurate tally of the number of slaves in the empire could be offered in May of 1888. Perhaps 500,000 blacks still remained in bondage. Yet the structure of the institution had become so fragile that this figure was misleading. Thousands of slaves were on the verge of manumission or were prepared to take exit if they did not receive the gift of liberty. As Senator Christiano Ottoni described the situation:

> In the beginning of 1888 slavery was abolished in fact, by revolution; those worked who wished; every slave who abandoned his master shortly found someone who would give him asylum; the authorities did not have force to apprehend them. . . . The characteristic of slavery—that is, forced and gratuitous labor—disappeared.[50]

With the foundations of the system crumbling, slavery was no longer a viable institution. In the light of these conditions, the Baron of Cotegipe admitted that the project for the immediate extinction of slavery represented "nothing more than the recognition of an already existent fact." [51]

On the Cabinet level, only the Minister of Justice, Ferreira Vianna, tried to soften the impending blow on the slaveholders. He received a barrage of criticism for his efforts. In expectation of the abolition law, Vianna sent a message to the provincial chiefs of police outlining the procedures they should follow to maintain order and prevent the freedmen from becoming disruptive. His suggestions had little effect after abolitionists denounced the statement as an offense to the idea of liberty.[52]

While members of Parliament prepared to convene, the Princess Regent made her contribution to the movement by taking a public position favorable to abolition. This action was not due completely to her antislavery sentiments, although her feelings on the subject were well known. After her father left

50. Moraes, *A campanha abolicionista,* pp. 391–92.
51. *Annaes do Senado* (1888), I, 34.
52. *A Redempção,* May 3, 1888, p. 2; *Província de São Paulo,* May 2, 1888, p. 1.

for Europe late in 1887, Isabel took charge and sat quietly on the throne during the period of the government's repressive policies. But she became noticeably impressed by the rapid march of events, especially the rise of national sentiment for abolition, the flights of slaves, the uncooperative attitude of the military, and the changing attitudes in Parliament. Then, in March 1888, Joaquim Nabuco cleverly arranged to put additional pressure on the Princess Regent. He cancelled a proposed trip to the United States and arranged to have an audience with Pope Leo XIII in Rome. Nabuco knew that a statement from the Pontiff would greatly impress the religious sentiments of the Princess Regent. The Pope's comments, which were published in *O Paíz,* included the following: "Slavery is condemned by the Church and it should have ended a long time ago. A man cannot be the slave of another man. All are equally sons of God, *des infants de Dieu.*" [53]

Nabuco's efforts may have been influential, for Isabel's "Statement from the Throne" of May 3 condemned slavery as "antagonistic to the Christian and liberal spirit of our institutions." In the speech, drafted primarily with the assistance of Ferreria Vianna, Isabel expressed confidence that abolition would be achieved "when the private interest comes spontaneously to assist Brazil in relieving itself of the unhappy inheritance which the needs of agriculture have maintained." [54] Isabel's sympathies with the abolitionists were now overt, but her "Statement from the Throne" still fell short of an outright, unequivocal endorsement of immediate emancipation. Some attributed her hedging to the influence of Vianna or other Cabinet members.[55] The editor of the *Gazeta do Povo* likened the disappointing speech to a wax nose that could be molded to

53. Duque-Estrada, *A abolição,* pp. 302–06; Nabuco, *Minha Formação,* p. 225; Notes and letters of Princess Isabel, March 1888; December 1888 (?), CXCIX–9030, Arquivo do Museu Imperial; J. Artur de Sousa Corrêa to Baron of Cotegipe, February 2, 1888; February 2, 1888; February 4, 1888, Instituto Joaquim Nabuco.

54. *Fallas do trono desde o anno de 1823 até o anno de 1889* (Rio de Janeiro, 1889); *Rio News,* May 5, 1888, p. 3.

55. *Gazeta da Bahia,* May 5 and 6, 1888.

fit any profile.[56] With the stage set for the last act, the final contribution to the cause of abolition would have to be made by the leaders in Parliament.

Rio de Janeiro was engulfed in excitement as Parliament opened its first session in early May. Huge crowds filled the streets approaching the Chamber of Deputies and the Senate. When the Princess Regent, Joaquim Nabuco, Souza Dantas, and other heroes of the day entered the buildings, the multitudes showered them with flowers. People jammed the galleries of Parliament cheering, hooting, and screaming for the vote. Outside the buildings, groups waited with musical instruments and rockets, ready to belt out the national hymn and create a noisy display of approval with the first word of abolitionist victory. The commotion had a profound effect on the delegates, keeping them constantly aware of the state of excitation over the issue.[57]

Only a few senators and deputies spoke out to defend slave proprietors against the abolitionist onslaught. They were led by the most notable of the Hard-Core Slaveholders, Andrade Figueira, Paulino de Souza, and the Baron of Cotegipe.

Andrade Figueira pleaded for the "cause of good sense in the face of excessive passions," and he complained that the noisy scenes before the opening of Parliament made discussion of the problem useless and impossible.[58] Then Figueira analyzed the reasons for the sudden acceptance of immediate abolition on a national scale:

> To what motive of public order do we owe, therefore, to this change of opinion, to this haste, such, which intends even to suffocate discussion?
>
> It is said that some disorders have been practiced, that it no longer is possible to maintain discipline on the agri-

56. *Gazeta do Povo,* May 5, 1888, p. 1.

57. *Rio News,* May 5, 1883, p. 2; *Gazeta de Notícias,* May 4, 1888; *Annaes da Câmara* (1888), June 7, p. 88; *Annaes do Senado* (1888), July 14, p. 153; *Cidade do Rio,* May 10, 1888, p. 3; *Gazeta do Povo,* April 29, 1888, p. 1; *Revista Illustrada,* May 3, 1888, p. 2; May 13, 1888, p. 6.

58. *Annaes da Câmara* (1888), I, 49.

> cultural establishments, from a certain time until now; the facts of São Paulo are cited; also isolated facts in the province of Rio de Janeiro, in Minas [Gerais] and in some other points of the empire are cited.[59]

Figueira explained that he could understand why the slave proprietors of São Paulo liberated their slaves after witnessing such widespread disorders, but he called these actions emancipation by "force" and "coercion." He then warned that abolition would mean the immediate loss of 600,000 workers to national production.[60] Senator Paulino de Souza called the proposed emancipation law "unconstitutional, uneconomic and inhuman." He deemed it unconstitutional because it destroyed legal property without allowing the slaveholders recompense, uneconomic because it would bring about the disorganization of work, and inhuman because it would break the slaves away from the paternal care of their masters and leave the old, the sick, and the orphans to their own fate. Paulino pointed out that slavery was the predominant labor system in the Paraíba Valley and that this region had been the source of national riches in the previous fifty years. To decree immediate abolition would upset the stability of the economy and society by setting loose thousands of individuals who were not prepared with education or habits of liberty.[61] The Baron of Cotegipe of Bahia blamed Antônio Prado for the collapse of the resistance movement. He charged that Prado's refusal to insist that the military apprehend fugitive slaves and his switch to immediate abolition brought the final downfall of the slaveholder interests. Cotegipe then suggested a compromise proposal that he had not been willing to accept during his own ministry. He recommended a three-year term of services similar to Prado's earlier plan.[62]

But it was too late for compromises. Many parliamentary

59. *Ibid.*, p. 50.
60. *Ibid.*, pp. 52–54.
61. *Annaes do Senado* (1888), I, 38–42.
62. *Ibid.*, pp. 33–37.

leaders had previously battled fiercely to delay emancipation, but now they capitulated before the wave of national sentiment for immediate abolition. One of these eleventh-hour emancipationists, the Minister of Agriculture, Rodriga Silva, reasoned:

> Whatever the horrors of my contradictions, whatever the injustices and cruelties of the concepts that I have been ingenuous to, it has been all well compensated for with what I did for the cause that is today the matter of general rejoicing in the country.[63]

An overwhelming majority of the deputies and senators were determined to pass a law with no strings attached. To be sure, many from both sides of the question desired additional provisions. Spokesmen for the slave proprietors wanted stipulations about location of services, indemnification, and bank loans to the planters; extreme abolitionists wanted provisions for minimum salaries for freed laborers and schools to educate the freedmen. But discussion of these matters would have delayed the settlement for many months. Members of Parliament could not afford to allow the crisis of Brazilian slavery to intensify further; the turbulence had already caused much anxiety among the population.[64]

The votes in the Chamber of Deputies and the Senate fell overwhelmingly in favor of the decree, which simply stated:

Article 1. From the date of this Law slavery is declared abolished in Brazil.

Article 2. All contrary provisions are revoked.

Slavocrats from the Paraíba Valley made most of the last cries of defiance. Of the nine votes against the law in the House of Deputies, eight were cast by representatives from the province of Rio de Janeiro.[65]

63. *Annaes da Câmara* (1888), I, 56–57.

64. *Província de São Paulo,* April 29, 1888, p. 1; May 5, 1888, p. 1; *Cidade do Rio,* April 28, 1888, p. 1; May 2, 1888, p. 1; *Annaes do Senado* (1888), July 14, p. 153.

65. Emília Viotti da Costa, *Da senzala à colônia* (São Paulo, 1966), p. 446.

The final solution was not determined on the basis of parties, although there were some grumblings from both political camps. While the Conservative Baron of Cotegipe blamed the Liberals for abolition, Liberal party partisan Silveira Martins denounced the Princess Regent for choosing the Conservative party to make the reform.[66] But Joaquim Nabuco reflected the attitude of most of the legislators when he said that abolition could not be a party issue. Nabuco judged that the Liberals had lost their chance to administer the reform when they divided over the Dantas plan in 1884.[67] Also, he and other Liberals recognized that only the Conservatives could pass the abolition law at that time. In order for the Liberal party to organize a new ministry, it would have to dissolve the Chamber of Deputies and hold new elections. This might delay the settlement, and the nation was too impatient to accept a postponement for political purposes.[68]

The celebration of abolition became a national holiday. Thousands of people in the cities and the countryside left their work to dance, sing, and shout to the glory of liberation. For ten days the state of excitation in Brazil seemed like an extended *carnaval*. Salutes were made to the heroes of the day—not only to those who had fought for many years against great opposition but also to the converted abolitionists such as Antônio Prado and João Alfredo. In the moment of rejoicing, the people were willing to forgive the eleventh-hour liberators for their years of resistance.[69]

Contemporaries acknowledged the reasons behind the government's hurried action to pass abolition. Leaders had been

66. *Annaes do Senado* (1888), I, 20; *Diário do Parlamento Brasileiro: Senado,* 13 de maio, 1888 (sessão de 12 de maio).

67. See Nabuco's speeches in the *Camara dos Srs. Deputados,* May 7 and 10, 1888.

68. *Gazeta da Tarde,* March 22, 1888.

69. Later, the editors of *Revista Illustrada* reminded readers that the true abolitionists were men like Antônio Bento, Joaquim Nabuco, João Ramos, João Cordeiro, João Clapp, and José Mariano—leaders who had been outspoken when it was dangerous to be called an "abolitionist" (August 7, 1889). Also see the article *"Risos e reflexoes"* in the *Província de São Paulo,* May 25, 1888, p. 1.

motivated by a fear of the "provocative new discussions and rancorous ferment that delay of the [emancipation] law would produce all over the country," explained the editors of the *Província de São Paulo.*[70] Postponement of a decision would only make conditions worse. The agitation of abolitionists and flights of slaves created "a dangerous and intolerable situation from which it was urgent to escape," said the president of São Paulo.[71] Observers thought rejection of the project for immediate abolition would increase racial hostilities, trigger an "inevitable" explosion of new slave insurrections and possibly throw the empire into a bloody, catastrophic conflict resembling the American Civil War.[72] "Only the blind would not see the effects of violent popular pressure," declared Joaquim Serra.[73] In the months following abolition, former abolitionists, emancipationists, and slavocrats agreed in assessing the primary factors which motivated the hasty and forceful decision of May 1888.[74] Christiano Ottoni gave one of the most dramatic descriptions. Who could deny it? he asked. Really, abolition had come "by revolution." [75]

The demise of slavery in Brazil was sudden, not gradual. Only after 1885 did figures for the total slave population drop precipitously, reflecting pressures of the abolitionist campaign and the concomitant upheaval. The *Lei Áurea* simply formalized the funeral for the institution which had reached its death throes in a year of turmoil. The foundations of slavery in Brazil

70. *Província de São Paulo,* May 13, 1888, p. 1.

71. *Relatório* of the president of São Paulo province, Pedro Vicente de Azevedo, January 11, 1889, p. 144.

72. *Revista Illustrada,* May 13, 1889.

73. *Ibid.,* May 13, 1888, p. 7.

74. *A Redempção,* August 18, 1888, p. 2; May 13, 1899, pp. 4–5; *Cidade do Rio,* April 13, 1888, p. 1; Notes of Princess Isabel (December 1888?), Arquivo do Museu Imperial; *Revista Illustrada,* May 13, 1888, pp. 4–5; *Falla* of the president of Alagoas, José Cesario de Miranda Monteiro de Barros, October 6, 1888, p. 43; Pierre Denis, *O Brazil no século* XX (Lisbon, n.d.), p. 158; *Annaes da Câmara* (1888), June 7, pp. 90–93.

75. C. B. Ottoni, *Autobiographia de C. B. Ottoni* (Rio de Janeiro, 1908), pp. 345, 348; C. B. Ottoni, *O advento da república* (Rio de Janeiro, 1890), pp. 62–63.

had collapsed by May 1888. "Gentlemen, servile labor is definitely finished," said deputy Lourenço de Albuquerque in a speech shortly before Parliament passed the emancipation law. "Already slavery does not exist in the empire; what exists is an apparition of slavery that is hindering the organization of free labor and maintaining a state of excitation that offers serious dangers." [76] Most political leaders saw the futility of continued resistance and feared that further delay of abolition might result in spreading anarchy or social revolution—consequences which they judged far more dangerous than simple emancipation of the slaves.

76. *Annaes da Câmara* (1888), I, 20.

10: The Aftermath of Abolition

THE ERA OF abolitionist controversy had seen much speculation about the possible consequences of abolition. Would the planters sink into economic ruin in the aftermath? Would the decision have repercussions on the political future of the empire? How would slaves behave once they won their freedom? Could they find a viable place in the economy and society? The history of the years following the decision of May 13, 1888, offers mixed answers. It shows that there was much substance to some of the fears expressed before abolition while other dire predictions did not bear out. But even the unrealistic expectations made an impact in the post-emancipation era, because persistent fears prevented many people from recognizing that their worst prejudices lacked foundation in fact. In time, the prejudices developed a force and logic of their own.

These conditions reveal the continuity of history—the important relationship between developments that occurred before abolition and the events that transpired after it. In the view of Brazil's eminent historian Sérgio Buarque de Holanda, 1888 was the most decisive date in the nation's development, a watershed which marked the beginning of a new epoch.[1] Indeed abolition helped to accelerate the new transformations in Brazilian society. Thus, the issues which came into play during the abolitionist controversy gave a good indication of which way the winds of Brazil's future were blowing.

1. Sérgio Buarque de Holanda, *Raizes do Brasil* (Rio de Janeiro, 1948), p. 138.

THE PLANTERS

Generally speaking, in the aftermath of abolition Progressive Planters found themselves in a boom economy, while the former Hard-Core Slaveholders sunk quickly into depression and the Traditional Planters continued to struggle along in a sluggish market that showed little sign of recuperation. Developments in São Paulo revealed that much of the late planter opposition to abolition there had been based on a conservative businessman's fear of change rather than a deep-seated belief that abolition would ruin the planters economically or politically. Paulista planters could adjust to the new situation in the midst of a coffee bonanza. The dislocations caused by abolitionist agitation had only a brief effect in São Paulo, where coffee production had been spiraling upward before the tumult of early 1888. The Paulista coffee economy recovered rapidly in the second half of 1888 and soared ahead of other areas. By 1892 exportation of coffee sacks from the city of Santos exceeded exportation from the city of Rio de Janeiro, and by 1900 the population of São Paulo state surpassed that of Rio.[2] The central zone of São Paulo—the region of Campinas, Piracicaba, and Itú—reached its highest point in the late 1880s.[3] As *fazendeiros* pushed into new, fertile, virgin lands, the western region became the state's nucleus of coffee production, and Riberão Prêto competed with Campinas as the boom city of the interior plantation society.[4] With São Paulo's leadership, Brazil produced more than 50 percent of the world's coffee in the 1890s.[5]

The situation was gloomy in other areas. Former Hard-Core

2. *Relatório* of the president of São Paulo, Pedro Vicente de Azevedo, January 11, 1889, pp. 144–45; Roberto C. Simonsen, *Aspectos da historia econômica do café* (Rio de Janeiro, 1938), pp. 38–40; Leóncio Basbaum, *História sincera da república, das origens até 1889* (Rio de Janeiro, 1957), p. 138.

3. Sérgio Milliet, *Roteiro do café e outros ensaios* (São Paulo, 1946), pp. 10–45.

4. Pierre Denis, *O Brasil no século xx* (Lisbon, n.d.), pp. 142–43.

5. Simonsen, *Aspectos da história econômica do café,* pp. 17–31.

Slaveholders who had held large numbers of bondsmen during a period of economic squeeze suffered severely. In Rio de Janeiro, for example, the coffee culture had begun a long-run decline in the mid-1880s, and abolition precipitated the drop. The *Lei Áurea* had entirely swept away the formal value of the human property in which they had invested so heavily in preceding years. Plagued by soil exhaustion, declining production, and lack of funds to pay wages to the freedmen, many desperate *fazendeiros* mortgaged their property to the banks.[6] Some who were still solvent recognized that the curtain was fast descending on the golden days of the Paraíba Valley and moved on to São Paulo to build new fortunes.[7] Production figures reflected Rio's rapid demise after decades of leadership in the fabulous coffee boom. While São Paulo pushed Rio out of first place in production in the mid-1880s, Minas Gerais pushed it out of second position in the mid-1890s.[8] Heavily in debt, and with little collateral to show that loans to them would be a safe investment, the former Hard-Core Slaveholders viewed abolition as a disaster which greatly exacerbated their already severe economic difficulties.

Former Hard-Core Slaveholders of Bahia suffered from similar problems. They had relied heavily on slave labor for manpower. Abolition brought temporary dislocation as freedmen left the plantations after the emancipation proclamation. When the ex-slaves returned, *senhores de engenho* lacked the capital to pay them. Traditional Planters were not caught off balance so severely by abolition, since they were already well along the way in making the transition to a free labor force. Still, the

6. *Ibid.*, pp. 30–31; *Relatório* of the vice-president of Rio de Janeiro province, Manuel Jacintho Nogueira da Gama, August 8, 1888; Stanley J. Stein, *Vassouras: A Brazilian Coffee County, 1850–1900* (Cambridge, 1957), pp. 277–79; Agenor de Roure, *A abolição e seus reflexos econômicas: Conferência realizada na segunda sessão de 1918, a 14 de Maio, no Instituto Histórico e Geográfico Brasileiro* (Rio de Janeiro, 1918), pp. 17, 27.

7. Afonso de Toledo Bandeira de Melo, *O trabalho servil no Brasil* (Rio de Janeiro, 1936), p. 84.

8. Roberto C. Simonsen, *A evolução industrial no Brasil* (São Paulo, 1939), p. 37.

long-range prospects for both types of sugar planters did not look good. Prices for the product were low, and most Bahian planters had maintained such antiquated production methods that they were not prepared to compete effectively. In many areas cane production seemed to stop completely as proprietors left the fields idle. Only the few sugar producers who had established *engenhos centrais* (central sugar mills) with modern equipment and free laborers fared with some success in escaping the dislocations of abolition.[9]

Repercussions varied in other sectors of the Bahian economy. Tobacco culture experienced some minor setbacks. The cereal and pastoral economies of the interior declined too, primarily because of the drought. Coffee and cacao planters of the littoral were not hurt much by abolition in part because of growing markets for their products and because they had not depended heavily on slave labor before abolition.[10]

By 1888 Pernambuco was well ahead of Bahia in modernizing sectors of its sugar economy through the development of *usinas* (central sugar factories), enterprises which had been established with the help of British capital. The *usinas* employed many free laborers and were not upset by abolition. But the over-all economic fortunes of Pernambuco remained in difficulty, not so much as a result of the emancipation of the slaves as from the low world price of sugar, foreign competition, lack of capital, and inefficient production of many planters.[11]

In the months following abolition, indemnification became the burning issue for planters who found themselves in difficult economic straits. Indebted planters began a concerted effort to obtain a transfusion of capital by forcing the government to pay them for the slaves they lost. They had considered

9. *Diário da Bahia,* May 9, 1888; Denis, *O Brasil no século* XX, p. 345; *Falla* of the vice-president of Bahia, Aurelio Ferreira Espinheira, April 3, 1889, pp. 156–58. Symbolically, the Baron of Cotegipe, an estate owner, died a poor man shortly after the abolition of slavery.

10. *Falla,* Aurelio Ferreira Espinheira, pp. 156–58.

11. *Relatorio* of the president of Pernambuco, Manoel Alves de Araujo, November 14, 1889, p. 8.

the demand before May 13, of course, but feared that an extended debate on the subject would increase the frustration of abolitionists and slaves, resulting in greater violence. Once the abolition law was passed, however, ex-slaveholders lost little time in organizing their campaign. Some gathered together to plan strategy even before the celebrations settled down.[12] As Parliament went back into session, they made indemnification the leading issue of the day, monopolizing much of the time in the debates of May, June, and July. The new drive received strong support from former Hard-Core Slaveholders of Bahia, Minas Gerais, and Rio de Janeiro. The Baron of Cotegipe (of Bahia) and Antônio Coelho Rodrigues (of Piauí) became active leaders of the movement in Parliament. Later, the chief minister of the government, João Alfredo, supported them, believing some recompense would help pacify the embittered planters.[13]

Cost estimates for indemnification varied greatly, depending on the determination of average slave values and the total slave population to be affected. Some thought indemnification would require an expenditure of 70,000 contos; others estimated the price as high as 600,000 contos or more. Whatever the final figure, many believed it would seem astronomical in the light of the financial state of the Imperial Government. Where would the money come from? Contemplating the problem nine years earlier, one deputy suggested that Brazil could not pay the bill unless it discovered a Potosí (the rich mountain of silver found by the Spanish in upper Peru during the colonial era).[14]

Large-scale indemnification would require taxes, an issue

12. *Annaes do Senado* (1888), July 14, 157; *Cidade do Rio,* May 10, 1888, p. 3.

13. *Gazeta Mineira,* June 22, 1888, p. 2; *Diário do Parlamento Brasileiro—17 de julho—sessão em 16 de julho*—Senado; André Rebouças, *Diário e notas autobiograficas* (Rio de Janeiro, 1938), p. 315; Melo, *O trabalho servil no Brasil,* p. 81.

14. *Annaes da Camara* (1879), March 5, p. 195; (1888), June 7, p. 95; *Rio News,* June 5, 1888, p. 2; Tobias do Rêgo Monteiro, *Pesquisas e depoimentos para a história* (Rio de Janeiro, 1913), p. 181.

that frightened many groups into active opposition. The commercial and industrial classes believed the heavy tax burden would fall on them, while planters would escape the levies almost completely. Paulista *fazendeiros* could not agree with this assumption. As the richest agricultural class, their activities could become a prime target for new assessments. Since they began to reap tremendous profits in the months following abolition, the prospect of paying for the economic problems of other planters did not appear attractive.[15] Moreover, the Paulistas had either freed or lost most of their slaves by May 1, 1888, the date by which the slave population would be calculated under one of the major proposals presented by the Baron of Cotegipe. Over-all, *fazendeiros* from São Paulo would have more to lose than to gain by a project for remuneration. Others agreed with the argument. Princess Isabel viewed the projects as costly plans which would help some planters pay their debts but do little for constructive improvement in agriculture.[16] Even the ex-slavocrat Andrade Figueira saw the folly of indemnification schemes. Ultimately, he thought, the planters would have to pay for their own compensation.[17]

The proponents of indemnification lost their battle in 1888. They could not secure enough votes to overcome the coalition of ex-abolitionists, Progressive Planters, and others who opposed the plans. The idea of compensating the proprietors received stinging criticism from individuals sympathetic to the freedom. A writer for the *Gazeta de Campinas,* for example, parodied the terse style of the emancipation decree and suggested that a new law go into effect if Parliament would pass an indemnification proposal: [18]

Article 1—The Government will indemnify the slaves of the empire with pay to the value of all the time they spent working gratis.

15. *Rio News,* May 15, 1885, p. 2; January 15, 1888, p. 3.
16. Notes of Princess Isabel, December, 1888 (?), Arquivo do Museu Imperial.
17. *Annaes da Camara* (1888), May 25, pp. 169–71.
18. Quoted in *Revista Illustrada,* June 30, 1888, p. 2.

Article 2—All contrary provisions are revoked.

Rui Barbosa expressed a similar view in a more serious vein, responding angrily, "If anyone ought to be indemnified, it should be the ex-slaves." [19]

The controversy remained alive, however. Many ex-slavocrats who felt that the government had let them down on both abolition and indemnification turned to the republicans, believing that remuneration might still be possible under a new form of government. The danger of rekindling the fires of the indemnification issue brought new concern for the significance of the slave registration materials still lying in government archives. During the Senate debates of July 1888, José Antônio Saraiva discussed the problem, suggesting, "If I had been Minister [when abolition was passed], I would have ordered, as part of the Law, the burning of all slave registration books so that no one would know who was a slave in Brazil." [20] Later, under the Republic, Minister of Finance Rui Barbosa implemented precisely this policy, ordering destruction of the government's records on December 14, 1890.[21] In the twentieth century writers described Barbosa's decision in romantic terms, as a symbolic gesture to help rid Brazil of the stigma of slavery. They overlooked the practical concerns which motivated the ex-abolitionist.[22]

The government continued trying to assist the troubled proprietors until the last days of the empire. João Alfredo encouraged creation of new banks to loan money to the planters.[23] After he resigned, the Emperor named the Viscount of Ouro Prêto (Affonso Celso of Minas Gerais) as the new Prime

19. Abdias do Nascimento, *et. al.*, *"80 Anos de abolição," Cadernos Brasileiros* (May–June 1968), p. 21; Frank Bennett, *Forty Years in Brazil* (London, 1914), p. 112.

20. *Annaes do Senado* (1888), July 14, p. 153; *Rio News,* July 24, 1888, pp. 2–3.

21. Edison Carneiro (ed.), *Antologia do negro brasileiro* (Rio de Janeiro, n.d.), p. 89.

22. Americo Jacobina Lacombe, *"Rui e a história política do império e da república," Revista do Instituto Histórico e Geográfico Brasileiro,* 1949, n.205, pp. 26–29.

23. *Revista Illustrada,* June 30, 1888, pp. 4–7.

Minister in June 1889. Ouro Prêto, a Liberal, quickly fell victim to pent-up grievances, as disaffected planters, military leaders, and urban citizens poured out their complaints. "Republicanism" became increasingly popular. With the intention of checking some of the growing sentiment against the monarchy, Ouro Prêto arranged new bank loans with easy credit and increased the amount of cash in circulation to help indebted planters to pay their workers.[24]

The ranks of republicans continued to grow. Abolition gave members of the small Republican party ardent new colleagues. In Paraíba do Sul, Rio do Peixe, and other zones which had been notoriously slavocrat, *fazendeiros* lined up behind the new banner.[25] The quick shift in the allegiance of these groups prompted a reaction from some of the ex-abolitionists who had long worked with urban republican organizations. José do Patrocínio's turnabout was especially extreme. As late as February 1889 he lambasted the monarchy as a bulwark of slavery. But the actions of Isabel and the defections of *fazendeiros* to the republicans changed his opinion. On the day of the emancipation decree, Patrocínio knelt down to kiss the feet of the Princess Regent. Later he scolded the new opponents of the monarchy, calling them "Republicans of May 14," and formed a Negro Guard to protect the Crown from its enemies.[26]

Dom Pedro probably recognized the political implications of abolition better than his daughter. For decades he had hedged on the slavery issue despite his personal sentiments against the institution and conveniently left the country when Parliament met to face critical questions. The Emperor was in Europe when legislators passed the abolition law, and after he received news of the *Lei Áurea,* he exclaimed, "What great people!"

24. *Rio News,* July 1, 1889, p. 2; José Maria Bello, *A History of Modern Brazil: 1889–1964* (Stanford, 1966), p. 44.

25. *Revista Illustrada,* June 2, 1888, p. 4; June 16, 1888, pp. 1–2; *Província de São Paulo,* April 30, 1888, p. 1; *Arauto de Minas,* May 31, 1888, p. 2.

26. Basbaum, *História sincera da república,* pp. 252, 310; *Rio News,* May 13, 1889.

When Dom Pedro returned to Brazil, however, and heard from the angry planters, he conjectured, "If I had been here, perhaps I would not have done what was done." [27]

For many years the strength of Dom Pedro's government rested on the support of the powerful planters particularly leaders from Rio de Janeiro and Bahia who "ruled the empire Britannically," as one observer described the system.[28] Despite their complaints, the Bahian statesmen tended to remain with Dom Pedro, afraid that a republic would precipitate their political decline to the advantage of the coffee *fazendeiros*.[29] But many Rio planters deserted the Emperor, joining the older and better organized planter-republicans in São Paulo. The Paulistas had been unhappy with the Imperial power structure for a long time because they lacked political power corresponding to their growing economic power. In the future would they have to pay for the needs of the rest of Brazil? Through the 1880s, Paulistas criticized the "centralized" power of the empire and the small number of deputies that represented them in Parliament. They suggested a policy of federalism which would allow more autonomy and power for the province. Some Paulistas wanted outright separation from the empire.[30]

By 1889 the republicans had broadened their base to include an amalgam of different groups and interests. The movement now claimed a strong complement of restive army officers, disgruntled *fazendeiros,* and ambitious urban citizens (including many ex-abolitionists who now viewed the antiquated political institutions of the empire, rather than slavery, as the principal obstacle to modernization). The Ouro Prêto ministry proposed a pot pourri of changes for Parliament's consideration—a comprehensive program designed to head off the movement of discontents. It included extension of the suffrage, autonomy for

27. Francisco José de Oliveira Vianna, *O ocaso do império* (São Paulo, 1925), p. 78.

28. Milliet, *Roteiro do café e outros ensaios,* p. 23.

29. Basbaum, *História sincera da república,* p. 254.

30. *Ibid.,* p. 183; *Revista Illustrada,* 1884, n.386, p. 2; 1887, n.451, p. 3; Joaquim Nabuco, *Conferencias e discursos abolicionistas* (São Paulo, n.d.), p. 240.

the provinces, abolition of life terms for senators, reorganization of the Council of State, improvement of education, land reform, and promotion of a credit system to aid the agricultural interests. On November 15, 1889, just five days before Parliament was to convene to begin discussing the program, army officers overthrew the government, sent the Emperor and his family off to Europe, and established the Republic.[31]

Military leaders were responsible for engineering the peaceful revolution of November 15; it had not resulted from a complete collapse of the empire or a groundswell of activity from the masses. Nor did civilian leaders play important roles in the coup.[32] Nevertheless, the importance of planter support in uprooting the monarchy cannot be overlooked. It is unlikely that the military would have executed its plans if it did not expect that leaders from the powerful planter class would watch with approval. The events of November 1889 validated the statement of the Baron of Cotegipe, who told Princess Isabel at the time of abolition, "Your Highness has redeemed a race but lost a crown." [33]

THE FREEDMEN

Unfortunately for the liberated bondsmen, the momentum of abolitionism died out after May 13. Abolitionists were not entirely to blame for the simplicity of the emancipation law which was not followed by attendant social legislation to bene-

31. Affonso Celso, *Visconde de Ouro Prêto (Excerptos Biograficos)* (Porto Alegre, 1935), pp. 42–51, 57; Austricliano de Carvalho, *Brasil colônia e Brasil império* (Rio de Janeiro, n.d.), II, pp. 805–06.

32. Percy Alvin Martin, "Causes of the Collapse of the Brazilian Empire," *Hispanic American Historical Review* (February 1921, pp. 4–48; June E. Hahner, *Civilian-Military Relations in Brazil: 1889–1898* (Columbia, 1969), pp. 1–33. For a review of the major historical controversies regarding the republican revolution, see George C. A. Boeher, "The Brazilian Republican Revolution: Old and New Views," *Luso-Brazilian Review* (December 1966), pp. 33–57.

33. João Pandia Calogeras, *A History of Brazil* (Chapel Hill, 1939), p. 259. For a provocative discussion of the ex-slaveholders' support for the Republic, see Richard Graham, "Landowners and the Overthrow of the Empire," *Luso-Brazilian Review* (December 1970), pp. 44–56.

fit the liberated.[34] The violence of the last years of slavery served as a catalyst to frighten proprietors into action and precipitate the fall of the servile institution. Ironically though, violence weakened the radical abolitionists' chances of effectuating related goals. The element of fear stimulated political leaders who had shown little interest in the plight of Negroes to jump on the antislavery bandwagon and declare themselves "abolitionists." The "Golden Law" was passed by legislators representing multifarious interests; it was not solely the product of hard-core abolitionists. After abolition, political power remained in the hands of the great *fazendeiros,* men who did not wish to bear the costs of the abolitionists' humanitarian programs and who saw serious threats in some of their more radical suggestions, such as the subdivision of large, landed estates. In the months following May 13, ex-abolitionists became preoccupied with new political battles fomented by the planters—namely, the issues of indemnification and republicanism. The few private benevolent organizations created by the reformers could hardly cope with the monumental task of elevating the condition of the liberated masses. Hence, rural proprietors succeeded in snuffing out the flames of agitation and discontent by destroying the most symbolic institution of bondage while leaving other forms of exploitation intact.[35]

34. Around the time of emancipation, abolitionists expressed considerably more hope about the future of the freedmen than the slaveholders, and they tried to prepare freedmen for a new, constructive role in society. In São Paulo and Bahia, for example, abolitionists responded to the coming of emancipation by establishing special schools to educate both children and adults, teach them their "rights and duties," and assist them in finding employment. *Província de São Paulo,* May 9, 1888, pp. 1–2; *Diário da Bahia,* May 10, 1888; May 26, 1888. Joaquim Nabuco voiced the concern of his cohorts a few days before passage of the emancipation law when he said, "Abolition directed only toward liberating the slaves without bothering to place them in the social and moral conditions of free men would prepare a sad future for the enslaved race. Fortunately, our form of abolitionism bases its cause on the present and the future of the Negro race, in slavery and in liberty, and, therefore, we need union and determination on the eve of the day in which their social state is going to be decided." *Gazeta do Povo,* May 2, 1888, p. 1.

35. Cardoso, *Capitalismo e escravidão: O negro na sociedade do Rio Grande do Sul,* p. 269; Nascimento, *et al., "80 Anos de abolição,"* pp. 3–8. Thirty years after abolition Rui Barbosa recalled the way in

The reaction of many ex-slaveholders to developments immediately subsequent to abolition suggested attitudes which would create great difficulties for emancipated blacks in the years to follow. Some former slave proprietors refused to greet Brazil's new emancipation law with resignation. For example, when the Campinas municipal legislature called a special session to honor abolition on May 14, Ricardo Gumbleton, Gaunt, a medical doctor, demanded that the ceremonies be canceled. He gained some support for his position but not enough to reverse the plans of the city officials.[36] More serious were the extraordinary actions of the embittered losers in São João de Principe, in the province of Rio de Janeiro. One *fazendeiro* in the area declared that he would not begin paying his freed laborers until the end of the coffee harvest. Until then, they would only receive wages for performing extra work on Saturdays and Sundays. Another planter from São João do Principe thrashed his slaves on May 13, describing the act as an appropriate send-off. When freedmen on a plantation in the area announced plans for a festival in the town to celebrate promulgation of the law, a police delegate ordered members of his force to load their weapons, then warned the blacks that he would receive them with gunshots.[37]

Some diehard *fazendeiros* tried to find loopholes in the abolition decree. They interpreted the law as non-binding with regard to *ingenuos* and freedmen who had been liberated on

---

which the freedmen had been left to themselves, describing the emancipation experience an "atrocious irony." See the introduction to Rui Barbosa, *Emancipação dos escravos; Obras Completas de Rui Barbosa* (Rio de Janeiro, 1945), XI, pp. xxxvii–xxxviii. Similarly, in 1885 Joaquim Nabuco noticed that slaves could no longer be found in the two freed provinces of Ceará and Amazonas, but "slavery" seemed to continue there in other forms. See Nabuco, *Conferências e discursos abolicionistas,* pp. 291–92. Nilo Odalia believes the planters' post-abolition fight for indemnification was a diversionary tactic to preclude discussion of measures to help the freedmen, particularly consideration of programs to redistribute land. *"A abolição da escravatura," Anais do Museu Paulista,* 1964, XVIII, p. 138.

36. Leopoldo Amaral, *A cidade de Campinas em 1901* (Campinas, 1901), p. 54.

37. *Província de São Paulo,* May 20, 1888, p. 2.

the basis of a term of services. This stratagem irritated the Imperial Minister of Agriculture, who circulated a letter explaining that no individuals were to be excluded from the effects of the law.[38] In a few distant localities, far from centers of communication, slaveholders succeeded in completely escaping from the immediate impact of the government's decision. By not informing their bondsmen of the *Lei Áurea,* some maintained slavery as long as four years after official abolition.[39]

The slaves' first response to news of emancipation seemed to confirm the worst fears of old slavocrats. Mass emigrations, which had plagued planters during the breakdown of the servile institution, continued at an accelerated pace after national liberation, as thousands of freedmen quickly left the estates. Excited by new opportunities of freedom and a chance to escape from authority, they wandered in the countryside, often looking for friends and relatives, or worked their way into the congested towns and cities to join the noisy festivities.[40] *Fazendeiros* watched in horror, complaining of "anarchy" on the plantations and a "paralyzed" economy. Ripe coffee beans dropped to the ground.[41] Desperate proprietors tried to arrange new contracts with freedmen only to find that the workers would break agreements and leave the fields at their slightest displeasure. Feeling proud but sensitive about

38. *Ibid.,* p. 2.

39. Luiz Luna, *O negro na luta contra a escravidão* (Rio de Janeiro, 1968), p. 205.

40. *Revista Illustrada,* June 2, 1888, p. 2; *Província de São Paulo,* April 5, 1888, p. 1.

41. Paulino José Soares de Sousa Jr. to Visconde de Paranaguá, June 4, 1888, 4.6.888, Arquivo do Museu Imperial; Florestan Fernandes, *A integração do negro na sociedade de classes* (São Paulo, 1965), I, p. 49; *Província de São Paulo,* May 1, 1888, p. 2; Celso Furtado, *The Economic Growth of Brazil* (Berkeley and Los Angeles, 1963), pp. 153–54; Roberto Simonsen, *"As consequências econômicas da abolição," Revista do Arquivo Municipal de São Paulo* (May 1938), p. 266; *Relatório* of the president of São Paulo province, Francisco de Paula Rodrigues Alves, January 10, 1888, p. 23; Nícia Vilela Luz, *"A administração provincial de São Paulo em face do movimento abolicionista," Revista de Administração* (December 1948), p. 94.

their new status, freedmen resisted subtle pressures on the job, which were designed to increase production or maintain discipline. They balked at mild forms of coercion, charging such treatment was an offense to their dignity and reminiscent of the old days of control by an overseer. Frequently, they quit their jobs, walking off in a huff. Those who remained worked at a leisurely pace, often taking long breaks to eat lunch, talk, smoke, or rest.[42]

Impatient *fazendeiros* viewed the situation as a nightmare turning into reality. They did not care to understand that generally the desire to evade work would be only a temporary reaction in celebration of liberty. They did not recognize that after a lifetime in slavery it was understandable that freedmen sought a "vacation" from the rigorous plantation routine.[43] Actually, most of the *libertos* terminated their wandering after a few weeks or months and began to seek employment. After sobering to the responsibilities of earning a living and to the need to obtain food and clothing, many signed contracts with *fazendeiros* and returned to work in the rural districts. Those who had fled during the time of slavery tended not to return to their old masters. They preferred to contract with different *fazendeiros* in places which would not provide a constant reminder of the days of slavery. Many never took extended leaves from the plantations. After marking a short time to celebrate liberty, they again fell into the work routine on their former masters' estates.[44]

Some ex-slavocrats were surprised by the behavior of their liberated slaves. After all their gloomy predictions, the results of emancipation proved satisfactory. When Paulino de Souza gathered his workers together to make the important announcement, he asked forgiveness. Immediately, one of the liberated stood up and gave a discourse, indicating that Paulino

42. *Província de São Paulo,* May 9, 1888, pp. 1–2; Fernandes, *A integração do negro na sociedade de classes,* I, p. 49.

43. *Gazeta do Povo,* March 19, 1888, p. 1.

44. *Gazeta do Povo,* March 16, 1888, p. 1; *Província de São Paulo,* April 5, 1888, p. 1.

did not need to ask forgiveness and that they would stay on the *fazenda.* With *vivas* to the abolitionists, Paulino's ex-slaves began their celebration. The results of abolition also impressed the notorious former police chief, Antonio Coelho Bastos. After all his workers remained on the plantation, he admitted to a friend, "The abolition law only proved advantageous to me." [45] Reports from provincial authorities in diverse points of the empire similarly indicated that many of the old fears had been exaggerated. With the exception of the popular festivities and some minor incidents, provincial leaders in São Paulo, Rio de Janeiro, Minas Gerais, Bahia, and Alagoas announced that the transition had been made without disorders and without need for major intervention by the authorities.[46]

As freedmen prepared to return to work, however, many were shocked to learn that planters no longer wanted them. This situation became especially noticeable in São Paulo, where in 1888 alone 92,086 immigrants entered the province, a number larger than the Paulista slave population at the beginning of the year.[47] Feeling renewed confidence in a seller's market, many *fazendeiros* turned the freedmen away, declaring that the ex-slaves' temporary absences were examples of "Negro ingratitude" in response to their masters' emancipatory actions. Proprietors in São Paulo announced their preference for foreign labor, viewing the freedmen as "vagabonds"—a group of "irresponsible" or even "useless" people.[48]

45. *Revista Illustrada,* June 2, 1888, p. 2.

46. *Relatório,* Pedro Vincente de Azevedo, p. 144; *Falla* of the president of Minas Gerais, Luiz Eugenio Horta Barbosa, June 1, 1888, p. 51; *Falla,* Aurelio Ferreira Espinheira, p. 95; *Falla* of the president of Alagoas, José Cesario de Miranda Monteiro de Barros, October 6, 1888, p. 4. Also see the *Relatório* of the Minister of Agriculture, Commerce and Public Works, Rodrigo Augusto da Silva, 1888, p. 25.

47. Simonsen, *Aspectos da história econômica do café,* p. 54.

48. Fernandes, *A Integração do negro na sociedade de classes* I, pp. 16–18, 32, 49, 55. *Província de São Paulo,* May 9, 1888, p. 1. For descriptions of similar attitudes in other sections of southern Brazil, see Henrique Fernando Cardoso, *Capitalismo e escravidão: O negro na sociedade do Rio Grande do Sul* (São Paulo, 1962), pp. 269, 276, 316; Octávio Ianni, *As metamorfoses do escravo: Apogeu e crise da escravatura no Brasil meridional* (São Paulo, 1962), pp. 264–65.

Emancipation did not result in any significant change in the position of free Negroes in the Brazilian social structure. In a society of rigid class lines, they were left on the lowest rung of the social ladder. The new, emerging order was a competitive society, and freedmen were ill-prepared to participate in it. The "school of slavery" had hardly developed occupational competence. Some women found urban jobs in the domestic services, and the few freedmen who had special skills acquired positions as artisans. Some well-mannered house servants retained privileged positions, and freedmen who were fortunate in obtaining land outside the cities succeeded in supplying the growing urban centers with fruit, vegetables, and eggs. But for the majority, particularly those who had been field hands, the opportunities were limited to temporary, insecure, and degrading jobs. As marginal men in the economy, they formed the occupational groups that worked for the lowest wages. Many who joined the exodus to the cities established *favelas* (shanty towns), while workers in the rural areas became tenant farmers or sharecroppers.[49]

Despite tremendous economic development in São Paulo in the decades following abolition, Negroes in the area were pushed out of the mainstream of employment. *Fazendeiros* directly substituted immigrants for freedmen or arranged contracts only with Europeans once they moved to clear new coffee lands in the western part of the state. By the twentieth century, observers noted that few blacks could be seen in rural areas once heavily populated with Negro laborers. In the cities Italians and other foreigners appealed successfully to white clients and quickly pushed Negroes out of artisan jobs. Recognizing the difficulty of competing in São Paulo, many vocation-

49. Stein, *Vassouras,* pp. 271–74; Bandeira de Melo, *O trabalho servil no Brasil,* p. 83; Fernandes, *A integração do negra na sociedade de classes,* I, pp. 3–4, 10, 31–32, 39–43, 49–50; Denis, *O Brasil no século xx,* p. 349; Fernando Henrique Cardoso and Octávio Ianni, *Côr e mobilidade social em Florianópolis: Aspectos das relações entre negros e brancos numa comunidade do Brasil meridional* (São Paulo, 1960), pp. xxix, 94, 151; Caio Prado Junior, *História econômica do Brasil* (São Paulo, 1949), pp. 255–57.

ally trained blacks moved to Rio de Janeiro, Minas Gerais, and other states where immigrants did not monopolize the occupational positions they desired.[50] Opportunities improved slightly beginning in the 1930s and 1940s with the waning of immigration, industrialization in the Vargas era, and Brazil's economic gains during World War II. The pace of internal migrations then increased as poor blacks from the Northeast and the interior moved to the cities in São Paulo and other Central-South and Deep South states to seek employment. But the reserve of these millions of poor always exceeded demands, and improvement in health service only exacerbated the problems by creating a population explosion.[51] The deep and persistent poverty of the Negro population from 1888 to modern times tended to reinforce the popular prejudices of the dominant classes which stereotyped blacks as lazy, shiftless vagabonds.

It appears that whites gave heightened attention to racial identification in the years immediately following abolition. Since the slave status was no longer a mark of inferiority, color increasingly became an identifying factor. Under the new conditions, Brazilian intellectuals became receptive to European racist ideas which related the technological advances of Western civilization to the alleged mental superiority of whites.[52]

Contemporaries reported many examples of racial discrimination in the 1890s. In 1895 an editor of *A Redempção* noted that many religious institutions and special schools did not enroll a single Negro, and even schools which usually offered two

50. Edison Carneiro, *et al.*, *O negro brasileiro* (*80 anos de abolição*) (Rio de Janeiro, 1968), p. 31; Denis, *O Brasil no século xx*, pp. 158–59, 337–39; Florestan Fernandes, "*Imigração e relações raciais,*" *Revista Civilisação Brasileira,* 1966, n.8, p. 78.

51. Fernandes, "*Imigração e relações raciais,*" pp. 79–89. Also, I am indebted to Professor Arthur F. Corwin for allowing me to see an early draft of his study "Afro-Brazilian Poverty: Myths and Realities."

52. I am indebted to Professor Thomas E. Skidmore for allowing me to see an early draft of his paper on this subject, "Brazilian Intellectuals and the Problem of Race, 1870–1930." Also see Cardoso, *Capitalismo e escravidão,* p. 316.

or three scholarships to the poor reserved the places for whites. The Episcopal Seminary in São Paulo, for example, passed a resolution stating, "Applicants for scholarships and partial scholarships should not be of black color." The police authorities also discriminated in their treatment of Negroes, handling them with severity while giving white immigrants preferential treatment. One disgusted observer claimed that "despite the presence of a thousand foreign criminals, one comes upon the scene of eight blacks locked up who had probably stolen some bread because of hunger!"[53] Moreover, whites continued to treat Negroes with overt condescension, as in the days of slavery, and continued to speak of them as *libertos* (freedmen), thus perpetuating their identity as ex-slaves.[54] In January of 1889 a writer for *Revista Illustrada* bemoaned the frequent association of the words "white," "mulatto," and "black" with specific groups when he had expected that the "Golden Law" would destroy old prejudices.[55] Sickened by examples "of a society full of ruinous prejudices originating from the institution of slavery," in 1895 Antônio Guimaraes Barroso sadly looked back on the shattered hopes of the abolitionists, saying, "I never believed, nor did it pass through my imagination, that with the extinction of slavery a new class of free-slaves would be created."[56]

In the twentieth century some Negroes and, particularly, mulattoes found positions of social and economic importance in Brazilian society. They never confronted institutions of racial prejudice as overt and harsh as those that troubled blacks in the United States in the same period. Yet the glaring reality remained that an extraordinarily disproportionate number of Negroes were locked in the culture of poverty, and, to a great degree, this problem could be traced to the heritage of slavery. Long after the servile institution was destroyed, its victims continued to suffer from the repercussions of the experience in

53. *A Redempção,* May 13, 1895, p. 2.
54. Cardoso and Ianni, *Côr e mobilidade em Florianópolis,* p. 126.
55. *Revista Illustrada,* January 12, 1889, pp. 4–5.
56. *A Redempção,* May 13, 1895, p. 1.

bondage. Without land, deficient in education, and stigmatized in the eyes of much of the white population, the ex-slaves and their descendants found their opportunities limited. Economic and social barriers were not easy to surmount. The legacy of the slave past cast a heavy shadow, hampering the efforts of Brazilian Negroes to challenge the obstacles.

The new era which many Brazilian groups had been anticipating during the time of debates over slavery began to materialize in the decades following emancipation. Establishment of the Republic, occurring just a year and a half after abolition, provided a shift in political power which was more in keeping with the recent shifts in economic power. The Paulista coffee *fazendeiros* eventually made their way to the helm, with other strong interests such as the cattle barons of Minas Gerais and Rio Grande do Sul also finding opportunities to press their influence in the federal republic. Brazil's military enjoyed the satisfaction of engineering the "revolution" of 1889 and, although it soon fell out of its official position of state control, the military remained a powerful force behind the scenes, capable of frightening politicians and turning elections in times of controversy. Also, important spokesmen for the urban groups enjoyed a brief tenure of influence in the governmental hierarchy, then lost much of their political power to the coffee planters. Though urban leaders became frustrated from the pattern of landowner-dominated regional politics which prevailed in the years to follow, the cities, nevertheless, continued to grow with expansion of the economy and slow advances in industrialization. The dream of making Rio de Janeiro a cultural and aesthetic landmark that would claim attention from the rest of the world got a helpful boost when the capital received an impressive, modernizing face lift in the early 1900s. Finally, the long-nurtured effort to attract European immigrants began to bring striking results, as tens of thousands of foreigners poured into the country in the years following abolition. It seemed that the prayers of many of Brazil's immigrationists were being answered: The influx of newcomers was "Europeanizing" and "whitening" Brazil.

The new, emerging order offered little to blacks. Abolitionism, as a movement in sympathy for the black population, disappeared quickly after the downfall of slavery. A decade after emancipation, Joaquim Nabuco lamented that "the abolitionist current stopped the day of abolition and receded the following day." [57] Indeed, the Afro-Brazilian seemed to sink into the background as an "invisible man" during the post-emancipation era. In Brazil, as in other countries where Negroes represented an important minority in the population, these were years of fettered freedom. Appreciation of the black man's contribution to the culture and the place he deserved in the society would be long delayed.

57. Joaquim Nabuco, *Minha formação* (São Paulo, 1934), p. 212.

Bibliography

Books: Primary Works

O abolicionismo perante a história ou o diologo das três províncias. Rio de Janeiro, 1888.

Alencar, Jose de. *Discursos proferidos na sessão de 1871: Câmara dos Deputados.* Rio de Janeiro, 1871.

Alferes, Barão do Paty. *Memória sôbre a fundação e costeio de uma fazenda na província de Rio de Janeiro.* Rio de Janeiro, 1860.

Amaral, Leopoldo. *A cidade de Campinas em 1901.* Campinas, 1901.

Araripe, Tristão de Alencar. *O elemento servil: Artigos sôbre a emancipação.* Paraíba do Sul, 1871.

Araujo, A. Pereira d'. *A incoherência da escravidão n'um paíz christão: Obra religiosa, moral e política.* Bahia, 1885.

———. *A monarchia brasileira se agarrando a taboa da escravidão.* Bahia, 1885.

Araujo, Carlos Benjamin da Silva. *A escravidão: Questão da actualidade.* Rio de Janeiro, 1871.

Azevedo, Arthur and Urbano, Duarte. *O escravocrata: Drama em 3 actos.* Rio de Janeiro, 1884.

B., F. L. C. *Memória analytica a' cerca do commércio d'escravos e a' cerca dos malles da escravidão domestica.* Rio de Janeiro, 1837.

Barbosa, Rui. *Abolicionismo,* in *Obras Completas de Rui Barbosa,* Vol. XIV, 1887, Tomo I. Rio de Janeiro, 1955.

———. *Emancipação dos escravos,* in *Obras Completas de Rui Barbosa,* Vol. XI, 1884, Tomo I. Rio de Janeiro, 1945.

———. *Emancipação dos escravos: Parecer formulado pelo deputado Ruy Barbosa (Projecto N.48).* Rio de Janeiro, 1884.

———. *Queda do império.* Rio de Janeiro, 1947–1949.

Barreto, Domingues Alves Branco Moniz. *Memória sôbre a abolição do commércio da escravatura.* Rio de Janeiro, 1837.

Barreto, Pais. *A abolição e a federação no Brasil.* Paris, 1906.

Bastos, A. C. Taveres. *Cartas do Solitario.* Rio de Janeiro, 1863.

———. *A Província: Estudo sôbre a decentralisação no Brasil.* Rio de Janeiro, 1870.

Bennett, Frank. *Forty Years in Brazil.* London, 1914.

Bocayuva, Quintino Ferreira de Souza. *A crise da lavoura.* Rio de Janeiro, 1868.

Brandão Junior, Francisco Antônio. *A escravatura no Brasil.* Brussels, 1865.

Brito, Peixoto de *Considerações geraes sôbre a emancipação dos escravos no império do Brasil. Indicação dos meios próprios para realisal-a.* Lisbon, 1870.

Bueno, José Antônio Pimento. (Marques de São Vicente). *Trabalho sôbre a extincção da escravatura no Brasil.* Rio de Janeiro, 1868.

Burgess, Wilson and Chandler, John. *Narrative of a Recent Visit to Brazil.* London, 1853.

Camara dos Deputados: Organisações e programmas ministeriaes desde 1822 a 1889. Rio de Janeiro, 1889.

Caminhoá, Luiz Monteiro. *Canna de assucar e café.* Rio de Janeiro, 1880.

Carneiro, Edison (ed.). *Antologia do negro brasileiro.* Rio de Janeiro, n.d.

Cartas do Imperador D. Pedro II ao Barão de Cotegipe ordenadas e annotadas por Wanderley Pinho. São Paulo, 1933.

Cartas de Miguel Lemos a R. Teixeira Mendes. Rio de Janeiro, 1965.

Carvalho, Augusto de. *O Brasil, colonização e emigração. Esboço histórico, baseado no estudo das systemas e vantagens que offerecem Os Estados Unidos.* Porto, 1876.

Celso, Affonso. *Oito anos de parlamento. Poder pessoal de D. Pedro II, reminiscencias e notas.* São Paulo, n.d.

———. *Reposta a uma impugnação.* Rio de Janeiro, 1885.

Chandler, John, and Burgess, Wilson. *Narrative of a Recent Visit to Brazil.* London, 1853.

Christie, W. D. *Notes on Brazilian Questions.* London and Cambridge, 1865.

Cincinnatus. *O elemento escravo e as questões econômicas do Brasil.* Bahia, 1886.

Coelho, José Maria Vaz Pinto. *Legislação servil—Lei N.3270 de 28 de setembro de 1885.* Rio de Janeiro, n.d.

Congresso Agricola: Collecção de documentos. Rio de Janeiro, 1878.

Conservador, Um. *Carta aos fazendeiros e commerciantes fluminenses sôbre o elemento servil ou refutação do parecer do Sr. Conselheiro Christiano Benedicto Ottoni acerca do mesmo assumpto.* Rio de Janeiro, 1871.

Costa, João Severiano Maciel da. *Memória sôbre a necessidade de abolir a introducção dos escravos africanos no Brasil.* Coimbra, 1821.

Coutinho, D. José Joaquim da Cunha de Azeredo. *Analyse sôbre a justiça do commércio do resgate dos escravos da costa da Africa.* Lisbon, 1808.

Couty, Louis. *Le Brésil en 1884.* Rio de Janeiro, 1884.

———. *L'esclavage au Brésil.* Paris, 1881.

———. *Pequena propriedade e imigração européia.* Rio de Janeiro, 1887.

Cunha, Francisco Xaxier da. *Reminiscências na imprensa e na diplomacia: 1870 a 1910, Propaganda contra o império.* Rio de Janeiro, 1914.

Demonstração das conveniências e vantagens a lavoura no Brasil pela introducção dos trabalhadores asiáticos (da China). Rio de Janeiro, 1877.

Denis, Pierre. *O Brasil no século xx.* Lisbon, n.d.

Dent, Hastings Charles. *A Year in Brazil.* London, 1886.

Os deputados republicanos na Assembléa Provincial de S. Paulo: Sessão de 1888. São Paulo, 1888.

Directoria Geral de Estatística—Relatório annexo ao do Ministério dos Negócios do Império de 1875. Rio de Janeiro, 1875.

Elemento servil: *Parecer e projecto de lei apresentados a Camara dos Srs. Deputados na sessão de 16 de Agôsto de 1870 pela commissão especial nomeada pela mesma câmara em 24 de maio de 1870.* Rio de Janeiro, 1870.

Fallas do trono desde o anno de 1823 até o anno de 1889. Rio de Janeiro, 1889.

Fonseca, Luís Anselmo da. *A escravidão, o clero, e o abolicionismo.* Bahia, 1887.

Furtado, J. I. Arnizaut. *Estudos sôbre a libertação dos escravos no Brasil.* Pelotas, 1883.

Galvão, Miguel Calmon Menezes de Macedo and Montmorency, Thomaz Deschamps de. *Parecer da secção de colonisação e estatística sôbre a questão: "Quaes os meios mais apropriados e convenientes para se obter o grande desideratum social de extincção da escravatura êntre nos?".* Rio de Janeiro, 1871.

Godoy, Joaquim Floriano de. *O elemento servil e as câmaras municipaes da província de São Paulo.* Rio de Janeiro, 1887.

Gonçalves, Domingo Maria. *A instrucção agricola e o trabalho livre.* Rio de Janeiro, 1880.

Guimaraes, Joaquim Caetano da Silva. *A agricultura em Minas.* Rio de Janeiro, 1865.

Hilliard, Henry W. *Politics and Pen Pictures at Home and Abroad.* New York and London, 1892.

Império do Brasil—Directoria Geral de Estatística—Relatório e trabalhos estatísticos. Rio de Janeiro, 1878.

Importação de trabalhadores chins. Memória apresentada ao Ministério da Agricultura, Commércio e Obras Públicas e impressa por sua ordem. Rio de Janeiro, 1869.

Jaguaribe Filho, Domingues José Nogueira. *Algumas palavras sôbre a emigração—Meios prácticos de colonisar.* São Paulo, 1877.

———. *Reflexões sôbre a colonisação no Brasil.* São Paulo and Paris, 1878.

Jardim, Antônio da Silva. *Memórias e viagens: Campanha de um propandagista, 1887–1890.* Lisbon, 1891.

Koster, Henry. *Travels in Brazil.* London, 1816.

Leal, Luiz Francisco da Camara. *Considerações e projecto de lei para a emancipação dos escravos sem prejuizo de seus senhores, nem grave onus para o estado.* Rio de Janeiro, 1866.

Leão, P. Lopes de. *Como pensa sôbre o elemento servil.* Rio de Janeiro, 1870.

Lemos, Miguel. *Immigração chineza.* Rio de Janeiro, 1881.

———. *O positivismo e a escravidão moderna.* Rio de Janeiro, 1934.

Magistrado, Um. *Analyse e commentário crítico da proposta do governo imperial às câmaras legislativas sôbre o elemento servil.* Rio de Janeiro, 1871.

Malheiro, Agostinho Marques Perdigão. *A escravidão no Brasil: Ensaio histórico-jurídico-social.* Rio de Janeiro, 1866–1867.

Martins, Almelia de Rezende. *Um idealista realizador: Barão Geraldo de Rezende.* Campinas, n.d.

Mattoso, Camara. *Discursos parlamentares sôbre questões econômicas.* Rio de Janeiro, 1890.

Mendoca, Salvador de. *Trabalhadores asiaticos.* New York, 1879.

Monteiro, Tobias do Rêgo. *Pesquisas e depoimentos para a história.* Rio de Janeiro, 1913.

Montmorency, Thomaz Deschamps de, and Galvao, Miguel Calmon Menezes de Macedo. *Parecer da secção de colonisação e estatistica sôbre a questão: "Quaes os meios mais apropriados e convenientes para obter o grande desideratum social de extincção da escravatura êntre nos?"* Rio de Janeiro, 1871.

Moraes, A. F. de Mello. *O Brasil, social e político: O que fomos e o que somos.* Rio de Janeiro, 1872.

Moura, João Dunshee de Abranches. *O Captiveiro, memórias.* Rio de Janeiro, 1941.

Nabuco, Joaquim. *O abolicionismo.* São Paulo, 1938.

———. *Campanha abolicionista no Recife.* Rio de Janeiro, 1885.

———. *Campanhas de imprensa, 1884–1887.* São Paulo, 1949.

———. *Conferências e discursos abolicionistas.* São Paulo, n.d.

———. *Discursos parlamentares: 1879–1889.* São Paulo, 1949.

———. *Um estadista do império: Nabuco de Araujo* (4 vols.), São Paulo, n.d.

———. *Minha formação.* São Paulo, 1934.

Netto, A. da Silva. *A Corôa e a emancipação do elemento servil.* Rio de Janeiro, 1869.

———. *Estudos sôbre a emancipação dos escravos no Brasil.* Rio de Janeiro, 1868.

———. *Segundo estudos sôbre a emancipação dos escravos no Brasil.* Rio de Janeiro, 1868.

Oliveira, Henrique Vellose de. *A substituição do trabalho dos escravos pelo trabalho livre no Brasil, por um meio suave e sem difficuldade.* Rio de Janeiro, 1845.

D'Oliveira, Luiz Rodriguez. *Algumas idéias sôbre a colonisação no Brasil.* Paris, 1871.

Ottoni, C. B. *O advento da república no Brasil.* Rio de Janeiro, 1890.

———. *Autobiographia de C. B. Ottoni.* Rio de Janeiro, 1908.

Pareceres do Conselho de Estado no anno de 1868 relativos ao elemento servil. Rio de Janeiro, 1871.

Peixoto, Manuel Rodrigues. *A crise do assucar: Os pequenos engenhos centraes, a colonisação e o problema servil.* Rio de Janeiro, 1885.

Pereira, J. Baptista. *Da condição actual dos escravos, especialmente após a promulgação da lei n.3270 de 28 de setembro de 1885.* Rio de Janeiro, 1887.

Pimentel, F. L. C. *Estatutos da Companhia Libertadora ou reparadora dos direitos da humanidade.* Rio de Janeiro, 1858.

Prado, Nazareth (ed.). *Antônio Prado no império e na república: seus discursos e actos colligidos e apresentados por sua filha.* Rio de Janeiro, 1929.

Proposta do governo sôbre a reforma do estado servil. Rio de Janeiro, 1871.

Protesto contra o acto do parlamento britannico sancionnado em 8 de Agôsto do corrente anno, que sujeita os návios brasileiros que fizerem o tráfico de escravos, ao Alto Tribunal do Admirantado e a qualquer tribunal de Vice-Admirantado dentro dos domínios de sua magestade Britannica. Rio de Janeiro, 1845.

Queiroz, Polycarpo de. *Transformação do trabalho.* Campinas, 1888.

Rebouças, André. *A agricultura nacional.* Rio de Janeiro, 1883.

———. *Diário e notas autobiográficas.* Edited by Ana Flora and Inácio José Veríssimo. Rio de Janeiro, 1938.

Rebouças, Antônio Pereira. *Recordações da vida parlamentar.* Rio de Janeiro, 1870.

Reis, Malvino da Silva. *Situação econômica do Brasil: Exposição apresentada a commissão especial nomeada pela assemblea geral da Associação Commercial em 2 de maio de 1884.* Rio de Janeiro, 1884.

Relatório Annual do Instituto Agronômico do estado de São Paulo (Brasil) em Campinas, 1892. São Paulo, 1893.

Relatório apresentado ao Exm. Sr. Presidente da Província de S. Paulo pela Commissão Central de Estatística. São Paulo, 1888.

Rezende, Francisco de Paula Ferreira de. *Minhas Recordações*. Rio de Janeiro, 1944.

Rodrigues, Antônio Coelho. *Manual de um subdito fiel ou cartas de um lavrador a sua magestade o Imperador sôbre a questão do elemento servil*. Rio de Janeiro, 1884.

Romero, Sílvio. *O evolucionismo e positivismo no Brasil*. Rio de Janeiro, 1895.

S, J.E.P. da *Memória sôbre a escravatura e projecto de colonisção dos europeos e prêtos da Africa no Império do Brasil*. Rio de Janeiro, 1826.

Sampaio, Antônio Gomes de Azevedo. *Abolicionismo: Considerações geraes do movimento anti-esclavista e sua história limitada a Jacarehv*. São Paulo, 1890.

Silva, J. M. Pereira. *Memórias do meu tempo* (2 vols.). Paris, n.d.

Smith, Herbert H. *Brazil: The Amazons and the Coast*. New York, 1879.

Soares, Antônio Joaquim de Macedo. *Campanha jurídica pela libertação dos escravos: 1867–1888*. Rio de Janeiro, 1938.

Soares, Caetano Alberto. *Memória para melhorar a sorte dos nossos escravos—lida na sessão geral do Instituto dos Advogados brasileiros*. Rio de Janeiro, 1847.

Souza, João Cardoso de Menezes de. *Theses sôbre colonização do Brasil: Projecto de solução as questões sociais, que se prendem a este difficil problema*. Rio de Janeiro, 1875.

Urbano, Duarte and Azevedo, Arthur. *O escravocrata: Drama em 3 actos*. Rio de Janeiro, 1884.

Viajante de Paizes Coloniaes. *Discurso histórico-refutatório-político sôbre a carta do leitor effectivo, que reprova a abolição da escravatura no Brasil*. Rio de Janeiro, 1825.

Vidal, Luís Maria. *Repertório de legislação servil: Lei n.3270 de 28 de setembro*. Rio de Janeiro, 1886.

Werneck, Luiz Peixoto de Lacerda. *Idéias de colonização, precedidas de uma sucinta exposição dos princípios que regem a população*. Rio de Janeiro, 1855.

Ypiranga. *Breves considerações histórico-políticas sôbre a discussão do elemento servil na Câmara dos Deputados*. Rio de Janeiro, 1871.

PAMPHLETS

Acta da conferência das secções reunidas dos negócios da Fazenda, Justiça e Império do Conselho de Estado. Rio de Janeiro, 1884.

Araripe, Tristão de Alencar. *25 de Março: O Ceará no Rio de Janeiro: Discurso Histórico do Conselheiro Tristão de Alencar Araripe*. Fortaleza, 1884.

Associação Commercial do Rio de Janeiro: Elemento Servil. Rio de Janeiro, 1884.

Barbosa, Rui. *Conferência abolicionista realizada a 7 de junho de 1885 no Theatro Polytheama da Côrte.* Bahia, 1885.

Boletim da Confederação Abolicionista. Paraná, 1888.

Câmara dos Srs. Deputados—Discurso proferido na sessão de 5 de setembro de 1883—Leopoldo de Bulhoes.

Club dos Libertos Contra a Escravidão. *Homagem a José do Patrocínio.* Rio de Janeiro, 1885.

Confederação Abolicionista. *A situação abolicionista: Conferência do Conselheiro Ruy Barbosa em 2 de agosto de 1885.* Rio de Janeiro, 1885.

———. *Homagem ao Patrocínio, Ministro Dantas. Sessão pública e solemne realizada no dia 7 de junho de 1885.* Rio de Janeiro, 1885.

Discurso proferido na sessão de 17 de julho de 1884 pelo deputado Dr. Affonso Celso Junior. Rio de Janeiro, 1884.

Discurso que tinha de ser proferido por occasião da primeira sessão magna da sociedade—Libertadora Cearense—no dia 27 de setembro de 1882, em um dos saloes do palácio da presidência por Diogo Cavalcanti de Albequerque. Pernambuco, 1882.

O eclypse do patriotismo. Rio de Janeiro, 1886.

Elemento servil—discurso proferido na Câmara dos Srs. Deputados pelo deputado Ruy Barbosa. Rio de Janeiro, 1884.

Emancipação dos escravos—discurso proferido no Senado por C. B. Ottoni, 30 de junho de 1883. Rio de Janeiro, 1883.

O êrro do Joaquim Nabuco. Rio de Janeiro, 1886.

Ferreira, Francisco Ignácio. *Projecto para abolição do elemento servil.* Rio de Janeiro, 1887.

Fuga de escravos em Campinas—Discursos pronunciados no Senado pelo Exm. Sr. Barão de Cotegipe. Rio de Janeiro, 1887.

Garantia nacional: Associação de interesses mutuos para a liquidação do capital empregado no elemento servil. Rio de Janeiro, 1875.

Homagem da Sociedade Emancipadora. São Paulo, 1883.

Jardim, Silva. *A patria em perigo—Conferência "meeting" sôbre a actual situação brasileira, realisada no cidade de Santos, em a noite de 28 de janeiro de 1888.*

Lemos, Miguel. *A incorporação do proletário escravo: Protesto da Sociedade Positivista do Rio de Janeiro.* Recife, 1883.

Malheiro, Agostinho Marques Perdigao. *Illegitimade da propriedade constuida sobre o escravo—natureza de tal propriedade—justica e conveniencia da abolição da escravidao; em que termos.* Rio de Janeiro, 1863.

Manifesto da Confederação Abolicionista do Rio de Janeiro. Rio de Janeiro, 1883.

Manifesto que vai ser apresentado ao corpo legislativo pela Sociedade Abolicionista Bahiana. Bahia, n. d.

Nabuco, Joaquim. *Circular aos eleitores do segundo districto da Côrte*. Rio de Janeiro, 1884.

———. *Conferência do Sr. Joaquim Nabuco a 22 de junho de 1884 no Theatro Polytheama*. Rio de Janeiro, 1884.

———. *O eclipse do abolicionismo*. Rio de Janeiro, 1886.

———. *Eleições liberaes e eleições conservadoras*. Rio de Janeiro, 1886.

———. *O êrro do imperador*. Rio de Janeiro, 1886.

———. *Nacionalisação do solo. Apreciação da propaganda para a abolição do monopólio territorial na Inglaterra*. Rio de Janeiro, 1884.

Penido, José. *A abolição e o crédito*. Rio de Janeiro, 1885.

Pinto, Elzeario. *Emancipação dos escravos: O. C. D. As Sociedades Maçonicas e abolicionistas do império*. Bahia, 1870.

Pitanga, Antônio. *A pena de açoites*. Recife, 1886.

Rebouças, André. *Abolição immediata e sem indemnisação*. Rio de Janeiro, 1883.

Silva, José Bonifácio de Andrada e. *Representação a Assembléa Geral Constituinte e Legislativa do Império do Brasil sôbre a escravatura* (reprinted by the Faculdade de Filosofia, Ciências e Letras de Santos). Santos, 1965.

Sociedade Brasileira Contra a Escravidão. *Banquete offerecido ao Exm. Sr. Ministro Americano Henry Washington Hilliard a 20 de novembro de 1880*. Rio de Janeiro, 1880.

BROADSIDES

Alerta Alerta!

A' S.A.I. O Snr. Conde D'Eu. Bahia, October 25, 1887.

Corra Sangue!. Fortaleza, 1881.

Ao exercito brasileiro. October 26, 1887.

Genese da escravidão segundo Lamennais: A Joaquim Nabuco. June 28, 1885.

13 de Maio: A S.A.I. a Sra. D. Isabel, Condessa d'Eu. May 13, 1891.

Manifesto Academico ao paíz. Recife, July 21, 1886.

Piracicaba: Avaliação de uma ingenua.

Um Voto de censura contra o procedimento do governo de S.A.I. A Sra. Princeza Imperante. Bahia, October 25, 1887.

NEWSPAPERS

O abolicionista. Rio de Janeiro. 1880–1881.

Arauto de Minas. São João d'El-Rei. 1888.

Brazil. Rio de Janeiro, 1884–1885.
Cidade do Rio. Rio de Janeiro. 1887–1888.
Correio Paulistano. São Paulo. 1887–1888.
O Cruzeiro. Rio de Janeiro. 1880–1881.
Diário da Bahia. Salvador. 1888.
Diário do Brasil. Rio de Janeiro, 1884–1885.
Diário de Santos. Santos. 1887–1888.
Gazeta de Campinas. Campinas. 1881.
Gazeta Mineira. São João d'El-Rei. 1888.
Gazeta de Notícias. Rio de Janeiro. 1880, 1883–1884, 1888.
Gazeta de Porto Alegre. Porto Alegre. 1884.
Gazeta do Povo. Campos. 1887–1888.
Gazeta da Tarde. Rio de Janeiro. 1880–1888.
Jornal do Commércio. Rio de Janeiro. 1880–1881, 1887–1888.
Jornal do Recife. Recife. 1888.
O Libertador. Fortaleza, 1881.
Novidades. Rio de Janeiro. 1887–1888.
O Paíz. Rio de Janeiro. 1884–1888.
Perseverança e Porvir. Fortaleza. 1883.
O Propulsor. Recife. 1883.
A Província de Minas. Ouro Prêto. 1888.
Província de São Paulo. São Paulo. 1880–1881, 1887–1889.
A Redempção. São Paulo. 1887–1891, 1893, 1895, 1897–1899.
Revista Illustrada. Rio de Janeiro. 1880–1889.
Rio News. Rio de Janeiro. 1879–1889.
A Terra da Redempção. Rio de Janeiro. 1883–1884.
Vinte e Cinco de Março. Campos. 1884–1885.

Journals

O Brasil Agricola. Recife. 1866, 1879–1882.

Parliamentary Records of the Imperial Government

Annaes da Câmara. 1871, 1879–1889.
Annaes do Senado. 1871, 1879–1889.

Reports of the Minister of Agriculture, Commerce and Public Works of the Imperial Government: 1873–1889.

Reports of the Provincial Governments (Including Reports of the President, Vice-President, Chief of Police and Other Officials)

Alagoas. 1887–1888.
Bahia. 1887–1889.
Maranhão. 1887.
Minas Gerais. 1887–1888.
Pernambuco. 1888–1889; 1890, 1893 (state government)
Rio de Janeiro. 1887–1888.
Sergipe. 1888.
São Paulo. 1880–1889.

Proceedings of the Provincial Legislature of São Paulo: 1878–1881, 1887–1888

Personal Correspondence

Araújo, Marcos Antônio de, Barão de Itajubá
Bueno, José Antônio Pimento (Marquês de São Vicente)
Celso, Affonso
Clapp, João
Chaves, José do Carmo Ferreira
Cordeiro, João
Corrêa, José
Cotegipe, Barão de
Coutinho, Erminio Cezar
Dantas, Manoel Pinto de Souza
Isabel, Princesa
Lacerda, Carlos de
Leão, Luiz Felippe de Souza
Malheiro, Agostinho Marques Perdigão
Mariano, José
Molinari, G. de
Moura, João Ferreira de
Nabuco, Joaquim
Paranaguá, Visconde de
Pedro II, Dom
Prado, Antônio da Silva
Rebouças, André
Ribeiro, Colonel F. Solon de Sampaio
Rio Branco, Visconde de
Santos, João da Cruz e
Saraiva, José Antônio
Silva, Rodrigo Augusto da
Sousa Junior, Paulino José Soares de
Souto, Teodureto Carlos de Faria
Souza, Francisco Belisario Soares de
Vianna, Antônio Ferreira

Books: Secondary Works

Alves, Henrique L. *Antônio Bento, O fantasma da abolição.* São Paulo, n.d.

Amaral, Braz do. *Fatos da vida do Brasil.* Bahia, 1941.

Amaral, Luís. *História geral da agricultura brasileira.* 3 vols. São Paulo, 1940.

Barbosa, Renalto. *Geração abolicionista.* Florianópolis, 1940.

Basbaum, Leôncio. *História sincera da república, das origens até 1889.* Rio de Janeiro, 1957.

Bastide, Roger and Fernandes, Florestan. *Relações sociais êntre negros e brancos em São Paulo.* São Paulo, 1955.

Beiguelman, Paula. *Formação política do Brasil.* Vol. I: *Teória e ação no pensamento abolicionista.* Vol. II: *Contribuição a teória da organização política brasileira.* São Paulo, 1967.

Bello, José Maria. *A History of Modern Brazil: 1889–1964.* Stanford, 1966.

Bethell, Leslie. *The Abolition of the Brazilian Slave Trade.* Cambridge, England, 1970.

Boehrer, George C. A. *Da monarchia á república: História do partido republicano do Brasil.* Rio de Janeiro, 1954.

Boxer, C. R. *The Golden Age of Brazil: 1695–1750.* Berkeley, 1962.

Brandão, Paulo José Pires. *A Princesa D. Isabel a Redentora.* Rio de Janeiro, 1946.

Burns, E. Bradford (ed.). *A Documentary History of Brazil.* New York, 1966.

———. *A History of Brazil.* New York and London, 1970.

———. *Nationalism in Brazil: A Historical Survey.* New York, 1968.

———. *Perspectives on Brazilian History.* New York and London, 1967.

Calmon, Pedro. *História do Brasil.* Vol. IV. São Paulo, 1947.

———. *A Princesa Isabel, a Redentora.* São Paulo, 1941.

Calogeras, João Pandiá. *A History of Brazil.* Chapel Hill, 1939.

Cardoso, Fernando Henrique. *Capitalismo e escravidão: O negro na sociedade do Rio Grande do Sul.* São Paulo, 1962.

———, and Octávio Ianni. *Côr e mobilidade em Florianópolis: Aspectos das relações êntre negroes e brancos numa comunidade do Brasil meridional.* São Paulo, 1960.

Carneiro, Edison. *Ladinos e crioulos: Estudos sôbre o negro no Brasil.* Rio de Janeiro, 1964.

Carvalho, Austricliano de. *Brasil colônia e Brasil império.* Vol. II. Rio de Janeiro, n.d.

Celso, Affonso. *Visconde de Ouro Prêto (excerptos biográficos).* Porto Alegre, 1935.

1st Centenário do Conselheiro Antônio da Silva Prado. São Paulo, 1946.

Cincocentenário da abolição em Pernambuco. Catologo da exposição realisada no Teatro Santa Isabel de 13 a 31 de maio de 1938. Pernambuco, 1938.

Costa, Emília Viotti da. *Escravidão nas áreas cafeeiras: Aspectos econômicos, sociais e ideológicos da desagregação do sistema escravista.* Universidade de São Paulo, 1964.

———. *Da senzala à colônia.* São Paulo, 1966.

Costa, João Cruz. *A History of Ideas in Brazil.* Berkeley and Los Angeles, 1964.

Cunha, Ciro Viera da. *No Tempo de Patrocínio.* 2 vols. São Paulo, 1960.

Curtin, Philip D. *The Atlantic Slave Trade: A Census.* Madison, Milwaukee, and London, 1969.

Dados para a história da immigração e da colonização em São Paulo. São Paulo, 1916.

Davis, David Brion. *The Problem of Slavery in Western Culture.* Ithaca, 1966.

Dean, Warren. *The Industrialization of São Paulo: 1880–1945.* Austin, 1969.

Degler, Carl N. *Neither Black Nor White: Slavery and Race Relations in Brazil and the United States.* New York, 1971.

O direito e a moral: Conferência realizada na sessão exotérica de 21 de março de 1932, na sede do Circulo Esotérico em S. Paulo, na Praça Almeida Junior n.20. São Paulo, 1932.

Docca, E. F. de Souza. *História do Rio Grande do Sul.* Rio de Janeiro, 1954.

Dornas Filho, João. *A escravidão no Brasil.* Rio de Janeiro, 1939.

———. *A influência social do negro brasileiro.* Curitiba, São Paulo, and Rio de Janeiro, 1943.

Duque-Estrada, Osório. *A abolição: 1831–1888.* Rio de Janeiro, 1918.

Elkins, Stanley. *Slavery: A Problem in American Institutional and Intellectual Life.* New York, 1963.

Fernandes, Florestan. *A integração do negro a sociedade de classes.* 2 Vols. São Paulo, 1964.

———, and Roger Bastide. *Relações sociais êntre negros e brancos em São Paulo.* São Paulo, 1955.

Ferreira, Herminio. *Depois da escravidão negra a economia no Brasil.* São Paulo, 1929.

Foner, Laura, and Genovese, Eugene D. (eds.). *Slavery in the New World: A Reader in Comparative History.* Englewood Cliffs, 1969.

Franco, Maria Sylvia de Carvalho. *Homens livres na ordem escravocrata*. São Paulo, 1969.
Freire, Jorge. *Notas à margem da abolição, Mossoró—Rio Grande do Norte*. N.p., n.d.
Freyre, Gilberto. *O escravo nos annúncios de jornais brasileiros do século xix*. Recife, 1963.
———. *Joaquim Nabuco*. Rio de Janeiro, 1948.
———. *The Mansions and the Shanties*. New York, 1963.
———. *The Masters and the Slaves*. New York, 1961.
———. *New World in the Tropics: The Culture of Modern Brazil*. New York, 1959.
———. *Ordem e Progresso*. Rio de Janeiro, 1959.
Furtado, Celso. *The Economic Growth of Brazil*. Berkeley and Los Angeles, 1963.
Genovese, Eugene D. *The World the Slaveholders Made*. New York, 1969.
Girão, Raimundo. *A abolição no Ceará*. Fortaleza, 1956.
———. *A escravidão no Ceará*. Fortaleza, 1956.
Goulart, Maurício. *Escravidão africano no Brasil: das origens à extinção do tráfico*. São Paulo, 1949.
Gouveia, Maurilio. *História da escravidão*. Rio de Janeiro, 1955.
Graham, Richard. *Britain and the Onset of Modernization in Brazil, 1850–1914*. Cambridge, England, 1968.
——— (ed.). *A Century of Brazilian History Since 1965*. New York, 1969.
Guerra, Flavio. *História de Pernambuco*. Rio de Janeiro, 1966.
Guimaraes, Alaor Malta. *Campinas: Dados históricos e estatísticos*. Campinas, 1953.
Guimaraes, João. *Patrocínio: O abolicionista*. São Paulo, 1956.
Hahner, June E. *Civilian-Military Relations in Brazil, 1889–1898*. Columbia, 1969.
Hanke, Lewis (ed.). *History of Latin American Civilization: Sources and Interpretations*. Boston, 1967.
Haring, Clarence H. *Empire in Brazil*. Cambridge, 1958.
Harris, Marvin. *Patterns of Race in the Americas*. New York, 1964.
Hoetink, H. *The Two Variants in Caribbean Race Relations: A Contribution to the Sociology of Segmented Societies*. London, New York, and Toronto, 1967.
Holanda, Sérgio Buarque de (ed.). *História geral da civilização brasileira*. Vol. V. São Paulo, 1966.
———. *Raizes do Brasil*. Rio de Janeiro, 1948.
Ianni, Octávio. *As metamorfoses do escravo*. São Paulo, 1962.
———. *Raças e classes sociais no Brasil*. Rio de Janeiro, 1966.
Ianni, Octávio and Cardoso, Fernando Henrique. *Côr e mobilidade*

em Florianópolis: Aspectos das relações êntre negros e brancos numa comunidade do Brasil meridional. São Paulo, 1960.

James, Preston. *Brazil.* New York, 1946.

José, Oliam. *Abolição em Minas.* Belo Horizonte, 1962.

Lins, Ivan Monteiro de Barros. *História do positivismo no Brasil.* São Paulo, 1964.

———. *Três abolicionistas esquesidos.* Rio de Janeiro, 1938.

Lowrie, Samuel Harman. *Imigração e crescimento da população no estado de São Paulo.* São Paulo, 1938.

Luna, Luiz. *O negro na luta contra a escravidão.* Rio de Janeiro, 1968.

Manchester, Allan K. *British Preeminence in Brazil: Its Rise and Decline.* London, 1933.

Marchant, Anyda. *Viscount Mauá and the Empire of Brazil.* Berkeley and Los Angeles, 1965.

Mariano, Olegario. *A abolição de escravatura e os homens do Norte: Conferência pronunciada na sessão inaugural do Auditório da Gazeta em S. Paulo, aos 3 de novembro de 1939.* São Paulo, 1939.

Melo, Afonso de Toledo Bandeira. *O trabalho servil no Brasil.* Rio de Janeiro, 1936.

Mendes, R. Teixeira. *Benjamin Constant.* Rio de Janeiro, 1936.

Mennucci, Sud. *O precursor do abolicionismo no Brasil: Luiz Gama.* Rio de Janeiro, 1938.

Milliet, Sérgio. *Roteiro do café e outros ensaios.* São Paulo, 1941.

Monbeig, Pierre. *Pionniers et planteurs de l'etat de São Paulo.* Paris, 1952.

Monográfia histórica do município de Campinas. Rio de Janeiro, 1952.

Moog, Clodomir Vianna. *Bandeirantes and Pioneers.* New York, 1964.

Moraes, Evaristo de. *A campanha abolicionista: 1879–1888.* Rio de Janeiro, 1924.

———. *A escravidão africana no Brasil: das origens à extinção.* São Paulo, 1933.

———. *A lei do ventre livre.* Rio de Janeiro, 1917.

Morel, Edmar. *A dragão do mar: O jangadeiro da abolição.* Rio de Janeiro, 1949.

———. *Vendaval da liberdade.* Rio de Janeiro, 1967.

Mörner, Magnus (ed.). *Race and Class in Latin America.* New York and London, 1970.

———. *Race Mixture in the History of Latin America.* Boston, 1967.

Morse, Richard M. *From Community to Metropolis: A Biography of São Paulo, Brazil.* Gainesville, 1958.

Moura, Clovis. *Rebellições das senzalas.* São Paulo, 1959.

Nabuco, Carolina. *The Life of Joaquim Nabuco.* Stanford, 1950.
Nascimento, Abdias do, et. al. *O negro brasileiro (80 anos de abolição).* Rio de Janeiro, 1968.
Nash, Roy. *The Conquest of Brazil.* New York, 1926.
Novaes, Maria Stella. *A escravidão e a abolição no Espírito Santo: História e foclore.* Vitória, 1963.
Octávio, Rodrigo. *Figuras do império e da república.* Rio de Janeiro, 1944.
Orico, Osvaldo. *Patrocínio.* Rio de Janeiro, 1935.
Petrone, Maria Thereza Schorer. *A lavoura canaviera em São Paulo.* São Paulo, 1968.
Pierson, Donald. *Negroes in Brazil: A Study of Race Contact at Bahia.* Chicago, 1942.
Pinho, Wanderley. *Política e políticos no império: Contribuições documentares.* Rio de Janeiro, 1930.
Pinto, Pedro A. *D. Pedro II e a abolição.* Rio de Janeiro, 1921.
Pires, Cornelio. *Conversas ao pé do fogo: Estudinhos costumes, contos, anedotas, cenas da escravidão.* São Paulo, 1921.
Porto, Mario Magalhaes. *A abolição da escravatura e o problema do negro. Niterói,* 1938.
Prado, Junior, Caio. *The Colonial Background of Modern Brazil.* Berkeley and Los Angeles, 1967.
———. *Evolução política do Brasil e outros estudos.* Rio de Janeiro, 1947.
———. *História econômica do Brasil.* São Paulo, 1949.
Prado Junior, Martinho. *In Memoriam: Martinho Prado Junior.* São Paulo, 1943.
Prado, Orlando de Almeida. *Em defenza da raça negra: O preconceito da raca não existe no Brasil.* São Paulo, n.d.
Queiroz, Maurício Vinhas de. *Paixão e morte de Silva Jardim.* Rio de Janeiro, 1967.
Ramos, Artur. *The Negro in Brazil.* Washington, 1939.
Rego, Alceu Marinho. *Nabuco.* Rio de Janeiro and São Paulo, 1951.
Rodrigues, José Honório. *Brasil e a Africa: outre horizonte.* Rio de Janeiro, 1961.
———. *Concilicão e reforma no Brasil: Um desafio histórico-político.* Rio de Janeiro, 1965.
Roure, Agnor de. *A abolição e seus reflexos econômicos: Conferência realizada na segunda sessão de 1918, a 14 de maio, no Instituto Histórico e Geográfico Brasileiro.* Rio de Janeiro, 1918.
Santos, José Maria dos. *Política geral do Brasil.* São Paulo, 1930.
———. *Os republicanos paulistas e a abolição.* São Paulo, 1942.
São Paulo e a sua evolução: Conferências realisadas no Centro Paulista em 1926. Rio de Janeiro, 1927.

Sayers, Raymond S. *The Negro in Brazilian Literature.* New York, 1956.

Schmidt, Afonso. *A marcha, romance da abolição.* N.p., 1941.

Schurz, William Lytle. *This New World: The Civilization of Latin America.* New York, 1964.

Simmons, Charles Willis. *Marshal Deodoro and the Fall of Dom Pedro II.* Durham, 1966.

Simonsen, Roberto C. *Aspectos da história econômica do café.* Rio de Janeiro, 1938.

———. *A evolução industrial no Brasil.* São Paulo, 1939.

Smith, T. Lynn. *Brazil: People and Institutions.* Baton Rouge, 1954.

Sodré, Alcindro. *O elemento servil, a abolição.* Rio de Janeiro, 1942.

Sodré, Nelson Werneck. *História da burguesia brasileira.* Rio de Janeiro, 1964.

———. *História militar do Brasil.* Rio de Janeiro, 1965.

———. *Panorama do segundo império.* São Paulo, 1939.

Stein, Stanley J. *The Brazilian Cotton Manufacture: Textile Enterprise in an Underdeveloped Area, 1850–1950.* Cambridge, 1957.

———. *Vassouras: A Brazilian Coffee County, 1850–1900.* Cambridge, 1957.

Stein, Barbara H. and Stanley J. *The Colonial Heritage of Latin America.* New York, 1970.

Tannenbaum, Frank. *Slave and Citizen: The Negro in the Americas.* New York, 1946.

Taunay, Affonso de Escragnolle. *Pequena história do café no Brasil.* Rio de Janeiro, 1945.

Thiollier, Reneé. *António Bento: Um grande chefe abolicionista.* São Paulo, 1932.

Turner, Charles W. *Ruy Barbosa: Brazilian Crusader for Essential Freedoms.* New York and Nashville, 1945.

Valladão, Alfredo. *Joaquim Nabuco, O evangelista da abolição.* Rio de Janeiro, 1950.

Verissimo, Inácio José. *André Rebouças através de sua autobiografia.* Rio de Janeiro, 1939.

Viana, Francisco José de Oliveira. *O império brasileiro, 1822–1889.* Rio de Janeiro, 1927.

———. *O ocaso do império.* São Paulo, 1925.

Vianna, Hélio. *Estudos de história imperial.* São Paulo, 1950.

Vieira, Hermes. *A Princesa Isabel no cenário abolicionista do Brasil.* São Paulo, 1941.

Viera, Celso. *Joaquim Nabuco, libertador da raça negra.* São Paulo, n.d.

Wagley, Charles. *An Introduction to Brazil.* New York and London, 1963.

Williams, Mary Wilhelmine. *Dom Pedro the Magnanimous, Second Emperor of Brazil.* Chapel Hill, 1937.

Woodward, C. Vann. *American Counterpoint: Slavery and Racism in the North-South Dialogue.* Boston and Toronto, 1971.

Articles

Adams, Jane Elizabeth. "The Abolition of the Brazilian Slave Trade," *Journal of Negro History,* X (October 1925), pp. 607–37.

Alexander, H. B. "Brazilian and United States Slavery Compared," *Journal of Negro History,* VII (1922), pp. 349–64.

Almeida, Benedito Pires de. *"Tietê, os escravos e a abolição," Revista do Arquivo Municipal de São Paulo,* XCV, No. 9 (1944), pp. 49–59.

Andrada, Antônio Manuel Bueno de. *"Depoimento da uma Testemunha," Revista do Instituto Histórico e Geográfico de São Paulo,* XXXVI (1939), pp. 211–24.

"80 anos de abolição." Cadernos Brasileiros (May–June 1968).

Calmon, Pedro. *"A abolição," Revista do Arquivo Municipal de São Paulo,* XLVII (1938), pp. 127–40.

Cardoso, Fernando Henrique. *"Condições sociais de industrialização em São Paulo," Revista Brasiliense,* XXVIII (March–April 1960), pp. 31–46.

Cardozo, Manoel. "Slavery in Brazil as Described by Americans." *The Americas,* XVIII (1961), pp. 241–60.

Castro, F. A. Viega de. *"Um fazendeiro do século passado," Revista do Arquivo Municipal de São Paulo,* XCVII (1944), pp. 25–44.

Conrad, Robert. "The Contraband Slave Trade to Brazil, 1831–1845," *Hispanic American Historical Review* (November, 1969), pp. 617–38.

Costa, Emília Viotti da. *"A proclamação da república," Anais do Museu Paulista,* No. 19, pp. 169–207.

———. *"Sôbre as origens da república," Anais do Museu Paulista,* XVIII (1964), pp. 63–120.

Davis, David Brian. "Slavery," in C. Vann Woodward, *The Comparative Approach to American History.* New York and London, 1968, pp. 121–34.

Dean, Warren. "The Planter as Entrepreneur: The Case of São Paulo," *Hispanic American Historical Review* (May 1966).

Degler, Carl N. "Slavery in Brazil and the United States," *American Historical Review* (April 1970), pp. 1004–1028.

Fernandes, Florestan. *"Imigração e relações raciais," Revista Civilisação Brasileira* (1966), n.8, pp. 75–96.

Frazier, E. Franklin. "A Comparison of Negro-White Relations in Brazil and in the United States," in E. Franklin Frazier, *On Race Relations* (Chicago, 1968), pp. 82–102.

Galloway, J. H. "The Last Years of Slavery on the Sugar Plantations of Northeast Brazil," *Hispanic American Historical Review* (November 1971), pp. 586–605.

Gigliotti, Adir. *"Libertação dos escravos foi a festa mais bonita a que alguem ja assistio!," Ultima Hora,* June 23, 1960.

Graham, Richard. "Brazilian Slavery Re-examined: A Review Article," *Journal of Social History* (Summer, 1970), pp. 431–53.

———. "Causes of the Abolition of Negro Slavery in Brazil: An Interpretation," *Hispanic American Historical Review* (May 1966).

———. "Landowners and the Overthrow of the Empire," *Luso-Brazilian Review* (December 1970).

Hamilton, Charles. "English Speaking Travelers in Brazil, 1851–1887," *Hispanic American Historical Review,* XL (1960), pp. 533–47.

Hill, Lawrence F. "The Abolition of the African Slave Trade to Brazil," *Hispanic American Historical Review, XI* (May 1931), pp. 169–97.

Ianni, Octávio. *"Capitalismo e escravadão," Anais do Museu Paulista,* N.19, pp. 137–45.

Jefferson, Mark. "An American Colony in Brazil," *The Geographical Review* (April 1928), pp. 226–31.

Kent, R. K. "African Revolt in Bahia: 24–25 January 1835," *Journal of Social History* (Summer, 1970), pp. 334–56.

Klein, Herbert S. "The Colored Freedmen in Brazilian Slave Society," *Journal of Social History* (Fall, 1969), pp. 30–52.

———. "The Internal Slave Trade in Nineteenth-Century Brazil: A Study of Slave Importations into Rio de Janeiro in 1852," *Hispanic American Historical Review* (November 1971), pp. 567–585.

Lacombe, Americo Jacobina. *"Rui e a história política do império e da república," Revista do Instituto Histórico e Geográfico Brasileiro,* CCV (1949).

Luz, Nícia Vilela. *"A administração provincial de São Paulo em face do movimento abolicionista," Revista de Administração,* VIII (December 1948), pp. 80–100.

———. *"O industrialismo e o desenvolvimento econômico no Brasil," Revista de História* (October–December 1963).

———. *"O papel das classes médias brasileiras no movimento republicano," Revista de História* (January–March 1964).

Manchester, Allan K. "The Rise of the Brazilian Aristocracy," *Hispanic American Historical Review,* XI (1931), pp. 145–68.

Martin, Percy Alvin. "Causes of the Collapse of the Brazilian Empire," *Hispanic American Historical Review,* IV (February 1921), pp. 4–48.

———. "Slavery and Abolition in Brazil," *Hispanic American Historical Review,* XIII (May 1933), pp. 151–96.

Nabuco, Carolina. *"O elemento servil—a abolição," Anais do Terceiro Congresso de História Nacional,* VI (1942), pp. 241–56.

Nogueira, Emília da Costa. *"O movimento republicano em Itú: Os fazendeiros do oeste paulista e o prodromos do movimento republicano," Revista de História,* XX (1954).

Odalia, Nilo. *"A abolição da escravatura," Anais do Museu Paulista,* XVIII (1964), pp. 121–45.

Pinto, Virgilio Noya. *"Ritmos da economia e dependência econômica em face dos mercados externos," Anais do Museu Paulista,* N.19 (1965), pp. 107–26.

Porter, Dorothy B. "The Negro in the Brazilian Abolition Movement," *Journal of Negro History* (1952), pp. 54–80.

Queiroz, D. Vitalina Pompeo de Souza. *"O levante," Escravidão em Campinas,* in the *Paço Municipal,* Campinas.

Reis, P. Pereira dos. *"Algumas considerações sôbre a imigração em São Paulo," Revista Sociologia* (March, 1961), N.1.

Revista do Instituto Histórico e Geográfico Brasileiro, CCIV (July–September 1949). A collection of articles about Joaquim Nabuco.

Riccardi, Adelino. *"Parnaiba, o pioneiro da imigração," Revista do Arquivo Municipal de São Paulo,* XLIV (1938), pp. 136–84.

Schwartz, Stuart B. "The *Mocambo:* Slave Resistance in Colonial Bahia," *Journal of Social History* (Summer, 1970), pp. 313–33.

Simonsen, Roberto. *"As consequências econômicas da abolição," Revista do Arquivo Municipal de São Paulo,* CXLVII (May 1938), pp. 257–68.

Skidmore, Thomas E. "Brazilian Intellectuals and the Problem of Race, 1870–1930," The Graduate Center for Latin American Studies, Vanderbilt University. Occasional Paper No. 6.

———. "The Death of Brazilian Slavery: 1866–1888," in Frederick B. Pike (ed.), *Latin American History: Select Problems* (New York, Chicago, San Francisco, Atlanta, 1969), pp. 133–70.

Stein, Stanley J. "The Historiography of Brazil, 1808–1889," *Hispanic American Historical Review* (May 1960), pp. 234–78.

Taunay, Affonso d'Escragnolle. *"Os representantes de São Paulo nos parlamentos do antigo regima, Senado e Câmara dos Deputados," Revista do Instituto Histórico e Geográfico de São Paulo,* XIV (1912), pp. 351–64.

Toplin, Robert Brent. "From Slavery to Fettered Freedom: Attitudes toward the Negro in Brazil," *Luso-Brazilian Review* (Summer, 1970), pp. 3–12.

———. "Reinterpreting Comparative Race Relations: The United States and Brasil," *Journal of Black Studies* (December 1971), pp. 135–55.

———. "Upheaval, Violence, and the Abolition of Slavery in Brazil: The Case of São Paulo," *Hispanic American Historical Review* (November 1969), pp. 639–55.

Williams, Mary W. "The Treatment of Negro Slaves in the Brazilian Empire: A Comparison with the United States of America," *Journal of Negro History,* XV (1930), pp. 315–36.

UNPUBLISHED MATERIAL

Conrad, Robert. "The Struggle for the Abolition of the Brazilian Slave Trade, 1808–1853." Ph.D. dissertation, Columbia University, 1967.

Corwin, Arthur F. "Afro-Brazilian Poverty: Myths and Realities."

Dean, Warren. "São Paulo's Industrial Elite, 1890–1960," Ph.D. dissertation, University of Florida, 1964.

Slave Population of Brazil: Provincial Totals

Province	1873	1875	1878	1883	1884	1885	1887
Amazonas	1,515	1,130	974	1,716	—	—	—
Pará	30,963	25,916	30,623	25,383	20,849	20,218	10,535
Maranhão	64,783	63,967	63,164	60,059	49,545	31,901	33,466
Ceará	31,975	33,409	25,773	19,588	—	—	108
Piauí	24,898	24,318	21,216	18,691	16,780	15,498	8,970
Rio Grande do Norte	13,165	12,858	10,282	10,051	7,209	7,209	3,167
Paraíba	27,651	26,033	25,596	25,817	19,165	18,824	9,448
Pernambuco	92,745	93,752	91,992	84,700	72,709	72,370	41,122
Alagoas	35,002	30,216	30,397	29,439	26,911	25,046	15,269
Sergipe	34,938	27,634	26,381	26,173	25,874	24,325	16,875
Bahia	169,766	165,403	116,108	165,403	132,822	132,822	76,838

Espírito Santo	22,286	22,659	21,216	20,717	20,216	19,762	13,381
Rio de Janeiro (Capital City)	47,084	44,775	43,409	35,568	32,103	29,909	7,488
Rio de Janeiro	303,810	278,212	289,239	268,831	258,238	250,896	162,421
Santa Catarina	13,547	13,884	12,829	11,049	8,371	8,221	4,927
Paraná	11,807	9,792	10,088	7,668	7,768	6,836	3,513
São Paulo	168,002	154,861	168,950	174,622	167,493	153,270	107,329
Minas Gerais	351,254	298,496	289,949	279,010	301,125	276,275	191,952
Rio Grande do Sul	100,549	77,633	75,937	68,703	60,136	27,242	8,442
Goiás	9,086	7,888	6,963	6,899	7,710	7,788	4,955
Mato Grosso	6,590	7,130	7,051	7,051	5,782	4,816	3,233
TOTAL	1,566,416	1,419,966	1,368,097	1,346,648	1,240,806	1,133,228	723,419

Source: *Relatórios* of the Minister of Agriculture, Commerce and Public Works

Slave Population of Brazil, 1872

Summary of Data from the 1872 Census

	TOTAL	PERCENT
Sex		
Male	786,575	53%
Female	689,992	47%
Marital Status		
Married	131,241	9%
Single	1,305,995	88%
Widowed	39,331	3%
Race		
Mulatto	446,054	30%
Negro	1,030,513	70%
Literacy		
Literate	1,338	—
Illiterate	1,475,229	99+%

Slave Registration in Brazil, March 30, 1887
Summary of Data *

	TOTAL	PERCENT
Sex		
Male	384,615	53%
Female	337,804	47%
Marital Status		
Married	76,804	11%
Single	632,210	87%
Widowed	14,105	2%
Occupation		
Agricultural worker	611,195	85%
Artisan	51,937	7%
Day laborer	60,287	8%
Residence		
Urban	71,191	10%
Rural	652,228	90%

* Source: *Relatório* of the Minister of Agriculture, Commerce and Public Works, 1888.

Index

ROBERT BRENT TOPLIN

Robert Brent Toplin is Assistant Professor of History at Denison University. Born in Philadelphia, Pennsylvania, in 1940, he received a B.S. from the Pennsylvania State University and an M.A. and a Ph.D. from Rutgers University. He has received fellowships from the Ford Foundation, the American Philosophical Society, the National Endowment for the Humanities, and Denison University, and has been a frequent visitor to Brazil. His scholarly articles have appeared in *Civil War History,* the *Hispanic American Historical Review,* the *Luso-Brazilian Review,* and the *Journal of Black Studies.*